PRAISE FOR *THE MONEY HACKERS*

"Until *The Money Hackers*, I didn't know who had created the fintech revolution and how transformative it is and will eventually be to every financial institution and transaction on Earth! Simon has written a fascinating, entertaining, and inspiring tale of the entrepreneurial outliers creating the revolution."
—Consuelo Mack,
Host of PBS's *Wealth Track*

"A brilliant book. Simon captures the essence of the crypto movement, highlighting its potential and its challenges, and artfully describes what it means in layman's terms."
—Michael J. Casey,
Senior Advisor to the MIT Media Lab,
Bestselling Author, and *Wall Street Journal* Columnist

"*The Money Hackers* is a marvelous account of how money became modern. For anyone who's wondered why they haven't written a check in a while or exactly how they were able to split a pizza on their phone, this is the book for you. Through a series of entertaining, at times hilarious, biographies of the luminaries behind the FinTech movement, Simon skillfully explains how technology has transformed your money forever."
—*The Financial Revolutionist*

"An instant classic. *The Money Hackers* is a funny and heartfelt account of the people and events that have shaped our understanding of finance today."
—Kabir Sehgal,
New York Times and
Wall Street Journal Bestselling Author

"*The Money Hackers* is a clever and curious story about the new pioneers of finance. Simon skillfully unpacks complex subjects by unearthing the basic ingredients that led to incredible innovations that have revolutionized the way finance is transacted."
—Stephen Tisdalle,
Creator of Fearless Girl and
CMO of State Street Global Advisors

"Finance is one of the largest components of the economy and the glue that holds much together. *The Money Hackers* is an amazing read that illustrates how the foundations of money are being reinvented not by the usual suspects but a new generation focused on solving real people's problems. It will wake you up and may even make you richer!"
—Rishad Tobaccowala,
Chief Growth Officer of Publicis Groupe and Author of
Restoring the Soul of Business: Staying Human in the Age of Data

"*The Money Hackers* is more than a book about finance or technology, it's a book about people. Through these unique perspectives—some funny, some heart-wrenching, all equally fascinating—Simon tells the story of how Fintech came to be and why you should care."   —Maria Deam, Head of Open Innovation at Citi FinTech
and Former Vice Consul of Fintech and
Banking Innovation at the British Consulate

"*The Money Hackers* is a powerful reminder that money touches everyone's lives differently. This book offers an approachable, inclusive, and entertaining take on how we interact with money and what it means for the future."   —Farnoosh Torabi,
Host of the podcast *So Money* and
Author of the bestseller *When She Makes More*

"Through a series of entertaining vignettes, Simon skillfully explains how technology has reshaped our money since the financial crisis and spotlights the fascinating individuals who have brought this innovation to life. Anyone who enjoys reading about disruptors, or dreams of being a disrupter themselves one day, would do well to read this book."   —Kara Goldin, Founder and CEO of Hint

"A smart, funny, and useful book, *The Money Hackers* documents with humor and clarity how the rise of mobile, social, and the network economy has reshaped so much of our financial lives."   —Mark Wetjen, Former Commissioner of the
U.S. Commodity Futures Trading Commission

"The current buzz is all about fintech and how mobile has taken over our lives. In a fast-paced and easy-to-read style, Dan Simon traces this seed change from its origins to the present. They are all here: the early adapters, the winners, the losers, the survivors, the techs, and the banks. Simon engagingly describes the tension between the "move fast and break things" mentality of the entrepreneurs vs. the "walk slow and play safe" of the banks. Pick this book up and disrupt your day. You won't put it down."   —David J. Cowen, Ph.D.,
President and CEO of the Museum of American Finance

"Tech has been major for my business—I mean I basically built my brand off of an iPhone. That's why I loved *The Money Hackers*. It tells the stories of others who have fused tech and finance to push the industry forward. I loved the book and it inspired me to name my next dog Bitcoin. Definitely read it!"   —Haley Sacks, *Mrs. Dow Jones*

"You don't need to be a Wall Street vet or an MBA grad to appreciate *The Money Hackers*. This unexpectedly human story chronicles the recent history of money with eloquence, simplicity, and soul."   —Chris Roush, Dean,
School of Communications at Quinnipiac University

"From bartering to bullion to banking and bitcoin—financial systems have evolved over the course of human history. Through approachable and at times hilarious storytelling, Daniel P. Simon profiles the most recent few chapters of that evolution and anticipates what the future of money might look like. Great context for how to position in a new marketplace." —Jenifer Brooks, CMO of Gerson Lehrman Group

"Before I created Mr. Skin, I worked in finance and it's incredible to see how far the industry has come in twenty years. At its heart though, *The Money Hackers* is a 'how-to' guide for aspiring entrepreneurs. How to spot opportunities others missed, how to create new markets and how to take on entrenched and established players and win! If you dream of starting the next Venmo (or even the next Mr. Skin) you should begin by reading this book." —Jim McBride, Founder and CEO of Mr. Skin

"Simon breaks down one of the more complicated narratives of history into a thrilling adventure. Regulations make innovating in this space full of unique problems and Simon explains it all in an approachable way. I loved learning the real stories behind the creators of new fintech products that better serve people who aren't part of the 1%. *The Money Hackers* weaves together an exhilarating tale of technology, change, and consequences." —Maia Bittner, Founder of Pinch

"Finance doesn't have to be complicated or exclusively for the elite. This book breaks down the evolution and innovation within the industry in a way that's both interesting and relevant to anyone who wants to get smarter about money." —Jon Zanoff, Head of Barclays Tech Stars US

"Beautifully written, this book simply and elegantly tells the stories of the people whose brilliant innovations gave us the financial technology we now take for granted today." —Jared Dillian, Author of *Street Freak* and *All the Evil of This World*

THE
MONEY
HACKERS

HOW A GROUP OF MISFITS TOOK ON WALL STREET AND CHANGED FINANCE FOREVER

DANIEL P. SIMON

HarperCollins Leadership
AN IMPRINT OF HarperCollins

Published by HarperCollins Leadership, an imprint of HarperCollins Focus LLC.

Any internet addresses, phone numbers, or company or product information printed in this book are offered as a resource and are not intended in any way to be or to imply an endorsement by HarperCollins Leadership, nor does HarperCollins Leadership vouch for the existence, content, or services of these sites, phone numbers, companies, or products beyond the life of this book.

Book design by Aubrey Khan, Neuwirth & Associates

ISBN 978-1-4002-1661-1 (Ebook)
ISBN 978-1-4002-1660-4 (HC)

Library of Congress Control Number: 2020930434

Printed in the United States of America
20 21 22 23   LSC   10 9 8 7 6 5 4 3 2 1

For Charlotte and Eleanor

"IF MONEY ISN'T LOOSENED UP,
THIS SUCKER COULD GO DOWN."
—President George W. Bush, September 25, 2008

"THERE'S AN APP FOR THAT."
—Apple, January 26, 2009

CONTENTS

Foreword by Peter Grauer   xiii

Fintech Timeline   xv

Prologue: There's No App for That   xxxi

Author's Note   xxxvii

CHAPTER 1   Making Money Move   1

CHAPTER 2   Giving Money to Strangers   15

CHAPTER 3   Aggregate and Automate   43

CHAPTER 4   Rise of the Machines   67

CHAPTER 5   Banking the Unbanked   89

CHAPTER 6   Border Crossings   105

CHAPTER 7   Mystery Money   121

CHAPTER 8 Distributing & Decentralizing   147

CHAPTER 9 The Empire Strikes Back   165

Epilogue: The Future   187

Acknowledgments   193

About the Author   195

Notes   197

Index   209

FOREWORD

Seventeen years ago, when I first came to Bloomberg, I invited Clayton Christensen to come talk about his book *The Innovator's Dilemma* and his perception of how companies reacted—or failed to react—to change.

Change in the banking industry has historically moved very slowly. People in finance get nervous about innovation. After all, a bank's first job is not to lose money: think of all those safe-deposit boxes and big locked vaults.

But a company like Bloomberg, a technology company, has no choice but to scan the horizon and try to identify the things that might disrupt our business model—and the disruption we've seen over the past decade has been staggering. People now buy, spend, borrow, and trade instantly, without touching money. Even my local pharmacy in rural Connecticut no longer wants my cash; it only takes payments electronically.

This is the "fintech revolution." It is a massive shift, it happened overwhelmingly fast, and most people inside the world of banking—distracted by the financial crisis and its aftermath—never saw it coming.

Now that it's here, everyone in the business of financial services has to be prepared to accept the fact that they're going to be disrupted. Why wouldn't they be? Nothing is the same. People from their mid-teens to their late forties are so confident in the power of technology, so fluent in its use, why should they be attached to the old way of doing things? Why should they use a check-book? Technology is going to continue to change the retail financial services industry.

The new, young financial technology companies—the "money hackers"—are either revolutionizing the old banking models or demolishing them altogether. Everyone inside the financial services industry will have to adapt—even at the expense of their existing businesses and cultures—or risk being left behind.

They can start by reading this book.

—PETER GRAUER,
chairman of Bloomberg LP

FINTECH TIMELINE

The history of financial technology is as old as money itself—money *is* technology!—but the phenomenon known as "fintech" got its start much more recently, with the rise of the internet and with the economic booms and busts of the 1990s and 2000s. What follows are some key moments that helped lead to fintech as it exists today.

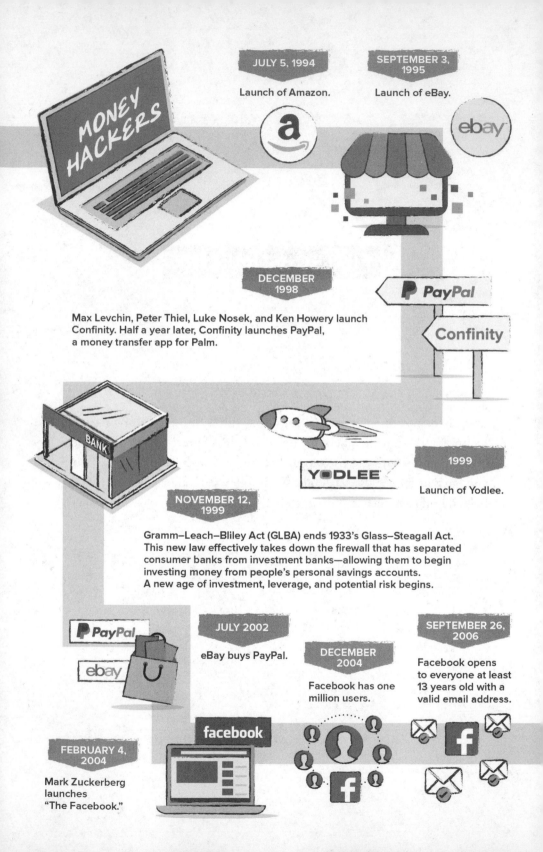

MONEY HACKERS

JULY 5, 1994

Launch of Amazon.

SEPTEMBER 3, 1995

Launch of eBay.

DECEMBER 1998

Max Levchin, Peter Thiel, Luke Nosek, and Ken Howery launch Confinity. Half a year later, Confinity launches PayPal, a money transfer app for Palm.

PayPal

Confinity

YODLEE

1999

Launch of Yodlee.

NOVEMBER 12, 1999

Gramm–Leach–Bliley Act (GLBA) ends 1933's Glass–Steagall Act. This new law effectively takes down the firewall that has separated consumer banks from investment banks—allowing them to begin investing money from people's personal savings accounts. A new age of investment, leverage, and potential risk begins.

PayPal

ebay

JULY 2002

eBay buys PayPal.

DECEMBER 2004

Facebook has one million users.

SEPTEMBER 26, 2006

Facebook opens to everyone at least 13 years old with a valid email address.

facebook

FEBRUARY 4, 2004

Mark Zuckerberg launches "The Facebook."

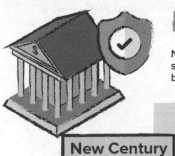

APRIL 2007

New Century, an American real estate investment trust specializing in subprime mortgages, files for Chapter 11 bankruptcy protection. The beginning of the subprime crisis.

New Century

MARCH 8, 2007

CreditKarma founded.

MARCH 2007

Kenya-based Safaricom launches a new mobile phone–based payment and money transfer service, known as M-Pesa, which moves money on the SMS network.

FEBRUARY 20, 2007

The Dow hits a peak level of 12,786. Home sales also peak this month and begin to decline.

NOVEMBER 2006

Wesabe, an online personal finance management tool, goes live.

JANUARY 9, 2007

Steve Jobs announces the iPhone at the Macworld convention, receiving substantial media attention.

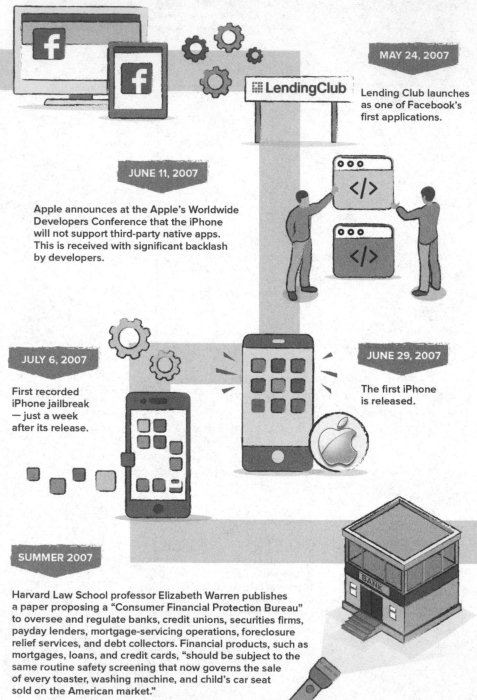

MAY 24, 2007

Facebook releases APIs called the Facebook Platform, which supports integration of Facebook services across the web and devices. Now third-party developers can use Facebook data for off-site applications.

MAY 24, 2007

Lending Club launches as one of Facebook's first applications.

JUNE 11, 2007

Apple announces at the Apple's Worldwide Developers Conference that the iPhone will not support third-party native apps. This is received with significant backlash by developers.

JULY 6, 2007

First recorded iPhone jailbreak — just a week after its release.

JUNE 29, 2007

The first iPhone is released.

SUMMER 2007

Harvard Law School professor Elizabeth Warren publishes a paper proposing a "Consumer Financial Protection Bureau" to oversee and regulate banks, credit unions, securities firms, payday lenders, mortgage-servicing operations, foreclosure relief services, and debt collectors. Financial products, such as mortgages, loans, and credit cards, "should be subject to the same routine safety screening that now governs the sale of every toaster, washing machine, and child's car seat sold on the American market."

Credit Karma
launches.

FEBRUARY 2008

Facebook settles with the Winklevoss twins
for $20 million and an estimated 1.2m shares
in the company. The twins quickly file to back
out of the settlement, demanding more.

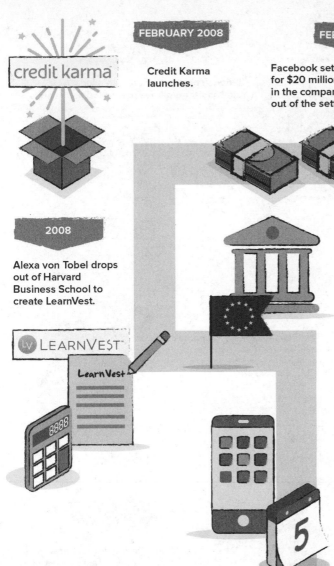

2008

Alexa von Tobel drops
out of Harvard
Business School to
create LearnVest.

DECEMBER 2007

The EU's "Payment Services
Directive" — new banking
regulations aimed at the
European banking sector
— goes into effect.

OCTOBER 2007

Apple reverses course
and announces a software
development kit for the
iPhone, to be available
by February 2008.

**SEPTEMBER
2007**

Mint.com is launched at TechCrunch40 conference (and wins
the conference's $50,000 first prize).

FEBRUARY 13, 2008

The Economic Stimulus Act of 2008 is enacted (including a tax rebate).

MARCH 6, 2008

iPhone software development kit is released, allowing third parties to develop native apps for iOS.

JUNE 2008

Yodlee gets $35 million investment from Bank of America.

MARCH 17, 2008

The Federal Reserve guarantees Bear Stearns' bad loans to facilitate its acquisition by JPMorgan Chase.

BANK OF AMERICA

YODLEE

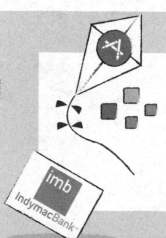

JULY 10, 2008

Launch of App Store. Apple goes from no apps to hundreds of apps overnight. The modern, mobile computing platform is born.

JULY 11, 2008

IndyMac fails and is seized by the FDIC.

imb
IndymacBank

JULY 30, 2008

The Housing and Economic Recovery Act of 2008 is enacted.

AUGUST 18, 2008

Bitcoin.org domain registered.

SEPTEMBER 16, 2008

The Federal Reserve takes over AIG. The Reserve Primary Fund breaks the buck.

SEPTEMBER 18, 2008

Treasury Secretary Henry Paulson and Fed Chairman Ben Bernanke propose a $700 billion emergency bailout.

"If we don't do this, we may not have an economy on Monday."

SEPTEMBER 15, 2008

Lehman Brothers declares bankruptcy, causing the Dow Jones to drop 504 points, its worst decline in seven years. Bank of America purchases Merrill Lynch.

SEPTEMBER 9, 2008

100 million downloads from App Store.

SEPTEMBER 7, 2008

Fannie Mae and Freddie Mac are taken over by the federal government.

SEPTEMBER 2008

The World Bank establishes the first international database of remittance prices, The Remittance Prices Worldwide Database, putting pressure on remittance service providers to improve their services.

Betterment

AUGUST 26, 2008

Facebook hits 100 million users.

AUGUST 25, 2008

Betterment founded.

SEPTEMBER 21, 2008

Goldman Sachs and Morgan Stanley convert to bank holding companies to increase their protection by the Federal Reserve.

SEPTEMBER 23, 2008

First commercially available Android smartphone, HTC Dream, also known as T-Mobile G1, is released.

SEPTEMBER 25, 2008

"If money isn't loosened up, this sucker could go down"

— George W. Bush

SEPTEMBER 26, 2008

Washington Mutual, with $307 billion in assets, begins a 10-day bank run on its deposits.

SEPTEMBER 29, 2008

The House of Representatives rejects the Emergency Economic Stabilization Act of 2008. The Dow Jones drops 770 points, its largest single-day decline.

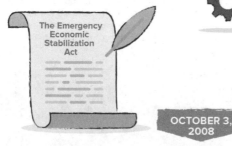

The Emergency Economic Stabilization Act

OCTOBER 3, 2008

The Emergency Economic Stabilization Act, which implements the Troubled Asset Relief Program (TARP), is signed into law.

OCTOBER 14, 2008

Lending Club announces it is the first peer-to-peer lender to be registered with the SEC.

FEBRUARY 17, 2009

Obama signs the American Recovery and Reinvestment Act, a $787 billion injection of capital with the goal of stimulating the faltering economy.

APRIL 2009

1 billion downloads from App Store.

JANUARY 26, 2009

"There's an app for that." — Apple ad campaign launches.

JANUARY 20, 2009

Inauguration of Barack Obama.

JANUARY 12, 2009

Cypherpunk Hal Finney receives 10 bitcoin in the first-ever transaction of cryptocurrency.

JANUARY 3, 2009

Launch of the Bitcoin network and the world's first cryptocurrency; Satoshi Nakamoto mines the genesis block of the first blockchain.

OCTOBER 31, 2008

Satoshi Nakamoto publishes a white paper, "Bitcoin: A Peer-to-Peer Electronic Cash System."

2009

BankSimple launched.

NOVEMBER 4, 2008

Barack Obama is elected President of the United States.

JUNE 2009

App Store lists 50,000 apps.

APRIL 2009

Venmo is founded.

JUNE 17, 2009

President Obama introduces a proposal for a "sweeping overhaul of the United States financial regulatory system, a transformation on a scale not seen since the reforms that followed the Great Depression."

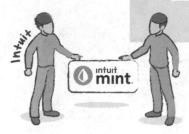

SEPTEMBER 13, 2009

Intuit acquires Mint. Mint's years-long partnership with Yodlee ends.

DECEMBER 2009

Venmo iPhone app.

NOVEMBER 2009

Launch of LearnVest.com, a personal finance site for people just out of college.

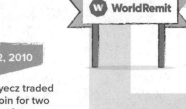

2010

WorldRemit founded by Ismail Ahmed.

MAY 22, 2010

Laszlo Hanyecz traded 10,000 bitcoin for two Papa John's pizzas.

JULY 21, 2010

Dodd-Frank signed into law, instituting new levels of bank regulation.

JULY 21, 2011

Consumer Financial Protection Bureau formed, to oversee consumer interests within banks, credit unions, securities firms, payday lenders, mortgage-servicing operations, foreclosure relief services, debt collectors, and other financial companies operating in the United States.

JUNE 19, 2011

Mt. Gox bitcoin exchange is hacked and 850,000 bitcoin are stolen or lost.

MAY 2011

Charlie Shrem co-founds BitInstant, the first way to quickly and easily buy bitcoin from retail locations.

JUNE 2011

The Winklevoss twins end their appeal to get more from their Facebook settlement.

MAY 2011

Kabbage begins making its first loans.

FEBRUARY 2011

Launch of black market ecommerce site Silk Road, which accepts bitcoin as its main currency.

zzz... zzz...

zzz...

JULY 31, 2010

Wesabe shuts down.

AUGUST 2011

SoFi founded.

SEPTEMBER 2011

Stripe founded.

SEPTEMBER 17, 2011

Beginning of Occupy Wall Street.

APRIL 2012

Braintree acquires Venmo.

NOVEMBER 15, 2011

Occupy Wall Street protesters are forced out of Zuccotti Park.

MAY 18, 2012

Facebook IPO.

SEPTEMBER 2012

Charlie Shrem becomes founding board member of the Bitcoin Foundation, a nonprofit aiming to increase the awareness and reputation of the cryptocurrency.

NOVEMBER 6, 2012

Barack Obama reelected President of the United States.

MAY 2013

BitInstant receives its first major investment, $1.5m, from Winklevoss Capital.

FEBRUARY 2014

The Winklevoss twins launch Winkdex, an online index showing the current price of bitcoin.

DECEMBER 2014

Charlie Shrem sentenced to two years in prison for conspiring to commit money laundering.

JANUARY 26, 2014

BitInstant CEO Charlie Shrem charged with money laundering.

JANUARY 2014

Vitalik Buterin, in conjunction with other members of the cryptocurrency community, releases Ethereum, a scripting language for blockchain.

2014

Digital Asset Holdings, LLC, is formed.

NOVEMBER 2013

Teenage hacker and Bitcoin enthusiast Vitalik Buterin writes Ethereum white paper.

OCTOBER 2013

Ross Ulbricht, AKA the "Dread Pirate Roberts" and the owner of Silk Road, is arrested on narcotics and money laundering charges.

AUGUST 9, 2013

Bloomberg gets Bitcoin ticker.

SEPTEMBER 2013

PayPal acquires Braintree.

MARCH 2015

Blythe Masters joins Digital Asset.

MARCH 25, 2015

Northwestern Mutual Life Insurance Co. announces acquisition of LearnVest.

OCTOBER 25, 2015

The Gemini Exchange, a cryptocurrency trading platform created by the Winklevoss twins, gets approval from the New York Department of Financial Services and goes live.

NOVEMBER 16, 2015

The Council of the European Union passes PSD2, giving member states two years to incorporate the directive into their national laws and regulations.

APRIL 15, 2016

Clarity Money is launched.

MARCH 2016

Charlie Shrem released from prison.

OCTOBER 2016

Goldman launches Marcus, online lending business.

NOVEMBER 8, 2016

Donald Trump elected president of the United States.

SEPTEMBER 14, 2019

PSD2 regulation goes into full effect in the EU.

OCTOBER 2019

Schwab eliminates all fees.

JUNE 5, 2018

Northwestern Mutual shuts down LearnVest.

MAY 24, 2018

The Economic Growth, Regulatory Relief and Consumer Protection Act exempts dozens of U.S. banks from the Dodd–Frank Act's banking regulations, removing some of the regulatory guidelines put in place after the 2008 crisis.

APRIL 2018

Goldman Sachs buys Clarity Money for "high eight figures."

SEPTEMBER 2017

Launch of Zelle.

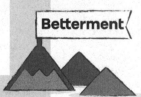

JANUARY 20, 2017

Inauguration of Donald Trump.

JULY 2017

Betterment surpasses 10bn A.UM.

APRIL 2017

Neobank Monzo receives a full banking license in the UK.

THERE'S NO APP FOR THAT

FIXING THE IPHONE'S FATAL FLAW

I n March of 2008, while Hank Paulson, Ben Bernanke, Tim Geithner, and all the bankers of New York were glued to their BlackBerry phones and the Bloomberg Terminal waiting to see if the failure of Bear Stearns would throw the world into economic collapse, Steve Jobs was onstage at the Town Hall theater of Apple's Cupertino campus, trying to save the iPhone.

The iPhone had been on the market for eight months. During the first weekend of its release, Apple sold 270,000 of them, and by Labor Day, just two months later, that number was up to one million. The media was gushing, and by the time Jobs took the stage in March, the "Jesus phone" had already captured 28 percent of the smartphone market share.

Things weren't exactly going badly for the iPhone.

But it did have one big problem, and the people in the room at Apple's spring event knew it.

It didn't have apps.

When the iPhone launched in 2007, all of its software came preinstalled and hermetically sealed: there was no way for a user to add apps. At the time, Jobs wasn't trying to create a new and revolutionary mobile computing platform; he was just trying to make a better phone. He said this no fewer than five times during the famous 2007 keynote where he introduced the product: "Today Apple is going to reinvent the phone."[1]

Jobs hated the existing market of cell phones. He hated the way they looked, he hated their software, and he hated their clumsy user experience. This sentiment only deepened after Apple tried partnering with Motorola on a phone they called the "Rokr"—a repackaged E398 candy bar phone that could sync with iTunes—which sold so badly that it was removed from Motorola's lineup only a few months later.

"I'm sick and tired of dealing with bozo handset guys," he told his internal team.

He knew he could do better.

In order to compete with other smartphones, Apple's phone would need to have texting, email, a camera, a way to manage its photos, and a web browser—and Jobs wanted all of these features to be better than anything else on the market.

And, because music was a core part of Apple's business at the time, he also wanted this phone to double as an iPod.

Finally, because he was Steve Jobs, he wanted all these things to operate together beautifully.

It was a huge design challenge that the team decided to solve by thinking of the new device less like a phone and more like a scaled-down computer, capable of running a lightweight version of Apple's macOS. But putting a computer in everyone's pocket was a *consequence* of their original goal, not the goal itself.

The goal was simply to make the best phone the world had ever seen.

The team added more hardware to the device, including Wi-Fi and an experimental new touch screen, and they enhanced the phone with other software capabilities—"widgets," they called them: a clock, a calculator, a way to check the weather, a way to check the stock market. They even worked with Google to add a map widget—despite the fact that their device had no GPS.

These were, as far as Jobs was concerned, just extras. "The killer app," he told his audience, "is making calls."

He first unveiled the iPhone at Apple's Worldwide Developers Conference: the people in the room were software engineers, and Jobs showed them a mobile computer platform that was more advanced than anything they had seen. If he had hoped to whet their appetites, it worked.

Then he told them they wouldn't be able to write software for it.

He didn't want anyone other than Apple creating software for the phone. "Jobs didn't trust third-party developers to offer the same level of aesthetically pleasing and stable experiences that Apple programmers could produce," Cal Newport wrote in the *New York Times*. "He was convinced that the phone's carefully designed native features were enough."[2]

Developers disagreed. They saw in the iPhone something that Jobs himself didn't quite yet see: that the untapped opportunities for a mobile, internet-capable computer were enormous. Apple wasn't going to invite them to write software for it, but that didn't mean they wouldn't try to crash the party.

The iPhone released to the world on June 29, 2007—and within a week, hackers had found their way into an iPhone's file system, installed a custom ringtone (something the original iPhone didn't allow), and posted a video on YouTube to prove they'd done it.

The age of iPhone "jailbreaking" had begun. Savvy coders cracked into their phone's software to get it out of the "jail" of Apple's restrictions and to experiment with and personalize the device and invent whatever they felt the out-of-the-box iPhone lacked. Some wanted to unshackle their phone from its exclusive link to AT&T's 2G EDGE network and switch it to another cell provider. Some wanted to add new capabilities—the ability to sync with Windows instead of just Macs or the ability to place calls over the internet. Some just enjoyed the challenge of breaking into the revolutionary technology.

But underneath the jailbreaking was a subtextual message to Apple: "This phone is ours, not yours. There are things we want it to do, and you can't stop us."

A month after the iPhone's release, unsanctioned developers were releasing the first native third-party iPhone apps and posting them online.

"In iPhone iOS 1.0, Apple didn't even have a f#$%ing game, right?" complained software developer Jay Freeman. "Every other phone had a copy of Snake, every phone had a copy of Hangman."[3] Freeman, also known by his hacker name "saurik," soon became one of the most famous jailbreakers of all when, on February 28, 2008, he released Cydia, a centralized platform for distributing and downloading third-party software for jailbroken iPhones. Soon, people were downloading installers for new iPhone features (many of which Apple later adopted, including ringtones, Do Not Disturb, and cut and paste)—and apps. Lots of apps.

Cydia—named after the worm that eats its way through an apple—was, effectively, the iPhone's first "app store."

Apps were new to the iPhone ecosystem, but the idea of them wasn't new to the software community. It was at the core of one of the oldest and most important modern computer platforms: Unix.

The creators of Unix, Ken Thompson and Dennis Ritchie, believed code should be lightweight, modular, and focused, and they designed their system around what came to be known as the Unix philosophy: "Write computer programs that do one thing and do it well."

THE APP MENTALITY
"Write computer programs that do one thing and do it well."

As desktop computers grew more powerful, and as software companies grew more reliant on repackaging their existing product lines, software became subject to "feature bloat," adding more capabilities and complicated code with each successive (and often crash-prone) release.

But smartphones like the iPhone didn't have anywhere near the computing power of a desktop machine, and suddenly programmers were facing new—or, rather, old—technological constraints: limited memory, small screens, and slow download times. If developers wanted to create software that would improve an iPhone, they would need to get back to Unix's original philosophy: think lean, and do one thing very well.

Unix is the platform that sits underneath Apple's own operating system, and anyone writing software for the macOS would have had an inherent understanding of the Unix philosophy.

The Unix philosophy became the app philosophy too.

Apple did everything in its power to fight back against the jailbreakers and the Cydia community: its internal iPhone team kept patching security holes, making jailbreaking harder, and sometimes even "bricking" the jailbroken phones, rendering them not just inoperable but also (because they'd been intentionally hacked) out of warranty.

"We want to make great products," Jobs said, justifying his tight control over the iPhone platform, "not crap like Android."[4]

But after each software patch, the jailbreakers found a new way to crack the iPhone, and the cycle continued. Apple was in an arms race against its own customers. Technology writer Saul Hansell commented, "There is something futile about the way Apple appears to be fighting some of its most ardent fans, those who want to use the full capabilities of the iPhone."[5]

Jobs was losing control of his ecosystem, and he knew it. He decided it was time to get ahead of the curve. On March 6, 2008 (eight days before the final collapse of Bear Stearns), at an iPhone event in the Town Hall theater, Apple released an "SDK," a software development kit that gave its developer community, finally, a legitimate way to write software for the iPhone. Four months later, on July 10 (and a day before the FDIC seized the mortgage company IndyMac), Apple launched the App Store—a way for those developers to distribute their software to iPhone users worldwide.

Steve Jobs had ceded total control. The future of the iPhone and mobile computing was no longer up to Apple. Now it was up to people everywhere—and their imaginations.

Who knew that it would start a financial revolution?

AUTHOR'S NOTE

When I was thirteen, my dad got very sick and lost his job. My family's world, which had been built on the cheap credit of the late 1980s, fell apart. We had to sell a lot of things, I got pulled out of my school, and my glamorous mom traded her sable coat for a polyester apron and took a job stacking boxes at the local supermarket. Dad went on benefits and drove a dry-cleaning truck to make ends meet.

People have faced greater hardships, but the experience left me with a lifetime of anxiety and a particularly complex relationship with money. I panic irrationally about basic things, like toothpaste running out. I buy more groceries than we can eat, I've never had a credit or store card, and my savings are mostly in cash, which means I sat out one of the greatest bull runs in stock market history.

The irony is that I chose to make a career out of telling stories about money, and I've made a lot of money doing it.

And as I've become more successful, the disconnect between my thriving professional interests and my personal financial infecundity has become more acute. I can tell you whether the Fed will raise or lower interest rates, but the thought of interest on a credit card leaves me in a cold sweat. I can explain how mortgage securitization led to the financial crisis, but the prospect of taking a mortgage for myself terrified me so much I wound up renting for ten years longer than I should have. A few years ago, the exasperated cofounder of my company finally stood over my desk and set up a 401(k) for me.

Oscar Wilde said, "Everything in the world is about sex except sex; sex is about power."

Money works the same way. Money is about literally everything except physical units of currency. It's about security, status, family, success, failure, health, and, yes, sex— everything except the numbers in the bank ledger. People are challenged by money not because they can't do basic math, but because they're frozen by their own psychology, by the burden of everything that money represents. Traditional finance works great for those who are born wealthy or financially confident. It sucks for the rest of us.

This book is about a group of people who felt the same.

The entrepreneurs profiled in this book all saw something fundamentally broken about the financial industry, beyond the obvious flaws that led to the crisis of 2008: that it had lost touch with its roots, yet simultaneously failed to keep up with the digital age; that it didn't have a solution for the majority of "regular" people who were struggling with money issues; that, while new tech giants were talking about connecting the world or making it a better place, financial services didn't have a stated purpose beyond simply moving money around or making more of it for fewer and fewer people.

These entrepreneurs—these "money hackers"—are all misfits and outsiders in their own way. Even the ones who have worked inside major financial corporations their entire adult lives were, by virtue of their gender, or color of their skin, or funny accent, playing the outside game.

As a misfit myself, I was drawn to them and I felt that their fascinating personal stories would serve as a neat gateway drug into a deeper exploration of the particular corners of finance they hoped to disrupt. Come for the innovator, stay for the innovation.

I wasn't looking for the first or the most famous name in each of their respective fields (not least because the closer you look for a "first" in technology, the harder it becomes to find: every innovation stands squarely on the shoulders of the innovative giants that came before it—and it's turtles all the way down . . .). I was looking, instead, for fascinating stories that could help tell the larger story of fintech.

But this book does not profess to be the *Encyclopedia FinTechia*. Sadly, I have had to leave a lot of amazing people and entire sub-industries out of the finished book: we didn't have time to cover commercial fintech (Square and Stripe) or the incredible developments in areas like real estate (PeerStreet/ Roofstock) or insurance (Lemonade/Corvus). We didn't talk enough about Europe and barely scratched the surface of China, perhaps the biggest global fintech player of them all.

Being entirely honest, availability was also a factor in deciding who is and isn't in the book. Some of these people were easier for me to reach than others; some were already acquaintances or former clients (though none were clients at the time of writing). I've strived to achieve a balance of voices and personalities, but some of your favorite names may be absent from the narrative, not because they were snubbed but because I'm still waiting for them to call me back.

Finally, they say anything can happen in a New York minute, and I'm acutely aware of the time delay between submitting my manuscript and its publication. Even as I'm writing this, Charles Schwab is announcing their decision to eliminate all fees on trading, creating a new era for online brokerage. I have no clue what will happen to Facebook's currency ambitions or indeed the wider market in Q1 2020. I have no idea if fintechs will take over the banks or be entirely subsumed by them (the latter being objectively more likely).

What I am confident about, though, is that regardless of the eventual fate of these individuals players, many if not most of the ideas that they have unleashed on the financial industry—that finance can serve more than the ultra-wealthy, that our industry should look more like the people it represents, that free can be a profitable price point—will live on inside whoever tomorrow's financial service providers turn out to be.

1 MAKING MONEY MOVE

HOW VENMO BECAME A VERB

When Iqram Magdon-Ismail and Andrew Kortina decided to disrupt the world of finance, it was because Iqram forgot his wallet.

This was 2009, and Iqram was spending a lot of time going back and forth to New York City from where he lived in Philadelphia. The trip was becoming somewhat routine for him: he would spend his weeks working at his day job and then spend his weekends in New York working with his friend Andrew on their new idea.

Iqram had met Andrew when they were freshmen at the University of Pennsylvania. They were randomly assigned together as roommates, and, unlike many of those random pairings, this one was a good match. The two of them shared the same interests and aspirations, and even some of the same computer science classes, so they got used to working side by side. By the time they were seniors, they were collaborating on a small business idea, a college classifieds site they called My Campus Post. They spent their afternoons doing grassroots marketing and their nights writing code. It was an exhausting, exhilarating first taste of the life they both wanted: creating an internet startup.

My Campus Post never took off, but it was a great learning opportunity. Most of all, it taught Iqram and Andrew that they wanted to keep working together. After graduating, they moved to New York and started working as programmers, hopping from startup to startup and collecting experience along the way. Then a company back in Philadelphia offered Iqram a position as vice president of engineering. He took the job, but he didn't want to stop working with Andrew. They'd recently turned their attention to something big, something with real potential—something they were calling "Venmo."

Venmo was a music app.

IQRAM MAGDON-ISMAIL AND ANDREW KORTINA,
"THE ROOMMATES"

They got the idea while they were at a jazz show. The music was so good, but they would never be able to hear it again. Wouldn't it be cool, they thought, if you could send a text message to the band and have a recording of the live show emailed to you?

The idea had promise, but figuring out how to implement it was taking a lot of time—and that meant, more weekends than not, one of them was on a train traveling to meet up with the other for a couple days of brainstorming and coding.

And one particular weekend, Iqram forgot his wallet.

Andrew told him not to worry about it. It wasn't the first time this sort of thing had happened to them, after all. They had been roommates for years, and over those years, they'd lent each other money for drinks, groceries, rent—and they'd always eventually gotten out a calculator, figured out who owed money to whom, and cleared their debt by writing each other checks.

How many times had they done this? Dozens? Hundreds?

But this time, the thought of their old system made Iqram laugh. A check? He wasn't even sure he knew where his checkbook was. He paid all of his bills online.

It was like a relic from a bygone era. If he could find that checkbook, he would scribble the amount onto that bank-issued piece of paper in barely legible handwriting and then have to mail the check to Andrew—which would mean buying a stamp and an envelope and finding a mailbox. Then, when Andrew received the check, he would have to find a bank branch, go there during its business hours, fill out one of those antiquated little deposit slips, and hand it to a bank teller along with some identification. Eventually— after a three- or five- or seven-day hold period—the money would be added to Andrew's account.

"Why are we still doing this?"

In 2009, people were doing everything from their mobile phones—except moving money. Somehow, this most fundamental, basic thing was a capability that hadn't been invented yet.

Why not?

Iqram and Andrew had come across a spot of what technologists and marketeers like to call "friction," the chafe that happens when someone tries to do something that should be easy but isn't. Imagine a visit to the DMV. That shudder that runs down your spine is because of friction.

Friction has been a driving force behind many of life's discoveries and inventions, and Venmo was no exception.

"Let's just try to solve this problem," they decided.

REMOVING FRICTION
"Let's just try to solve this problem."

Iqram and Andrew began work converting their mobile music app, Venmo, into a tool that people could use to exchange money.

Why is it so hard to move money across the internet?

In 2009, moving money on the internet wasn't new. Amazon and eBay had been up and running for nearly fifteen years. Every major retailer had some version of an online shopping cart on its website, and, according to the US Census Bureau, e-commerce was generating more than $130 billion a year in sales.[1]

And e-commerce wasn't just for people with credit cards, either. Banks were issuing debit cards that worked just as well for online purchases.

Why was it straightforward to move money to Amazon and eBay but not to individual people?

PAYMENT GATEWAYS

ONLINE SHOPPING HAS become so commonplace that people don't think about how complicated it is. You hit the BUY NOW button and it works.

Magic.

But there are a remarkable number of complicated steps that go into making that magic, and the steps are collectively known as a "payment gateway."

First, anyone who wants to receive credit card information on the internet has to follow guidelines spelled out by Visa, Mastercard, and the other members of the Payment Card Industry; their technology has to be what is called "PCI compliant."

PCI compliance requires the use of bank-level data security: established cryptographic protocols for encoding sensitive information; safeguards for protecting that information where it is stored; and maintenance and testing to make sure those systems are, and stay, secure.

Bank-level security isn't easy and it isn't cheap. The expense is a justifiable investment for big online retailers, but for small businesses—or for individuals who want to pass money between each other—it is completely out of reach.

And PCI compliance is only one part of the process. Once the credit card data is sent securely across the network, the receiving end has to translate those sixteen numbers into an actual payment. Is this string of data attached to a Visa, a Mastercard, a Discover, an American Express? Before the merchant can check to see if the credit card number is real, verify that it belongs to the person who submitted the order, and confirm there is money available in the account, the merchant must first figure out which credit card company to ask. The software that does this, a "payment switch," interprets the data and handles the connection with the issuing bank.

Then that credit card company—the issuing bank—goes through its own verification process. Debit card transactions get routed through the account holders' banks. Security checks run to protect against fraud.

The average credit card transaction goes through roughly a dozen individual steps before it can be approved—and these steps all happen in the two or three seconds between pushing the Buy Now button and seeing the confirmation screen.

Like magic.

All Iqram and Andrew wanted to do was create an app that could transfer money from a personal bank account to someone else's. Their banks had websites that showed them how much money they had—so they knew this data was already in a digital format. Why was it so hard to access?

And more to the point, why hadn't the banks created this functionality themselves?

One answer is the banks just didn't care. Banks had a long history of developing new technologies, but their idea of innovation was always aimed at making their own processes better and more efficient. Innovating the customer experience wasn't something that would have occurred to them, and even if it had, it wouldn't have been a high priority, least of all during the lean years that followed the market crash.

But for a software developer, creating a good user experience is paramount.

Even if banks had wanted to build a tool for transferring money, it wasn't as straightforward a problem as it might seem. In 2009, according to the FDIC, the United States had just shy of seven thousand banks.[2] Getting the banks to talk to one another was hard enough, but getting their databases to talk to one another—when each one had been built to its own custom specifications—was somewhere between infeasible and impossible. It would have taken a lot of work, and banks had no incentive to do it.

But Iqram and Andrew did—so they got to work.

Building the prototype, it turned out, wasn't especially hard. They were soon passing money back and forth to each other, leaving a long trail of SMS receipts of their transactions: "Iqram 20" quickly evolved into "Kortina paid you $20 for Thai lunch at Nooch."

It was working.

What wasn't working, though, was getting funding.

They took one meeting after another, but couldn't get anyone to take them seriously: they had no track record, no user base, and a prototype cobbled together on top of Google Voice—not enough to reassure a venture capitalist. One investor interrupted Iqram and Andrew's presentation to tell them he was only interested in "billion-dollar, home-run opportunities."

"This will be a trillion-dollar company," Iqram shot back.[3]

The investor wasn't convinced. Most investors hadn't heard of this thing called "fintech," a field that wasn't quite finance and wasn't quite technology. There was no reason to believe that, as a sector, it would be profitable. What was their plan to monetize? How was this little tool for trading small amounts of cash between friends ever going to make a substantial profit?

Iqram and Andrew didn't have clear answers. But that didn't change their commitment to the app. They continued to find ways to make the user experience more seamless, improving it one iteration after another, sending countless text messages back and forth across the system.

Then they noticed something.

Their collection of text receipts was starting to paint a vivid, if accidental, picture of their lives. The list of transactions showed where they liked to eat and drink, what bands they liked to see, who they were spending their time with. Every time someone passed money to someone else, it was because there was something interesting going on—and, collected together, all of this information about a person's transactions started to tell a unique story.

What they had created, by pure accident, was a social news feed.

Venmo wasn't just a way of moving money. It could also be a social network, broadcasting real-time data information about its users.

This could be huge.

If only they could get some money.

BILL READY KNEW a thing or two about money.

He was an unlikely dot-com entrepreneur: he had never even used a computer until he arrived at college. But he was a quick study. He dove into software engineering, and before he turned thirty, he was president of an online bill payment company called iPay. When iPay sold for $300 million, Bill moved on to take over one of the most important internet companies you've probably never heard of: Braintree.

For Braintree, being next to invisible to its users is a feature, not a bug.

Founded in 2007, Braintree became the digital expert at taking all of the various steps that make up an e-commerce transaction—the ten to fifteen different handshakes and data submissions and switches and verifications—and bundling them up so they can be integrated easily into a website.

Bill's goal for Braintree was simple: "How can we democratize access to the tools that have been the exclusive domain of only the biggest e-commerce players and give them to everybody? How do we take the fire from the top of the mountain and give it to the masses to make sure that it benefits the many rather than benefiting the few?"

Braintree's software allowed merchants who wanted to accept payments online to offer their customers an easy, frictionless shopping experience, just as good as Amazon or eBay. Braintree could handle all of the technical and regulatory complexity so that merchants could focus on the products they wanted to sell.

Braintree created, in essence, a plug-and-play shopping cart that the whole internet could use.

For anyone running a small business online, this was revolutionary.

But when Bill took over Braintree in 2011, the company pivoted in a direction that no one else saw coming and created the innovation that would power so much of the fintech and e-commerce we have today.

BILL READY, "THE FIXER"

Bill thought Braintree should start building a platform for mobile shopping.

In the first years of the iPhone, people weren't using them much for shopping. The experience was just too terrible. By 2011, the iPhone had been out for four years and the App Store had been open for three, and three of its bestselling apps were Angry Birds, Skee-Ball, and The Moron Test.[4] The bleeding-edge smartphone of the day was the iPhone 4, which ran on a still-being-developed 3G network that was slow and unreliable. Smartphones weren't being used for serious things, including serious shopping.

If people did want to shop on their iPhones, they had to visit websites that hadn't yet been optimized for mobile—so they would have to pinch and zoom just to see what they were buying. Then they would have to type in their credit card information with their thumbs—all of it: name, billing address, the sixteen digits of the credit card, the CVV number.

By 2011, Amazon had implemented 1-Click purchasing on its site, but generally, websites weren't saving credit card credentials; they were asking users to type in their card information every time they made a purchase. Collecting and storing credit card data always carries some risk, and storing this data with PCI compliance requires ongoing expense and care. There just weren't enough reasons for most vendors to go to all that trouble. As long as people were shopping through their desktop and laptop computers, they had access to full-size keyboards, and typing in their payment details each time didn't seem like much of a bother.

On a mobile device, it was a pain in the ass.

In those rare cases when consumers did go to the trouble of all that thumb typing, they would have to hope that, when they hit the Submit button, the 3G network didn't drop their connection—because if it did, they would have to start the whole transaction over, without knowing whether or not the first one had gone through.

With all those deterrents to mobile shopping, the e-commerce industry didn't believe smartphones were worth the investment of their attention or, more importantly, their money.

Bill Ready thought otherwise.

"I started looking at our traffic logs, and I'd see a half percent, one percent, one and a half percent of our traffic was coming from mobile." He started thinking about Moore's Law, the famous principle that computing power doubles every two years, and he realized: in just a few more years, phones were going to become the main way people did their shopping.

He knew he could have Braintree build out the tools to make this possible—but to justify the company's expense, he also needed customers who would be willing to buy those tools.

And convincing them wasn't easy.

"I would say, 'Someday, people are going to buy TVs and clothing—everything you buy on e-commerce, you will buy on your phone.' And I'd get laughed out of the room."

TRUE BELIEVING

"I would say, 'Someday, people are going to buy TVs and clothing—everything you buy on e-commerce, you will buy on your phone.' And I'd get laughed out of the room."

Bill Ready also didn't have any data to prove his point. He was seeing into a future that hadn't happened yet. "When we did our first native mobile payment APIs, we literally had tick marks on the wall for each transaction. We would literally count them, because there was nobody trying to do that."

It was a vicious cycle: as long as the consumer's experience was bad, people wouldn't shop on their phones. But until people started shopping on their phones, merchants didn't see any need to improve the mobile experience.

Bill knew he was going to have to find a way to break the cycle. He was going to have to improve the customer experience on his own.

Braintree was one of the main go-to companies for any small business that wanted e-commerce, on a mobile phone or not, and the company already had relationships with most of the early mobile winners—Uber, Airbnb, Dropbox, and Angry Birds. All of them told Bill the same thing: their biggest falloff in the customer acquisition funnel—the place where they were most likely to lose prospective customers—was the point where the person had to type in credit card information. As long as they could get customers to enter their card info that first time, then the apps could save the information, so users would never need to enter it again and would be able to make future purchases with the push of a button.

But customers *really* didn't want to enter all that information, even that first time.

Bill knew something that these customers didn't: the credit card information that they thought was being saved by Uber or Airbnb (founded in 2009 and 2008, respectively) or Dropbox or Angry Birds was actually being saved by Braintree. "We had the payment credentials. So, imagine a user that would sign up for Uber, sign up for Airbnb, sign up for Dropbox, go play Angry Birds. They would be asked to reenter their payment information for each app. And that would be this huge pain point in every single one of those apps. But we already had the payment information for that user. We knew who that user was. We had the technical ability to make it such that, when you went from one of those apps to the next app, we could just pop your payment information there if we wanted to—at a technical level."

But Bill knew he couldn't do that. "The user would have completely freaked out."

Braintree had been so successful at making itself transparent to customers, at hiding its brand and its whole existence from the shopper, no one knew that half the e-commerce sites on the internet were running on the platform and capable of sharing payment information across different brands.

"Braintree had millions and millions and millions of credit cards on file and known users and known devices. But what we needed was a consumer network. We needed a way for the consumer to understand when they came to that next app, how in the heck did their payment information become available."

He needed to make his invisible brand visible so consumers wouldn't get freaked out.

He needed a social network.

When Bill found Venmo, it had just three thousand users, all of them in New York—and had roughly that same number of dollars in the bank. The company had just notified its employees that they were planning to shut the doors. "They had run out of money, and they didn't have a monetization model."

But Bill thought they might be exactly what Braintree needed.

Venmo is a "peer-to-peer" service that connects people directly to other people. "There's an inherent virality in P2P services. If somebody sends you money, you sign up. You have a strong incentive." As more people use it, more people sign up—and you build a mass of users who have opted into the service.

Bill imagined merging Venmo's users with Braintree. "That could be a way to go build the consumer network and have people understand how their payment details were available in the next place." If people knew that they had signed up for Venmo, and their Venmo information was suddenly available to them across the entire network of Braintree apps and sites, they would understand that their credentials had jumped from site to site because of their membership on Venmo.

In 2012, he decided that he was going to buy Venmo.

"I had to wire them money to make payroll so there [would still be] employees there when we finished closing the deal."

Bill also knew the key to monetizing the platform. It costs money to send money—to interact with banks and PCI-compliant payment gateways. "Customers don't want to pay for those services. But if you bring a consumer to a merchant, the merchants are happy to pay for those services. That's how payments have been working for a long time. We can monetize from the merchant side of this."

With the addition of Venmo to Braintree's arsenal, the company was able to offer a "push-button" buying experience that would work not just in a single app but across any app that used Braintree's payment gateway—literally millions of merchants.

Mobile shopping was about to get a lot easier.

The following year, Braintree processed $12 billion in e-commerce transactions and a third of them were on smartphones. As Bill had predicted, Braintree was able to monetize Venmo while also rapidly growing its user base.

That's when he got a call from John Donahoe, the CEO of eBay and its subsidiary, PayPal.

In the world of online payment, PayPal was and always had been the giant gorilla. Founded in 1998 and one of the great IPOs of the dot-com boom, the company grew every year after, and by the time Donahoe reached out to Bill, PayPal had 137 million active user accounts and was processing almost 8 million payments every day.

But, like just about everyone else, the company had failed to see the coming importance of smartphones. "We know we need to rebuild PayPal for native mobile," Donahoe told Bill. "We want you to bring your technology here."

PayPal bought Braintree, and Venmo along with it, for $800 million in cash.

As of 2019, mobile payments make up more than 40 percent of PayPal's business: people used it to transfer money over their phones to the tune of $19 billion in the last quarter alone.

With the push of a button.

Shopping and sending money with our phones has become commonplace. This change didn't happen because of banks, though banks had all the technology they needed to do it. It happened because a few people outside of the banking industry saw what the banks weren't seeing, and they seized the opportunity.

But banks see it now.

In 2016, a consortium of some of the biggest banks in the United States—JPMorgan Chase, Bank of America, Wells Fargo, PNC, and others—formed a joint venture called Early Warning Services. The following year, the company released Zelle, a mobile app that lets users send money to other Zelle users—directly competing with Venmo.

Because Zelle has direct access to all of its banks' members, its network has grown quickly, reaching 27.4 million US users and processing $75 billion in payments in 2018.[5]

And because Zelle is operated directly by the banks, it is able to move the money instantly, without Venmo's one-to-three-day delay.

The only thing Venmo has that Zelle doesn't have is a social feed—and to some Zelle users, this is an improvement: many people are resistant to the idea of broadcasting their financial transactions out into the world.

But this, too, might be something that is shifting beneath the banks' notice, because plenty of people—especially younger people—*do* prefer the social feed. "Thirty percent of all Venmo payments use emojis," Bill Ready said of his service, "and that number is growing."

It's hard to know what to make of this. Maybe the idea of an emoji-based social feed that broadcasts our spending is a fleeting moment in history. But it absolutely reflects a fundamental shift in the way our society is interacting with, and talking about, money. Thanks in part to Venmo, there are people who will never walk into a bank branch, because they can beam each other money from their phones. And after centuries of taboo around the idea of talking about finances, people are willingly transmitting this information out to the world. A generation ago, this would have been unthinkable. Even in 2010, it was practically unthinkable.

Cultural change is happening right in front of us, incredibly quickly.

And it's not yet clear if the banks will be able to keep up.

2 GIVING MONEY TO STRANGERS

THE INVENTION OF PEER-TO-PEER LENDING

"**G**ood afternoon. My name is Renaud Laplanche, and I am the founder and CEO of LendingClub."

The 2008 Finovate Conference had assigned Renaud an afternoon slot, right after lunch, and it showed: the handful of people in the conference room at the back of New York's Crowne Plaza hotel were heavy with digestion, drained from their morning, and saving what was left of their energy for the mingling and cocktails that lay ahead.

No matter. Renaud looked out at his small audience with an easy, almost chipper confidence. He clipped the bulky microphone to his blue Oxford shirt and stepped up to the podium.

He had come to Finovate to make a big announcement.

In 2008, the Finovate Conference was in its second year, and, except for the insiders of this nascent industry—the new intersection between consumer finance and technology that some people were starting to call "fintech"—no one really knew what the conference was. Bankers had banking conferences; technologists had technology conferences; Finovate was a conference for the handful of strange misfits who were both and neither.

LendingClub's chief operating officer, John Donovan, had attended Finovate's inaugural conference in 2007 and shown off their just-launched product—something they were describing as "peer-to-peer lending."

But that same weekend, LendingClub's biggest competitor in the new peer-to-peer lending sector, a company called Prosper, did a demo of their own and stole LendingClub's thunder, even winning the title as one of the conference's Best of Show.

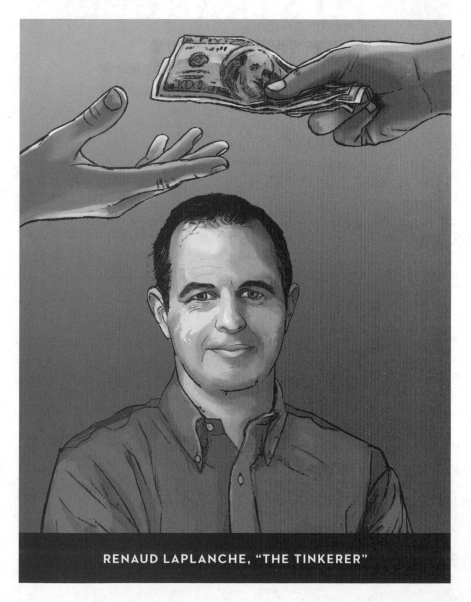

RENAUD LAPLANCHE, "THE TINKERER"

In the months that followed, both companies grew—but Prosper grew faster. Then something happened: LendingClub went silent, while Prosper kept gaining more name recognition and market share.

By Finovate, though, Renaud knew that was about to change.

Renaud had never set out to be a banker or a software mogul, but had always been savvy in business. He had received a law degree from the Université de Montpellier and an MBA from the London Business School, and then he took a job as a securities attorney in the Paris office of the international law firm Cleary Gottlieb, working on mergers, acquisitions, and corporate investments. When the firm sent him to New York for a six-month project, he liked it so much, he told them he didn't want to leave. "There are too many exciting things happening here."

During his years with Cleary Gottlieb, Renaud worked with a lot of tech companies, and the more he learned about them, the more curious he became. He always liked to tinker with things, to see how they worked and to see if he could make them work better. Software and the startup companies that created software both appealed to his tinkerer's mind.

So, Renaud decided to start a tech company of his own.

He cofounded a venture called TripleHop Technologies, which was in the midst of designing enterprise database software when the work was interrupted—on September 11, 2001. TripleHop's office was in the North Tower of the World Trade Center. The attacks destroyed a lot of the company's in-progress software and all of its hardware.

Undeterred, Renaud bought a new set of computers on his credit card, and the company got back to work, releasing such impressive software that Larry Ellison's company, Oracle, soon acquired TripleHop.

Renaud—suddenly a very rich man—found himself with unexpected free time. He decided he'd take a one-year sabbatical and begin coming up with a new business idea.

But it didn't take him a year. Seven weeks after his sabbatical began, he was already at work on the project that would become LendingClub.

·   ·   ·

DISINTERMEDIATION
"When you're an entrepreneur and you see a big spread, you immediately think, 'Big opportunity.'"

"I was on vacation. I was opening my mail. I clearly had too much time on my hands, because I actually read my credit card statement, which is not something I normally do." Renaud noticed, maybe for the first time, that his bank was charging him an interest rate of 18.99 percent. That seemed to him exorbitantly high, "especially considering the low risk I felt I represented to the bank."

The next piece of mail he opened was also from his bank—a statement that showed him his "high-yield" savings account, which he noticed was earning him 0.5 percent yield.

He realized that when he put money into his savings account, he was essentially lending it to his bank for half a percent of interest, and then, when he used his credit card, his bank was lending it back to him at nearly 19 percent—a spread of 18.5 percent.

Where was all that money going?

"When you're an entrepreneur and you see a big spread," Renaud said, "you immediately think, 'Big opportunity.'"

The opportunity that he saw here was an opportunity to *disintermediate*.

He understood that the reason banks were taking such a large margin— apart from greed—was that they needed to cover their infrastructure costs. For a bank to take your money, maintain your savings account, and offer you a credit card, it has to sustain a vast network of branches, tens of thousands of employees, legacy computer systems, ATMs, advertising, and so much more. It's expensive to run a bank, especially a national or multinational one.

But something nagged at Renaud. In this age of technology, where people are paying for transactions on the internet with their credit cards, he wondered how necessary these extensive banking infrastructures really were. Did we really need the branches? Did we need all the employees acting as intermediaries? The old clumsy computer systems?

The more he thought about it, the more he wondered—do we need the bank, at all?

"Would there be a more efficient way to allocate capital between the people who have the money, who put it in a deposit account, and the people who need it, who borrow from the bank?"

It would be much more efficient, he realized, to use technology to connect willing investors directly to people who needed to borrow money—and cut the bank out of the process.

The idea for LendingClub was born.

To understand the insight of LendingClub, it helps to think about how traditional bank lending works—and for that, it helps to remember everyone's favorite banker, George Bailey, from Frank Capra's *It's a Wonderful Life*.[1]

In the movie, George runs a small community bank. When the hardworking people of Bedford Falls want to put their money in a safe place, they take it to George at Bailey Building and Loan. George takes their money and keeps a ledger of how much they've deposited. Periodically, he adds a little extra to their balances in that ledger—interest—as a sort of thank-you to each person for depositing the money in his bank.

When these bank customers have bills to pay and they want some of their money back, they return to Bailey Building and Loan and make a withdrawal. George gives them the cash they want and updates his ledger to show how much money they have remaining.

What the people of Bedford Falls don't fully understand is: *George is not keeping their money in the bank.* The bank doesn't hold the money. "You're thinking of this place all wrong," he explains, when they storm his doors and demand the return of their deposits.

George doesn't keep a vault in the back of his building with all of Charlie's money and all of Tom's money and all of Randall's money stored away for the day that they decide they want to close their accounts. Instead, he keeps only a small portion of that money—his "reserves." It's enough to make sure that he can cover the transactions of a normal workweek, plus a little extra to be safe.

The rest of it, he gives away.

George Bailey's main business isn't holding on to people's money. His main business is selling loans to the people of Bedford Falls. When they need extra cash to cover their rent or to mortgage a house, they come to George and ask to borrow money. He lends them the money they need, and they agree to pay him back over time, plus interest. This interest is how a bank makes a profit. It is how George pays for all of the bank's expenses, and how he pays for his own salary.

So, where does George get this cache of money that he is lending out?

The money is Charlie's money and Tom's money and Randall's money. It's the combined assets of all of the people who leave their deposits at the bank. It's the money that George is *not* keeping in the vault.

"Your money's in Joe's house that's right next to yours, and in the Kennedy house and Mrs. Macklin's house and a hundred others," George tells his customers. "You're lending them the money to build, and then they're going to pay it back to you as best they can."

You are lending them the money, George tells them. The borrower may sign a promissory note with the bank, but George makes it clear to his customers that he thinks of *them* as the investors. George is just an intermediary, a person who draws up the contracts and keeps the ledger.

And George's ledger, that book that shows how much money each person has in a savings account, is not an inventory of the cash sitting in George's vault. It's an IOU to each of the investors.[2]

The idea of peer-to-peer lending is simple:

What if Charlie just lent money directly to Joe?

If borrowers and investors could bypass the bank, then that would mean none of their money would go toward paying for the bank and its infrastructure. By cutting out the middleman, Charlie can offer a loan to Joe at a lower rate than the bank could have offered, and he can make a higher return on his investment than he would have made if he had kept a savings account at the bank. Both of them are getting a better deal if they cut out the middleman.

So why don't we do this?

One big reason is risk. If we lend our life savings to a stranger and then the stranger defaults on the loan, we're ruined—ruined, and probably humiliated for having trusted our wealth to a complete stranger.[3]

This was the first challenge Renaud's idea of LendingClub would have to solve: how to convince potential investors like Charlie and Tom and Randall that peer-to-peer lending would be a good, safe place for them to put their money.

One easy step that LendingClub took to help investors feel safe was to give them the option to diversify their investment. Instead of "peer-to-peer lending," the model became "peer-to-peers." That is, rather than an investor having to give an entire chunk of savings to a single borrower, LendingClub could help spread the investment across a number of different borrowers, lending twenty-five dollars to one person and twenty-five dollars to another. This way, even if one borrower defaulted, the entire investment wouldn't be lost.

Adding this feature to LendingClub definitely helped reassure lenders. But it still didn't get to the real root of LendingClub's problem.

THE POWER OF SOCIAL MEDIA
"We were essentially asking you to lend money to strangers on the internet."

"We were essentially asking you to lend money to strangers on the internet. We didn't present it that way! But that's what we asked people to do. And lending money to strangers on the internet sounded borderline crazy."

People were used to the idea of giving their money to banks. That's because banks have always gone to a lot of trouble to make sure that their customers feel safe. If you look at the names of the old bank buildings on your town's street corners, you'll see the same words come up again and again:

Fidelity.

Security.

Trust.

There's a reason for that. It's the same reason that banks have long been built out of granite and limestone and marble, with architecture that looks like a fortress: people want to believe their money won't be lost.

The infrastructure that banks have been building for hundreds of years has been designed around collecting people's deposits and ensuring that the money can be held safely—with fidelity, with security, with trust.

This has been one big source of banks' infrastructure costs—they have to pay for all of those castle-like bank branches—and, for the most part, this has paid off: with a few notable historical exceptions, people have generally believed their money is safe in the bank.

But a bank's strong walls and reassuring name are mostly just for show. The main thing that the bank does to protect our investments is assess and measure risk.

Banks won't lend our money to just anyone. They lend it to people who they believe are likely to pay back their debts—people who are "creditworthy."

If you go back to, say, a time more like *It's a Wonderful Life*, bank managers knew their customers. These people walked into the bank every week, and whenever they deposited money or took it out, the bank manager would write the transaction into his ledger. This meant the bank had ample opportunity to develop a very holistic understanding of a person's creditworthiness. If someone came to the bank asking for a loan to renovate a restaurant, the bank manager likely knew the restaurant owner, had probably eaten at the restaurant, and had seen firsthand how busy the place was. If it was packed every night and the restaurateur never missed a day of work, then the bank manager could easily assess that this loan would be a safe risk for the bank. But if the place was empty every Saturday except for the owner and his poker buddies, who reliably drank through their inventory of cellared wine, then the bank manager could guess that this loan would be a riskier investment.

Creditworthiness used to be very personal. But as banks grew and became more corporate, they lost their direct day-to-day contact with their customers. People went into bank branches less. When they did go in, they saw a different teller each time, or they used an ATM and saw no teller at all. It became hard, maybe impossible, for bank managers to decide a person's creditworthiness based on personal acquaintance.

Banks needed a more systematic way to gauge whether or not a loan would be a high or low risk. The solution they adopted was credit scores.

In the United States, three main credit bureaus—Equifax, Experian, and TransUnion—track records of every person's borrowing history. They track how much debt we have taken on and how quickly and reliably we have paid back that debt. Based on this data, each credit bureau uses an algorithm to assign each of us a score. For years, credit bureaus experimented with their own patented scoring systems, but now they all share the same one: FICO, a metric introduced in 1981[4] by (and named after) the data analytics firm now known as Fair Isaac Corporation, which assigns people a credit score between 300 and 850.

A person with a higher FICO Score—usually 640 or higher—is considered "prime," very creditworthy.

Anyone with a score below that is considered "subprime."

This FICO Score helps investors estimate the risk presented by any particular borrower. Low-risk borrowers are generally offered low-interest loans, and subprime borrowers usually have to pay a higher interest rate to help offset the risk that they might default on the loan.

By offering a standardized way of evaluating risk, FICO has made it easier for lenders to feel safe about their investments.

But it also has its shortcomings. Because the FICO Score is based only on past transactions, a person who has never had debt has no FICO Score. That person doesn't have a bad credit history, just *no* credit history—making it nearly impossible to get a loan. Someone else, a person who has always had a stable, reliable income and paid the bills on time, might have a high FICO Score—but that score completely fails to tell a prospective lender if this person *currently* has a source of income.

FICO Scores are an accurate measure of what borrowers have done in the past but not necessarily what they will do in the future.

And the score gives no measure at all of what those borrowers are like as people. Long gone are the days when a bank manager like George Bailey could size someone up and say, "I can personally vouch for his character."

KEN LIN/CREDIT KARMA

JUST DOWN THE hall from Renaud Laplanche at Finovate 2008, there was someone else who was thinking about consumer lending and credit scores: Ken Lin, the founder of Credit Karma.

When Ken launched Credit Karma in February 2008, he had one simple goal: to give people access to their credit scores, for free.

"I tried a credit monitoring service and couldn't understand why it was so expensive to monitor my own score. I mean, it was my score. Why should I have to pay for it? With that experience, I set out to find a better way to provide consumers access to their credit scores."

Ken grew up around money, but not in the sense that people usually mean: when he was four, his parents emigrated from China to Las Vegas. His parents worked as dealers at the blackjack tables, and Ken grew up watching people assess risk and borrow cash on the hope of higher returns. In some ways, he has always been thinking about credit.

Through his years working in the credit card industry and online lending, Ken saw that people knew very little about their credit and its effect on their lives. A credit rating doesn't just determine what loans you can get and the interest rate on your credit card. "It is pervasive. It affects everything, from your ability to rent a home to your ability to take out auto insurance."

Ken made it his mission to help people become more aware of their credit scores and how to improve them. Credit Karma offers a Credit Score Simulator to show how certain choices affect a person's credit rating, and it makes targeted recommendations for financial products suited to a user's credit rating. "A good credit score could save average consumers over $1 million in interest over their lifetimes. On Credit Karma, our goal is to show consumers how to optimize their credit scores and achieve those savings."

DEMOCRATIZATION

"The 99 percent are most vulnerable, and that's where technology can really step in."

Of course, like any "simple" idea, launching Credit Karma wound up being not so simple: just days away from the company's public release, Ken almost had to shut the whole thing down.

"It's kind of a funny story . . ."

After a year of nonstop work, in early 2008 Ken and his team launched a beta version of the Credit Karma site—still in testing and only available to a small set of invited users—and then Ken took a quick, much-needed vacation to Thailand.

While he was away, their new site received some unexpected publicity: a write-up in *American Banker*. "We didn't want to have any press. We were still in beta. But it was fine."

But the *American Banker* article led to even more press coverage— and then, while Ken was on his eighteen-hour flight back from

Thailand, someone leaked the registration code to the beta site. Because the site was still in testing, it was sending Ken an email for each new registration. When his plane touched down from Thailand, he had six thousand new messages.

All the hype in the press had also garnered some unexpected scrutiny; without warning, one of the three credit bureaus the site was using to provide consumer credit data decided to terminate their contract.

KEN LIN, "THE ADVOCATE"

Credit Karma was on the brink of launching a site that offered one single service—free credit scores—and a company they contracted to provide the credit scores had decided to pull the plug.

Getting that contract in the first place had been a small miracle. "Nobody wanted to work with us. There was already a proven business model that was generating a billion dollars of revenue, and here we were, a company [saying], 'Oh, we're going to give the service away for free.'"

A lot of Ken's prior year had been spent setting up that agreement, convincing the credit bureaus that his company wasn't a threat to their business model.

But once he got the contracts signed, everything seemed good with the credit bureaus.

Until they read the *American Banker* article.

"We didn't realize you were going to do *that*—give away credit scores for free." They worried that this would ruin their relationships with all of their existing partners, many of whom charged consumers for credit scores.

Ken and the Credit Karma team had never hidden their intentions: they had said up front that they wanted to give credit scores away for free.

"Yes, you put it right in your application," the bureaus told him. "We just didn't read it."

Ken was told he had thirty days until the termination went into effect. Credit Karma had one month to live.

"For twenty days, I called everyone I knew, everyone in the industry, every venture capitalist, every connection I could find, and to no avail." Then he caught a lucky break: someone gave him the name of the person at the credit bureau he needed to contact, the person who could overrule the termination decision.

"I wrote him a cold email. I didn't know him. I said, 'Hey, I'm the CEO of Credit Karma, the service that I think you turned off. I think it's a mistake, and I'd like to tell you why.'"

After seemingly endless minutes, the man wrote back: "Why don't we have breakfast?"

"It was the most sleepless night of my life. We were at seven days from termination. In the morning, I was going to have a meeting that was—it was going to be the only lifeline."

Over the course of that breakfast, Ken was able to persuade the man that Credit Karma would be a valuable customer for many years to come.

"These are amazing partners today," he said recently, looking back.

For Ken and Credit Karma, the credit score is a small piece of something much more important. "When consumers are looking for credit scores, they're actually looking for the options the credit scores provide them." These options may include credit cards, car loans, or the ability to refinance debt. "That's been our niche. We're a technology company focused on the needs of consumers, specifically around their finances."

Since its public launch in 2008, Credit Karma has continued to add other services: the aforementioned Credit Score Simulator; a spending tool that aggregates users' banks info to help them track how their money comes and goes; and online tax preparation—with the promise that all services will always be free.

Renaud wasn't looking to replace the FICO Score: it remained a useful and time-tested way to evaluate risk. But for LendingClub to work, it would need to find a way to build trust between investors and borrowers—to make lending money to strangers on the internet feel less "borderline crazy."

"We decided we needed some sort of connection between people to soften the blow."

What Renaud wanted was a technology that could bring some of that interpersonal, George Bailey–style evaluation back into the lending process, a technology that could use the power of networks to vouch for a person's character.

Luckily for LendingClub, there was this thing called Facebook.

By the end of 2006, Facebook was no longer just for college students; it had opened up registration to the general public, and its user base was growing threefold with every passing year.

By 2007, Mark Zuckerberg and his team were about to expand into something new they called the Facebook Platform. They were developing software libraries that would allow third-party websites to integrate Facebook user data into their own applications, outside Facebook.

Given Facebook's user base—roughly twenty million people—the capabilities of this Facebook Platform were potentially enormous.

But before they rolled it out to the public, they wanted to work with a few handpicked case studies that they could show to the world as a proof of concept—and Renaud approached them about partnering with LendingClub.

"The goal," he explained, "is not to get friends to lend to friends, but to use the Facebook platform to enable lenders to find borrowers within shared networks, like groups or schools. You're not going to lend money to complete strangers. You lend money to a friend of a friend or someone who went to the same school or someone who is in the same small town—some sort of connection."

Facebook liked the idea. They were trying to find ways to differentiate themselves from Myspace, and they wanted to show that the Facebook Platform could be used for something more meaningful than just games.

LendingClub became one of Facebook's first five case studies, and it launched to the public alongside the Facebook Platform on May 24, 2007.

LendingClub's site included a feature called "LendingMatch," which might as well have been a dating site, but for money: it allowed users of the site to browse anonymized profiles of people who were looking for loans, view their relative creditworthiness, see whatever social network connections they shared, and, with the click of a button, authorize LendingClub to initiate a loan.

The site was meant to appeal to borrowers who were carrying a balance on a high-interest credit card. "Credit cards," Renaud thought, "are very convenient payment mechanisms, but they are terrible credit instruments. When you charge a credit card, if you carry the balance to the next month, you'll be paying an interest rate of 17 or 18 percent. We can refinance these balances at an average rate of 12 percent."

On the investor side, LendingClub wasn't looking for high-rolling bankers or hedge-fund managers to do the lending, just any individuals who wanted to get a higher rate of return than they would get on their savings accounts. Investments could start as low as $1,000.

Partnering with Facebook helped Renaud put LendingClub on the map. In its first hundred days, LendingClub helped Facebook users invest and borrow over a million dollars.

But the shortcomings of the platform quickly became apparent.

Facebook in 2007 was growing, but it was still a platform used predominantly by college students and young adults, and it was known mainly for apps like Scrabulous, SuperPoke!, and Mob Wars. This wasn't a place where serious investors were looking to build out their portfolios.

"It was a really good idea in terms of adding PR and really helping us be more successful in the long run," Renaud says. "It was a bad idea in terms of generating loans."

But Facebook was the least of LendingClub's problems. A bigger one was the Securities and Exchange Commission—the SEC, the government body that regulates securities trading in the United States.

Renaud had been thinking a lot about the SEC—mainly because he didn't know what the SEC was thinking about peer-to-peer lending. His industry was so new, no one yet knew how—or if—it should be regulated. This gave LendingClub and other peer-to-peer lenders the freedom to innovate and create a whole new sector from scratch. But it also left them in constant danger of getting blindsided by a regulatory hammer.

Renaud didn't want to run afoul of the SEC—but he also didn't want to kick a hornet's nest if he didn't have to, especially if the government regulators were going to subject his company to laws written in the 1930s that had never anticipated the idea of internet-based peer-to-peer lending. The culture of banking, and especially the culture of Washington that regulated banking, wasn't set up to keep pace with rapidly evolving technology.

"Something I find really interesting," Renaud said, "is the reconciliation of 'fin' and 'tech.' It's almost a dual culture that a fintech company has to reconcile: On one side, [there are] people who are very innovative, who are always thinking of making the world better. And on the other side, [there are] financial services people who understand the constraints that you need to work with, the responsibility that comes with getting people's money, and the compliance and regulatory framework and intellectual rigor that needs to come with a financial services product. Making these two types of people understand each other and work well together is really a key factor of success for any fintech product."

Renaud, a veteran of securities law but also the creator of a very successful software company, was himself a bit of both fin and tech—and, because of this, he decided to pick up the phone and call the SEC. It would be better, he figured, for him to get ahead of this and be a part of helping to create the regulatory framework.

It turned out that he was right to call, because the SEC had a fundamentally different understanding of what peer-to-peer lending was than Renaud did.

LendingClub was originally conceived as a way for lenders to connect with borrowers, plain and simple. In that transaction, the company acted as a matchmaker: it connected the two parties much in the way that Etsy might connect a jewelry maker with a customer. LendingClub didn't own its loans any more than Etsy owns the jewelry that artists sell on its platform.

In the simplest version of peer-to-peer lending, one individual makes a loan directly to another individual. But this isn't a great investment, because it leaves the lender very exposed: if the borrower defaults, the lender loses everything. LendingClub's customers needed the ability to diversify investments, spreading them out across many different borrowers. LendingClub had built this functionality into the platform.

Giving lenders the ability to spread $10,000 investments out into increments as small as $25 was, to LendingClub's thinking, a natural progression of peer-to-peer lending. It didn't substantially change the way Renaud and his team thought of their business; it just made the business safer for everyone involved.

But the SEC saw it differently. From their point of view, as soon as LendingClub split up its loans and started selling them in tranches, the company had stopped acting as a simple matchmaker and had moved into the business of selling securities. This meant LendingClub needed to be regulated like any other securities exchange.

The trouble was, the SEC had no idea how to regulate peer-to-peer lenders. Before LendingClub could file an SEC registration—a complex and time-consuming process under the best of circumstances—the agency needed to decide what the company should register *for*.

Over the next few months, LendingClub worked in close cooperation with the SEC to determine how, exactly, this new industry should be regulated. On June 20, 2008, LendingClub filed for registration with the SEC.

And then they waited.

An SEC filing comes with a mandatory "quiet period," during which LendingClub was unable to do new business. The company's existing loans stayed in place, but LendingClub couldn't take on new lenders until the SEC finished its protracted, bureaucracy-heavy registration process—and there was no assurance that, at the end of this quiet period, LendingClub's registration would be accepted.

Meanwhile, Prosper—which had decided not to register with the SEC—continued to grow.

By the time Renaud stepped up to the podium at the Finovate Conference in October 2008, he knew two things that the rest of the room didn't.

First, LendingClub had just received its completed registration from the SEC and was legally allowed to sell securitized peer-to-peer loans.

Second, none of LendingClub's competitors could say the same thing.

It soon became obvious that Renaud's decision to preemptively approach the SEC had been the right one, because on November 24, 2008, Lending-Club's competitor Prosper was issued a cease and desist order for violating the Securities Act of 1933. This was a costly setback and exactly the sort of thing Renaud had been steering his company to avoid. It took Prosper nine months and $10 million in court settlements to get an SEC registration in place and eventually reopen for business.

There was something else going on in the financial sector during the autumn of 2008: a meltdown. In September, the subprime mortgage crisis had blown open. The investment bank Lehman Brothers, the fourth largest in the world, filed for bankruptcy, setting off a chain reaction that destabilized capital markets in ways that hadn't been seen since the Great Depression. The stock market crashed, the country plunged into recession, and banks were suddenly strapped for cash—and not very inclined to lend it out.

The subprime crisis became a credit crisis.

UNDERSTANDING THE FINANCIAL CRISIS

IF YOU'RE TRYING to understand the rise of "fintech"—that is, if you're trying to understand how technologies like Venmo and Lending Club emerged to change the ways we interact with banks and money—then it's easy to see the importance of the iPhone, the mobile web, and our growing use of social media in bringing about these changes.

It's harder to see the importance of the financial crisis.

The 2008 financial crisis began as a "subprime mortgage crisis." As we learned from George Bailey, mortgage lending is an important part of a bank's balance sheet: banks lend money to would-be home-owners, and homeowners pay this money back with interest, in regular installments that show up as reliable profit for the bank. Mortgages are among the safest loans a bank can make, because the homeowner puts up their house as collateral. Borrowers want to keep their homes, so they do their best to make payments even during times of eco-nomic hardship; and in the event that a borrower does default, the bank comes into possession of the house. Historically, for the bank, this has been win-win.

But during the first decade of the twenty-first century, this changed. Mortgage lenders began offering bigger and bigger loans to more and more borrowers—including people who didn't have the income to pay back these loans.

The reasons for this were myriad. Relatively low interest rates during the 2000s made it easier for people to afford mortgages—including people who might have been priced out of the housing market in a higher-interest environment. The federal government helped push this trend through programs like the Community Reinvestment Act, which was designed to reduce discrimination in mortgage lending by encour-aging banks to make loans in lower-income neighborhoods. Meanwhile, banks, eager to compete for this business, relaxed their lending stand-ards and incentivized their employees to sell more mortgages. This led to more people buying houses, and this in turn drove up housing prices, which then led to even bigger mortgage loans. The cycle fed itself.

These conditions alone would have been enough to create a bub-ble in the housing market, and that bubble would have burst sooner or later. But what made the 2008 crisis particularly and uniquely cat-astrophic was securitization.

Since people tend to pay back their mortgages and since mort-gages are collateralized, these are relatively low-risk loans, and this allowed banks to bundle up large sets of mortgages into something called a "mortgage-backed security," which could be sold to investors with the assurance that they were safe and profitable investments.

The housing boom of the 2000s created a great appetite among investors for these mortgage-backed securities, and to keep up with demand, investment banks created all sorts of innovative investment products—not just bundles of mortgages, but bundles of those bundles, and bundles of *those* bundles. These investment products were bets placed on bets placed on bets—all dependent on the underlying bet that the housing market would continue to rise and that people would continue to pay their mortgages.

Every one of the world's biggest investment portfolios, including retirement and pension funds, were tied up in these bets on mortgage-backed securities.

Unfortunately, the bet was lost. By 2007, subprime borrowers were defaulting on their mortgages in growing numbers, and when the banks foreclosed on these homes, this flooded the market and deflated housing prices.

This didn't just create a problem for homeowners—it created a problem for anyone who was holding a mortgage-backed security. Investors rushed to sell off their mortgage-backed securities only to find there were no buyers. Investment banks discovered that their balance sheets were full of unsellable assets with no practical value—and if they couldn't sell them, that meant banks were also incapable of getting the cash they needed to pay their debts. Almost overnight, every major bank found itself in a liquidity crisis—and the banks caught holding the most mortgage-backed securities and the least cash were looking at immediate bankruptcy.

This is what happened to Lehman Brothers on September 15, 2008—and other banks would have soon followed, if it hadn't been for government intervention. The Troubled Asset Relief Program, signed into effect on October 3, allowed the US Treasury to buy up these otherwise unsellable mortgage-backed securities and injected much-needed liquidity back into the market.

For the banks, these bailouts came at a steep price. First was public sentiment: whatever goodwill banks might have had before the crisis was wiped out when Wall Street received a $700 billion check from the government. According to Gallup, by October 2010, trust in banks had reached a historic low.

But there were tangible costs too. In exchange for the bailout, the government required investment banks to restructure as "bank holding companies"—and that meant the banks would need to set aside a substantial amount of money as a "reserve requirement," just like commercial banks, to prevent future liquidity crises. Money that the banks used to be able to invest would now have to be locked safely away in case of emergency.

The investment banks, which had just taken a haircut of the worst sort, now needed to be a lot more careful in investing the money they had left. The time of high-stakes gambling and risky lending was over; instead, banks became stingy about all but the safest of loans. They were in no mood for innovation. To their thinking, innovation had gotten them into trouble in the first place: the creation of experimental financial instruments that too many people traded but too few people understood. After 2008, banks reasoned that the best way for them to recoup their losses would be to stick with tried-and-true business practices and steer clear of anything that seemed remotely innovative.

During the exact time that Silicon Valley was starting to explore the ways that new, emerging technologies might appeal to everyday banking consumers, Wall Street was focused elsewhere: on itself.

LendingClub found itself positioned to fill a void, both for borrowers, who could no longer get bank loans, and for investors, who were eager to put their money somewhere more lucrative than their now 0 percent savings accounts. During 2009, the rate of return for LendingClub's investors outperformed Treasury bills, CDs, the S&P 500, and the Nasdaq—and people noticed.

Peer-to-peer lending was proving to be a reliable way to make money, and investors—individuals, but also institutional investors like pension funds and asset managers—put more and more of their money into LendingClub. In 2010, the company issued more than 2,500 loans worth over $126 million. The following year, those numbers jumped to 21,721 loans and $257 million, and the year after that, they more than doubled again: 53,367 loans worth almost $718 million.[5]

Other peer-to-peer companies emerged to service distinct sectors of the lending marketplace: SoFi for student loan refinancing; Kabbage for small business loans; PeerStreet for real estate. Combined, the peer-to-peer lending sector in the United States brought in over $3 billion of revenue in 2018.

An industry that didn't exist in 2006 has become a significant part of the global economy.

KATHRYN PETRALIA'S MODELING CAREER

KATHRYN PETRALIA WANTED to become an English professor; instead she became (according to *Forbes*) one of the most powerful women in the world.[6]

Kathryn is cofounder and head of operations at Kabbage, a fintech lending company that was created in 2008 and is now worth more than $1.2 billion.[7]

Kabbage has thrived by providing quick, easy business loans up to $250,000. As a rule, small businesses depend on loans and lines of credit for "working capital"—the cash they need to, say, purchase inventory, cover payroll, and invest in growth while they wait for their own payments to come in. Without liquidity, it's hard for any business to maintain its operations.

But banks had trouble making money on small business loans. The biggest reason was paperwork: vetting a business, determining whether or not it was creditworthy, and ascertaining the risk of each loan took time—and from a bank's perspective, this time was better spent offering larger and more profitable loans to bigger companies. Small businesses, even creditworthy ones, were left largely underserved.[8]

This created what entrepreneurs like to call a "white space," an unmet need in the marketplace—and it was one that Kabbage rushed to fill.

Any sort of small business might need to borrow money, but when Kabbage launched, it focused on a very specific kind of small business:

eBay vendors. "An underserved market inside an already underserved market," Kathryn said.

The reason was data. In 2008, eBay was fighting against counterfeiting and fraud on its platform, and the company built software to allow third parties to view the real-time transaction data of its sellers—to see how long a merchant had been selling on eBay, how many satisfied or dissatisfied customers it had, the growths and slumps in the

KATHRYN PETRALIA, "THE READER"

business, and so on. eBay released this data to help buyers on the site assess the risks of making a purchase from any particular vendor.

When the founders of Kabbage saw this wealth of data, they wondered if they could take it a step further: Could they use the eBay data to assess the risk of lending to these vendors? Could they use the eBay data to make automated, algorithmic judgments about the creditworthiness of the businesses—and begin offering loans?

It turned out they could.

"Only because of that data," said Kathryn, "were we able to serve a population that was previously unserviceable."

Figuring out how to use the data wasn't easy. Though Kabbage was able to access businesses' complete eBay history, that didn't make it obvious which businesses would be able to pay back their debt and which ones wouldn't. There was no existing model for how to translate an eBay vendor's data into a measure of creditworthiness. Kabbage had to build one from scratch.

The way to do that, Kathryn explained, is "you get a lot of people not to pay you back." Kabbage's early years were spent making educated guesses about who would or wouldn't pay back their loans. "Our first model was a simple formula that even I, an English major, could have written."

The Kabbage team lent out money and waited to see how good their guesses had been. Whenever a business had trouble repaying, the team knew they had guessed wrong—but each failed loan represented new data—and new data provided a new opportunity to learn. "You can't build a risk model without giving some bad loans. So, you risk-adjust the pricing, and you keep going, and then you see performance improvements," she said. "That's it. That's all there is to it."

Before long, Kabbage had created data models that allowed the company to offer profitable loans to eBay vendors—some of the smallest, most volatile, and least predictable businesses in the marketplace. "If you can make a portfolio of eBay businesses profitable," Kathryn said with a laugh, "you can frankly do just about anything."

From there, the company expanded to include Amazon vendors and then brick-and-mortar businesses too. Each time Kabbage added a new set of customers, that meant new sets of data—and this new data resulted in the design of even better models. "Now we have all kinds of machine learning and a team of data scientists rounding out the edges, making it better. This helps us extend into new markets and offer better pricing—and our pricing has certainly come down to customers; that's one place where you see all of those analytic skills bearing fruit."

All this data modeling has led Kabbage to some surprising discoveries. "Social data is more predictive than credit data," Kathryn said. "Our customers use Facebook the way big businesses use Salesforce, as a customer-relationship tool. They use [social media] to communicate product information and promotions and resolve disputes—so it's a measure of reciprocal engagement. A lack of activity is potentially negative, and a lot of activity is potentially positive," she explained. "I would never make a stand-alone decision on Facebook data; but our data finds tended to build a stand-alone Facebook model that was more predictive than a stand-alone FICO model."

Sometimes the patterns identified by the machine learning are easy to understand, and sometimes they're not. "We built a UPS model that is more predictive than FICO, and we found this funny thing: our customers who were shipping to California addresses were better businesses than those who weren't. There are like eighty million reasons why this could be."

The data doesn't lie, but it also doesn't tell a complete story. "You want to understand why. Letting the machines do all the work unsupervised is problematic. You need somebody who can correlate the results you're seeing with the real cause that's in the world. Ultimately, it's a human thing," she said, like an English major. "You have to read to understand."

Letting the machines do *some* of the work has allowed Kabbage to automate many of its processes: most Kabbage customers are approved for loans and given access to funds in under ten minutes. This automation has cut the company's administrative costs and allowed it to do what banks were unable or unwilling to do: make big profits on small-business loans.

But has the peer-to-peer lending industry lived up to its promise?

No doubt, it has resulted in better rates for its investors and for its borrowers during historically low-yield years.

But to ensure those high rates of return, most peer-to-peer lenders have turned away all but the safest borrowers: LendingClub declines 80–90 percent of its loan applicants,[9] and the average FICO Score of its customers hovers somewhere around 700. These are people who could get loans anywhere. Meanwhile, people with poor credit—the people who have been most underserved by banks and might have benefited most from alternative forms of lending—won't find much recourse in LendingClub and its peers.

And as LendingClub attracts more institutional investors, it strays further from its original idea of "social lending." In 2007, LendingClub might have been a place where Charlie could lend money to Joe. Now it's more "H2P" than P2P: a place where hedge funds and banks can invest in low-risk, high-yield securities. The company's board members include former Treasury secretary Larry Summers, former Morgan Stanley CEO John Mack, and former Visa president Hans Morris. The culture has become decidedly more "fin" and less "tech."

In May of 2016, LendingClub's two cultures of fin and tech collided spectacularly when the company's board announced that they had "accepted the resignation of Renaud Laplanche as Chairman and CEO."[10]

The circumstances of this decision were a bit convoluted. Days before the release of a quarterly earnings report, an internal investigation started by Renaud himself revealed several irregularities that alarmed the board. First, LendingClub had sold $22 million in loans to the investment bank Jefferies, despite the fact that these loans didn't meet the bank's required specifications. "The financial impact of this $22 million in loan sales was minor," the board said in its statement—but, especially on the eve of the earnings report, they wanted to avoid anything that gave even the appearance of irregularities. "A violation of the Company's business practices, along with a lack of full disclosure during the review, was unacceptable to the board."[11]

The probe also alerted the board that Renaud was invested in a fund called Cirrix Capital, a vehicle that owned $114.5 million of LendingClub loans. Renaud had disclosed this investment to the proper channels within his company, though some members of the board were caught unaware by the probe's findings and claimed he hadn't. Again, LendingClub's board of directors worried about the appearance of impropriety. They decided that, for the good of the company, the company's founder should resign.

The experience was "incredibly frustrating and disappointing," Renaud said, made up mainly of "mistakes and miscommunications."

Mark Zuckerberg coined a motto to describe Facebook's—and much of Silicon Valley's—innovation: "Move fast and break things." This motto has been a driving force behind a lot of the decade's fintech: try something that has never been done before, see how it works, and fix it whenever it breaks. But moving fast and breaking things is anathema to bank regulators, whose job is to ensure that the financial system doesn't get broken. They prefer to "walk slow and play safe"—and this thinking becomes part of the culture of bank executives, even the ones who wind up joining growing fintechs.

This brings us back to Renaud's explanation about the need to reconcile "fin" and "tech." "When you innovate in a regulated industry," Renaud explained, "you are faced with a set of regulations that weren't meant to apply to what you are doing. They were meant to apply to things that were entirely different, because what you're doing didn't exist previously. So, it's a lot of trying to put a square peg into a round hole."

This is a big part of what seemed to happen during his last weekend as LendingClub's CEO. "There were a series of decisions being made in the heat of the moment by people who were applying, I think, the wrong framework. Instead of applying the innovation framework to problem solving, which was, 'Oops, we broke something; let's fix it,' and then learning to make sure it didn't happen again, they applied the framework of bank regulators and Wall Street, looking for fraud and conflicts of interest. I think there was none of that."

Days after LendingClub announced Renaud's resignation, the SEC opened an investigation to look into the series of incidents, and Renaud eventually made a settlement with the agency that neither admitted nor denied wrongdoing. "I am glad," he said in a statement, "that we can now put these issues behind us and focus on the important goals of making credit more affordable to consumers."[12]

One way that he is moving on: he has founded a new online lending company called Upgrade. "We had a long list of things where we said, if we had to do it all over again, we would do it differently—all the learnings over the last ten years, all the feedback we got from the investors, borrowers, partners. There was enough there that we thought, yeah, it's worth building a new platform from scratch."

Silicon Valley might think of it as a "Version 2.0."

Many of LendingClub's original backers jumped at the chance to support Renaud's new venture: Upgrade's $60 million series A funding was the largest ever for an American fintech startup. Notably, the very first company to buy loans from Upgrade was the investment bank Jefferies—the bank that had bought the problematic loans that led to Renaud's removal from LendingClub.

These days, Renaud is more keenly aware of the cultural differences between West Coast innovators and financial regulators. "At Upgrade, we have this amazing chance of getting a better balance, not just in terms of people and culture but also operating principles and processes."

He likes running fast—but that doesn't mean he's eager to break things. "Banking is regulated for good reason, so it's really important to get that balance. A lot of younger fintech founders don't necessarily have the benefit of our dual culture and seem to underestimate the importance of regulations, compliance, and so on."

BALANCING INNOVATION WITH REGULATION

"Banking is regulated for good reason, so it's really important to get that balance. A lot of younger fintech founders don't necessarily have the benefit of our dual culture and seem to underestimate the importance of regulations, compliance, and so on."

His story is a cautionary tale to any in fintech. "I am worried," he said, "that these issues might repeat themselves."

3 AGGREGATE AND AUTOMATE

FRESH-MINTING PERSONAL FINANCE MANAGEMENT

When Aaron Patzer was twenty-five, he decided he wanted to disrupt an industry he hadn't previously given much thought.

Aaron had gone to college—Duke—for a triple degree in computer science, electrical engineering, and computer engineering. Afterward he'd enrolled in an engineering PhD program at Princeton. He'd gotten as far as passing his "quals," the qualifying exams that decide whether or not a student can continue in the program, when he met Sandy Fraser.

Alexander G. "Sandy" Fraser had been the chief scientist at Bell Labs, the storied research company responsible for inventing, among many other things, the transistor, the laser, and the UNIX operating system. Fraser had recently left Bell Labs to start his own company, Fraser Research—and he offered Aaron a job.

The offer, and the peek into Sandy's remarkable life, helped Aaron to see that he didn't want to be an academic; he wanted to be an entrepreneur. He dropped out of Princeton to start work in the private sector. "It was probably the best move I ever made."

Entrepreneurship wasn't new to him. He had created his first company when he was sixteen, building websites to save up money for college. He'd learned the ins and outs of running a business, sometimes the hard way: "I was sort of comingling my personal and business finances." To get better organized about his money, he did what any tech-savvy kid in 1997 might have done: he went to the store and bought a copy of Quicken.

Quicken, the personal finance software created by Intuit, was one of the first consumer fintechs—a fintech before anyone called it "fintech." First released in 1983, it launched with two separate and completely incompatible versions, one for MS-DOS (because this was before Windows) and one for the Apple II

AARON PATZER, "THE AUTOMATOR"

(because this was before the Macintosh). Quicken was essentially a spreadsheet that people could use to enter and track their finances, adding labels for different categories to help get a better handle on their spending habits.

"I was pretty religious about it," Aaron said. "I would manage my finances every Sunday afternoon for about an hour each Sunday to make sure all of my accounts would balance." He kept this up—week after week, year after year, all through college, and during his jobs with Fraser Research and IBM.

Then he started working at a startup called Nascentric, and he got busy. Very busy.

"I was working eighty to a hundred hours a week, and I didn't open Quicken for probably five months." By the time he went back to the software and imported his bank data, it was a total mess. "I could see all my transactions, true, but in order to see where my money went, I had to sit there and categorize almost every one of them." Quicken had a feature that was supposed to be assigning a category (groceries, utilities, travel, etc.) to each transaction automatically, but more often than not, the software would assign the wrong category, requiring the user to undo all of the automated work and redo it by hand.

"At this point, I could have invested an afternoon into categorizing transactions. But . . . I took a different tact: I started a company to make personal finance effortless."

That was the impetus behind Mint.com—to create an alternative to Quicken and Microsoft Money that was easy to set up and easy to use, where the automation actually helped people instead of just promising to help people.

By 2006, Aaron was at work on the idea. First, he mulled over the problem of transaction categories with his engineer's mind and realized, "I could categorize these transactions much more accurately by using the Yellow Pages." He wasn't being sarcastic: the phone book was essentially a list of vendors, already sorted into different categories. "I got a database of twenty million merchants and got the categorization accuracy to about 90 percent."

What he didn't have was the other part of the puzzle: people's personal bank data. For his new website to be actually useful, he was going to need to connect it to real-life data—and he had no idea how to do this. How do you get access to privileged bank information?

Banks wouldn't give access to their customer data without a customer's permission. So, if he was going to have customers, he would need to earn their trust the same way Intuit had and get the customers to provide him with their private account info.

Solving that trust issue wouldn't be easy—but that problem seemed small to Aaron compared to the larger problem of the data itself. Even if he could get a customer to provide him with access to a bank account, he would have to write software that was able to retrieve that data—and the software would only work for that one bank. In 2006, the United States had over seven thousand banks, and most of them had their own proprietary software systems, each one a little different.[1]

So this wasn't a problem Aaron would need to solve once. It was a problem he would need to solve seven thousand different times.

His heart sank. Even if it were possible, it would take years. It could take a decade.

That's when he learned about Yodlee.

BY THE TIME Aaron Patzer was thinking about Mint, Yodlee had been at work for just under a decade. During the early years of the dot-com boom, Yodlee's founders—Venkat Rangan, Sam Inala, Srihari Sampath Kumar, P. Sreeranga Rajan, Ramakrishna "Schwark" Satyavolu, and Sukhinder Singh—worked at software giants like Microsoft and Amazon and also in academia. Between the six of them, they had more than eighty published works and thirty patents.[2]

In 1999, they got together to try something different.

The internet had become, during recent years, an enormous sprawl, growing from under three thousand websites in 1994 to over three million by 1999.[3] People were coming to rely on dozens of different websites for the information they were using to navigate their daily lives. The team at Yodlee wanted to create a place where all of this diverse, fluid, ever-changing information could be gathered in one single place. "Instead of a user going to over a dozen sites," Rangan said, "we make sure these sites come to you."[4]

Yodlee was an early entrant into an emerging field called "aggregation."

According to the company's longtime CEO, Anil Arora, "Where Yodlee really innovated was this idea of software bots, very similar to the crawl agents that search companies like Google use, software agents that mimicked what a consumer would do." The Yodlee founders studied hundreds of sites to see how data was being displayed, and then they created software agents to "scrape" data from various websites and deliver that data to a single aggregated website where a user could find relevant information consolidated in one customized place.

"It was meant to grab all your personal data," Yodlee founder Sukhinder Singh said. "Your frequent-flier miles were scraped. Your bills were scraped. Your bank account information was scraped. Any rewards programs you had. If you had an account, Yodlee could scrape it."

SUKHINDER SINGH, "THE CONNECTOR"

The effect would be to create a single dashboard where users could go, a page that would cut through the internet maze and become people's default starting point every time they logged on to a web browser. "If Yahoo is your source of all your news information, Yodlee's the source of all your personalized information," Singh described. "That was the original plan for the company."

That plan didn't last long.

Teaching software agents how to scrape, interpret, and redisplay so many different kinds of data from so many disparate sources was very labor intensive and not inherently lucrative. But Yodlee found one sector that wanted to implement this technology—the financial sector.

"We had this small competitor out of Atlanta called VerticalOne, and we knew that they were in conversations with Citigroup and Intuit about being a white-label aggregator for those companies," Singh said. "What happens if we don't pitch for that business? What happens if they win Citigroup and they win Intuit? Then we're here on this consumer vision, but they're going to have a leg up on us."

Why would a bank hire a company to scrape its own customer data?

By the turn of the millennium, banks were already deeply invested in computer technology: they had been using custom-built "core banking" software to manage their customer transactions for as long as thirty years. As their products and needs evolved, so did the software, and the banks—especially the bigger banks—were staffed with vast teams of computer programmers who maintained these complicated, aged systems, year after year. Any update or revision to a bank's software had to be done without breaking the software's legacy functionality, so the code grew more complex and arcane, with workarounds built on top of workarounds that made future revisions even more difficult.

In short, the banks were stuck with decades-old platforms that were getting harder to use and harder to change.

But the technology that Yodlee was developing—the ability to scrape a webpage and parse its content—offered the banks a kind of fresh start, a way to get clean data from their messy systems without having to do an expensive and complicated overhaul of their underlying software.

"If you wanted to be in a long enterprise transformation project, you could spend hundreds of millions of dollars at the bank to go build systems integration to marry up all your customer records," Singh said, "or you could just take

Yodlee and, say, go through the front end. If you can get consumers to give you their passwords, awesome, and go scrape the data."

Yodlee got the Intuit contract, and then the Citigroup contract too. "We were off to the races. We became an enterprise company *de facto*."

And it really did become a race—because banks didn't just want to see customer bank data from their own systems. They also wanted to see the accounts that their customers had at other banks.

"The average US consumer," Yodlee's former CEO, Arora said, "has fourteen different accounts. You get a checking account. You may have a savings account. You typically have six credit cards, on average. You get a mortgage. You get an auto loan. You start saving for retirement through a 401(k). You get an investment account. You have kids and you start saving for your kids' education. And so on. You have pieces of your financial life fragmented all over the place." This is what analysts at Forrester call the "fractured banking model."

WHOSE DATA IS IT?

"The average US consumer has fourteen different accounts. . . . You have pieces of your financial life fragmented all over the place."

Citigroup wanted to get a more complete view of its customers' total financial life, and this required data not just from its own sites but also from its customers' accounts at the other banks too. "Why would a bank want to see what accounts you have at other places?" Singh asked, rhetorically. "You know why. Because theoretically, if they know they don't have your credit card business, they can go sell it to you."

But why would customers give Citigroup the login info to all of their *other* bank accounts? It was for the same reason they might have given that earlier version of Yodlee access to their frequent-flier accounts and their billing accounts and their reward programs: because it was much more convenient to see it all in one place.

"The people who hated Yodlee were like, 'Wait a second. You're taking my customers' data and you're putting it somewhere else? Isn't that illegal?' And we would say no: the consumer has signed up to these terms of service. You think you control consumers' data, but they control their own data, and they are going to decide on what site they want to aggregate it. If consumers decide they want to take advantage of Citigroup's service to aggregate data, and they put in a password and they set it up . . . then wherever they want to see a picture of it, on whatever third-party site, that's okay."

Citigroup believed that having access to its customers' other accounts would ultimately benefit the customers too: if you were willing to show Citigroup all of the loans and credit cards you had with other banks, then in turn Citigroup could offer you better loans and credit cards.

"That seminal offering was very disruptive," Singh said. "If no bank had wanted it, Yodlee would never have existed. But if one bank had Yodlee's technology, then it became an arms race, because if you're Citigroup and you can use data aggregation to understand your customers' financial relationships with other banks, does Bank of America think that's an acceptable outcome? No. Now [Bank of America needs] technology to do the same thing."

As a result, the first few hundred of Yodlee's customers were banks.

It turned out, even when a bank *wanted* Yodlee to access its data, the data was a bit of a mess. "There were billions of variations of the data," Arora remembered. "You could have a single stock, let's say Microsoft. One company would say: 'Microsoft.' Another one would say the ticker symbol, 'MSFT.' Another one would have Microsoft's CUSIP number. Another one would say: 'MSFT Company.'"

Then there was the problem of volume. "There were thousands of banks, and many banks had dozens of different products and account types. Large banks, on average, had fifty, sixty different types of accounts: one for mainstream users, one for wealthier clients, one for private banking, one for credit card users, one for mortgage users, one for auto loan users, and so on and so forth. So, it's thousands of banks, but hundreds of thousands of account and product types. And we had to cleanse and normalize all of this data."

This took a lot of work. For the next four years, Yodlee worked around the clock building out this massive capability, and they got very good at programming bots that could scrape a bank's account page and translate the information on it into useful data.

Then, a funny thing happened.

Every minute of every day, Yodlee's software bots were crawling the web-sites of banks to scrape data—and this started to put a tremendous opera-tional load on these websites. The banks had no choice but to keep increasing their capacity for web traffic, buying and installing web servers and paying for more bandwidth.

Since many of these banks were also Yodlee's customers, they were having regular conversations with the software company about this growing prob-lem—the ongoing drain on their web servers and need for expensive band-width—and, eventually, Yodlee suggested a different solution: "Why don't we *not* do software crawling? Why don't we build a direct connection to your database?"

Up until then, Yodlee had been taking the long way around the block to get to the customer data, scraping the front end of a bank's website, where the data was displayed, instead of going straight to the data itself.

Now it was asking to enter through the front door.

Initially, the banks resisted the idea: giving Yodlee access to their customer-facing websites was one thing. Giving it access to their back-end da-tabases was something else altogether. But, Arora argued with them, Yodlee was going to keep collecting this data either way; the company was under con-tract by the banks themselves to do it. So, the banks might as well offer a more direct way to do so.

Consequently, Yodlee evolved most of its work away from scraping and to-ward "APIs."

An API—"application programming interface"—is software that allows one website or database to interact directly with the data from another web-site or database. Using an API to get bank data directly from the bank was faster, more efficient, and less error prone than the scraping that Yodlee had been doing to retrieve its data. APIs allowed Yodlee to draw directly from the source, like collecting water straight from a well instead of from an old rusty faucet.

It's impossible to overstate the importance of APIs on the growth of fintech and on the internet more broadly as we know it today. APIs are the tools that allow useful information to get passed around and used in different contexts—granting remote websites the ability to retrieve data feeds or complete transac-tions across different websites.

Yodlee still had the problem that every bank was using a different data system—and each data system would require a unique API. The task of creating these APIs was extraordinarily labor intensive. But by now Yodlee had long relationships with the banks and could work with each bank directly to learn how its system was put together.

What really sold the banks was when Yodlee assured them that they wouldn't have to change a thing about their own internal systems. "The prior attempts by Microsoft and Intuit focused on trying to establish standards," Arora said of earlier efforts to get the banks to share their data back and forth. "We at Yodlee said, 'It doesn't matter what format your standard is. You, as a banker, won't need to invest in redoing your entire technology or database platform. We can take your data in whatever format it's in, and we'll do the dirty work of taking all the different formats and all the different standards and normalizing them.'"

Bank by bank, they came around and hired Yodlee to develop APIs. With slow, diligent work, Yodlee built up the tools to retrieve customer data—always with the customer's permission—from nearly all of the country's banks. Yodlee then reformatted the data so it was in one standardized, "normalized" format, which, using the APIs, could be aggregated, passed around, and shared with other apps. "Around 2003, it really started moving," Arora says. "Now it's somewhere between 70 and 85 percent of our banking data comes from direct data feeds."

Yodlee's complex data puzzle was, more or less, solved.

"What happens when you take away the back-end pain? What happens when a service like Yodlee on the data side makes the back end easy?" Singh pondered. "All of the innovation shifts to the front end."

That's when Yodlee was contacted by a startup called Mint.com.

JASON PUTORTI FIRST heard of Mint.com in 2006. He had just moved to the Bay Area from Pittsburgh when a man he met at a café offered him a job.

The man was Noah Kagan, and he was Mint's first head of marketing.

"Uh, okay," Jason answered. "Maybe."

By the time Jason joined Mint, Aaron Patzer had moved the young company out of his living room and into an office in Sunnyvale. Jason became Mint's fifth employee. "I basically came in and I didn't really even know what my role was going to be." In Pittsburgh, he had been running his own web design shop and doing everything—designing, coding, creating databases, making billboards, whatever needed to be done. "I showed Aaron my work, and he pegged me as a designer, so I became a designer."

A designer was what Mint needed.

Ever since Aaron had found Yodlee and licensed the use of its bank data, he had been working on the part of the project that was his area of expertise: its algorithms. He coded ways to process a user's data, categorize it, and parse it out into the sort of dashboard he had always wanted from Quicken. He built this into a working prototype that could spit out real data, and he was using the prototype to demo Mint to potential investors.

"But it was a pretty rough product," Jason remembered. "It was pretty busy. It was really a proof of concept prototype." Aaron asked him to "skin" the website—to "make it prettier, because we know that it looks terrible right now."

"That's such an engineering thing to say," Jason said with a laugh.

He started to deconstruct the prototype and think about it conceptually, to think about the real goals of the site. The goals of the site were a big part of why Jason had agreed to start working with Mint in the first place, even before he knew what his role would be. "Mint's fundamentals to me made a lot of sense. There was real value being created. It solved a real problem." He wanted to come up with a design that lived up to the promise of Mint's original idea. "If you can't fundamentally and easily answer the questions that the users have or give them actual insight and real value, then you haven't really done anything, right?"

USER-CENTERED DESIGN
"If you can't fundamentally and easily answer the questions that the users have or give them actual insight and real value, then you haven't really done anything, right?"

But the more he dug into the prototype, the more he felt that a simple visual update wasn't going to do the trick.

"Adding all of your bank accounts was really important," Jason knew. So, the first challenge the site was going to face would be to persuade customers to enter in their confidential banking information. Once they entered their data, customers could easily see the value of Mint firsthand. But if the site couldn't convince them to type in their information, then it would never work.

How were they going to earn the user's trust?

"Trust comes from a number of different places," Jason said. "Number one is brand. You go to the Citigroup website, 'Okay, I know Citigroup. They've been around for a hundred years.' We didn't have that. We didn't have the one-hundred-year-old brand to fall back on. So, people tend to judge credibility and professionalism on appearance."

But in 2007, when Jason was designing Mint, the brand of the old banks wasn't exactly synonymous with "trust." This was the beginning of the subprime mortgage crisis. That same summer, a mostly unknown Harvard law professor named Elizabeth Warren published a paper arguing that the United States needed a "Consumer Financial Protection Bureau" to crack down on some of the rampant predatory practices of the financial industry. The sentiment about those hundred-year-old banking brands was changing at the precise moment that people were gaining trust in companies like Amazon, LinkedIn, and Facebook.

This created a real opportunity for a young, innocent tech company with a cheery populist design. Jason had no way of knowing what was around the corner—the collapse of the financial sector, the bailouts, and the complete depletion of people's trust in the banking system. But he knew the feeling he needed Mint's web design to convey—something that mixed the clean professionalism of the banks with a friendlier, kinder, and more human aesthetic.

This wasn't going to be a "skin." This was going to be a complete redesign.

He went back to the team and convinced them that they would all need to rebuild the user interface from scratch. This was a big ask: the site was scheduled to launch as part of TechCrunch40—a contest between seven hundred different startups hoping to win a high-profile $50,000 prize. That was in September. It was already March. That meant just half a year to come up with a visual identity, a new interface, and all the computer code they'd need to make it work.

But Aaron could tell that Jason understood the true intentions of the site and gave him the go-ahead.

Jason started with the color green. The prototype had been built in a deep, dark green—the color of money. Jason knew it didn't feel quite right. "I actually hate the color green. Like forest green just turned me off aesthetically. So, I'm like, all right, we've got to make this a little lighter, a little more approachable. I did a lot with airbrushing and tried to give it a calmer feel." After some trial and error, he found a shade he liked, and he used it as the centerpiece of Mint's new visual identity.

Then he moved on to the user interface. "We needed to build a UI that, in initial setup, encouraged people to add multiple cards at the same time before the first one finished. Otherwise you'd end up waiting a really long time, and people could bounce out. If there's any kind of friction, people will just leave. So, getting people to flow through the setup really quick was maybe the most important design challenge there was."

Some of this needed to be solved at the engineering level: the site needed to be able to support the simultaneous addition of different accounts. But the design also needed to make it clear to users that this was an option.

"I came up with a clickable card, which would just keep encouraging you to add. There are a bunch of empty slots, and there's big text on the card saying 'Click me, click this one, click that one.' People would just keep doing it, and they finally understood that you could do a lot at that same time."

He worked through the entire site like this, trying to anticipate and solve for every user need and bit of friction. "We actually removed a lot more than we added. It was about making a smaller feature set that was easy to understand, easily digestible." He streamlined the user experience with the "app mentality" so that Mint would to do one thing, very well—accept people's banking information and aggregate it clearly and simply.

The site launched, as scheduled, in September 2007, as part of the inaugural "TechCrunch40" event. It survived the first round of the contest and advanced into the top fifty semifinalists, and then it went on to win the overall competition. It quickly gained fifty thousand new users and kept growing up to a hundred thousand by December.

By the time Mint presented at the Finovate Conference in 2008—the same conference where Renaud Laplanche launched Lending Club and Ken Lin launched Credit Karma—the site had already won raves from PCWorld, *PC Magazine*, the Webby Awards, and *Time* magazine (which called it one of the "50 Best Websites of 2008") and was up to five hundred thousand users.

A year after that, in September of 2009, now with a user base of 850,000, Mint.com sold to Intuit—the makers of the Quicken software that had frustrated Aaron in the first place—for $170 million.

"It's the way of the internet," Sukhinder Singh mused. "A startup creates a . . . simple set of consumer tools in a beautiful front end. I don't want to diminish what Aaron does. Aaron creates a *very* consumer-friendly dashboard. Theoretically, should Intuit have done that themselves? For sure. That, unfortunately, is the history of the internet: the guys who should have built it didn't build it—the big guys. And then some startup comes along, with not that much technology, builds what the big guys should have built, and gets acquired for that competency." She added, "And then, often, it gets shut down."

Jason seems to agree. "The state of fintech was so bad in 2006 that for us it wasn't really particularly hard. But Mint pretty much died at the basic insight stage of combining everything into one UI and giving you the number and making it very easy. We sold pretty fast, and we never really hit that milestone of making people smarter and teaching them stuff they didn't realize before—helping them make better future decisions, helping them plan better, helping them understand the consequences of their actions."

Marc Hedlund, creator of a competing product called Wesabe that shut down in 2010, came to a similar conclusion: "I am anything but an unbiased observer," he freely admitted on his blog, "[but] no one, in my view, solved the financial problems of consumers. No one got even close."[5]

Mint, now under the banner of Intuit, claims to have more than twenty million users. But the promise of Mint—and where it could have gone if it had managed to become a smarter recommendation engine for its users—was never realized. According to Jason, "It pretty much died."

But the evolution of personal finance software didn't end with Mint.

ADAM DELL DIDN'T imagine himself working at Goldman Sachs. He isn't a banker. He doesn't think of himself as one, and, most days, he doesn't dress like one either: his jeans, ribbed sweater, broad chest, and rugged salt-and-pepper beard make him look something like a cross between a backwoods lumberjack and a stoic philosopher.

Nonetheless, through some twists of fate, Adam is now a partner at one of the most powerful banks in the world.

If he is atypical among bankers, then he seems just as out of place in the other world he inhabits: the world of the celebrity gossip columns. The attention he gets from tabloids is a consequence of a few things they find endlessly fascinating—it is not, he knows, the result of his success as a venture capitalist (he invested in more than fifty companies including Hotjobs.com, Connectify, Ingenio, and OpenTable), and it doesn't even have anything to do with the inescapably long shadow of his big brother, that other Dell, Michael, who

ADAM DELL, "THE VENTURE CAPITALIST"

founded Dell Computer and went on to become one of the richest people in the world.

No. Gossip columnists are interested in him because of his years-long on-and-off relationship with celebrity chef, model, author, and actress Padma Lakshmi. The otherwise serious Adam Dell has been referred to as "Padma Lakshmi's baby daddy."[6]

Twists of fate, indeed.

For years, Adam used Mint to help him manage his personal finances, but ultimately, the software left him frustrated. His complaint was the same as Marc Hedlund's: Mint didn't *do* anything.

"It was really a dashboard about your past and didn't do a good job of helping you think about what decisions you should be making and how those decisions could impact your financial well-being." The software was great at making pie charts to show how you were spending your money. But it didn't do much to help you improve your situation.

Adam's long experience in venture capital taught him a very specific way of seeing the world: "When I look at an industry, I think about what's inevitable given what technology enables, and I try to jump four or five years ahead and plant a flag into that space where I think the market will evolve."

SEEING THE FUTURE

"When I look at an industry, I think about what's inevitable given what technology enables, and I try to jump four or five years ahead and plant a flag into that space where I think the market will evolve."

Adam foresaw some technological inevitabilities that were coming to disrupt the world of finance—and he didn't think Mint was ready for them.

So he decided to plant a flag of his own.

WHAT IS A VENTURE CAPITALIST, AND WHAT THE !@#$ DO THEY DO?

A VENTURE CAPITALIST ("VC") is an early-stage investor in a business. VCs are sometimes individuals—called "angel investors"—who put their own personal money into the venture. But more often, the VC is acting on behalf of a venture capital firm, investing larger pools of money from pensions, insurance companies, or endowment funds, for instance.

In exchange for this investment, VCs usually receive a sizable share in the nascent business: they will make a return on their investments if, and only if, the company grows and becomes profitable.

Venture capitalists are expected to make higher rates of return than other types of investors—and this means they have to make riskier investments, hoping for the promise of a higher yield. But this can be a long game. For instance, when Peter Thiel became Facebook's first angel investor in 2004, he invested $500,000 in exchange for a 10.2 percent stake in the company. By 2012, when Thiel first sold some of his shares, the company's market valuation was around $100 billion, making Thiel's share worth, at the time, $10.2 billion—a pretty good rate of return. (Thiel has since sold off most of his shares in the company, at a much lower value.)

The VC's payday generally comes in one of two ways. If a startup is acquired by a larger company, then the owners of the company split the proceeds of the sale, and the VC earns a percentage based on his or her share of the company. The other way for a VC to make a return on the investment is to sell his or her stake in the company. This will often happen during a company's "IPO"—its initial public offering as a publicly traded stock, the first opportunity for the company's owners to sell their shares on an open market.

The first inevitability that Adam foresaw was the rise of mobile. "People are making profound economic decisions on their smartphones," he said, citing Rocket Mortgage, a fully digital mortgage lender that lets borrowers contract thirty-year home loans by clicking on the buttons of their phone. "There has been a real shift around mobile as a medium for helping people think about how to interact with their financial lives."

Second, he believed that people were going to begin to want their apps to take action. "It's one thing for me to tell you the value of putting aside money every month. It's another thing for me to give you a button to press that will cause that to happen." Mint did a good job of providing its users with clear information about the state of their finances, and that was good. It was a perfect realization of Pearson's Law, the principle that says, "When performance is measured, performance improves." Just by measuring users' spending patterns and reporting these back to them, Mint was causing people to adjust their behaviors for the better.

But an app designed to actively empower people to change and improve their financial lives—one that could make recommendations and offer appropriate resources—would be even better.

The third inevitability that Adam saw coming was artificial intelligence. "In a machine-learning world, where Amazon knows what you want to buy and Netflix knows what you want to watch, consumers are going to begin to expect that digital assistants will help them navigate financial choices, and that those digital assistants will be their advocates. They will be on the side of the consumer. They will be able to analyze an individual's financial situation and discern insights and recommendations that are in the best interest of the consumer rather than in the best interest of the bank."

He set out to create what he imagined would be the future of "PFM" (personal finance management) software: a platform that incorporated mobile, the ability to take actions, and AI-powered consumer advocacy.

The result was an app he called Clarity Money.

Adam started by doing research. He met with people who had deep experience in the space, like Mint's designer Jason Putorti and Yaron Samid, one of the founders of BillGuard, an app that scans users' credit card transactions to detect possible billing errors and fraud. From them, he tried to learn more about the decision-making that went into the PFMs that Adam considered best-in-class.

But he also sought the advice of a whole other set of professionals: Clarity Money's advisory board is made up of three different behavioral economists—Dan Ariely, Niall Ferguson, and Eric Johnson.

Behavioral economics is the study of how human psychology affects economic decision-making. Adam had become keenly aware of the importance of behavioral economics during his work with OpenTable, an online service designed to take the friction out of making restaurant reservations. You might think restaurant reservations are a relatively low-key endeavor, without a lot of emotional stress attached—but you would be wrong. It turns out the process of making a reservation at a restaurant causes people inordinate anxiety—and most of this anxiety has its root in finances.

Behavioral economics wound up being central to OpenTable's entire business. "The vast majority of Americans live in fear of an inability to pay their bills. And among those people, going out to eat is, without question, one of the most luxurious experiences they are going to have that month."

This makes going out to eat an acutely heightened experience. "Consumers are fearful when they go to a restaurant, particularly a fine dining restaurant. 'Is my reservation going to be there? Are they going to sit me next to the kitchen? Is it going to be too expensive?' A whole cacophony of cascading fears unfold in their minds."

OpenTable was designed specifically to disarm people's fears by putting more information—and thus, more power—into the hands of the consumer. "At OpenTable, we were obsessive about the democratization of eating out. Here are the available options for you at the price point you're comfortable with. We put the power in the hands of the consumer and that was a very powerful notion." And judging by the app's success—it was acquired in 2014 for $2.6 billion—it has largely been able to address those fears.

But if this is what people feel when they talk to a waiter or maître d' then how much more frightening is it when they talk to their credit card company or their bank manager?

"Money is an extremely emotional thing, more so than most people appreciate. Even though it shouldn't be, individuals believe it is a reflection of self-worth. Most people can't face that emotional reality. They would rather just not think about it. So, inertia takes hold, and many fail to address the issue of retirement, having a nest egg, or setting up an emergency fund."

And consumers who are looking to improve their financial situation can find it incredibly difficult to get the information they need to do so. "Banks and credit card companies, insurance companies, mortgage companies, even cable companies thrive on obfuscation. They make it hard to cancel your account. They make it hard to figure out what your APR is on your credit card. When you talk to consumers about their money, two things happen: (1) They think you are going to try and sell them something, and (2) They are convinced, with good reason, that it's going to get complicated very quickly."

Adam wanted to create PFM software that did for people's anxieties about finances what OpenTable had done for their anxieties about restaurants. He wanted to design an experience that would help people not only face their financial fears but also eventually eliminate them—to begin to feel ownership of their financial lives.

"I had a very specific intention with Clarity, and the name embodies this. We wanted to make it clear that we are on your side. So, Clarity Money is about transparency, simplicity, and advocacy. By giving consumers a tool that makes them feel as though they have a partner who can help them navigate their finances, we knew we could build relationships of trust.

ADVOCACY
"We wanted to make it clear that we are on your side."

One easy first step is saving. "Everybody knows they should save, not everybody does it—so we knew this was something that had to be really simple and easy to do." In designing the app, the team at Clarity added a button to let users set up a savings account with just a few clicks. Then they partnered with Acorns, a fintech that allows its users to round up debit and credit card transactions to the nearest dollar and deposit that difference into an investment account. With these features, in a matter of minutes, Clarity Money takes people from knowing that they should be saving to actually doing it.

Another way that Clarity helps users save money is by looking for any subscriptions they might have and offering a one-click option to unsubscribe. "Subscriptions are one of those things that nag at you. No matter how wealthy you are, virtually everyone has recurring charges that they just don't need but have failed to cancel. Even though you know you should."

The app scans a user's spending history to identify recurring charges like Hulu or Audible or a *Men's Health* subscription that's getting mailed to an old address, or a gym membership leftover from a New Year's resolution sometime in the last decade. With the click of the CANCEL button, the recurring payment will never be paid again.

In addition to helping people save money, Adam says this feature enables something even more important to happen for users psychologically. "It puts power in the hands of the consumer to say you are in control of your financial life. You can tell us what you want and don't want, and we will help make that happen."

Once the app builds a picture of a person's finances, its AI kicks in. Clarity uses Spectral Analysis of spending patterns and techniques from Natural Language Processing and Anomaly Detection to get a better understanding of a person's habits and needs, and then it begins offering financial advice the same way that a bank manager might. For example, it can see that you have three high-interest credit cards but that you also have a prime FICO Score—and at that point it can recommend that you switch to a lower-interest credit card. Eventually, the app may begin to make more sophisticated financial suggestions, too, to help consumers pick the best ways to invest their 401(k)s.

Adam's hope is that PFMs act as a gateway to better financial health—that people who use them become more financially literate, get a much clearer picture of their spending habits, and are empowered to make better choices. "A remarkably high percentage of our customers open up a savings account, open up an investment account, get an insurance product or a credit card."

It's easy to see why a tool designed around the idea of consumer advocacy would find a loyal audience, and during the first year after its launch, Clarity Money did exactly that. It was Apple's number one finance app and was listed by Apple as one of the "New Apps We Love"; it was nominated for a Webby award; and—most important of all—it gained more than a million users.

But consumers weren't the only ones who noticed the app: after it launched, it raised $14.5 million in new investments, and before long, there were some very major companies competing to partner with the firm—an eclectic list that included PayPal, Comcast, and Goldman Sachs.

"What's interesting about that," Adam said, "is how different all three of those businesses are."

He sold Clarity Money to the bank—but swears he picked it not just because of the money. He picked Goldman because there was another technological inevitability that he wanted to get ahead of—and this one was much bigger than Mint.com:

Banks, as we know them today, are done for.

"The internet is fundamentally changing the margin structure of banking. It's very similar to what Amazon has done in retail. By eliminating bricks and mortar and focusing on technology, scale, and logistics, there is an opportunity to remove cost and pass that savings along to the consumer."

Yet in this age of internet-led disintermediation, banks have thrived. Jamie Dimon, the head of JPMorgan Chase, called it a "golden age of banking," the most profitable time in the history of the industry.

Adam has a less-than-glittering view of this "golden age."

"We've been in a no-interest-rate environment for nearly ten years. Think about that: banks charge consumers high interest rates when they borrow, they offer consumers very little interest on their savings, and they charge the consumer $150 a year in fees to do very little for them."

He said that age is at its end. "As I look at it, it is inevitable that banking is going to be disrupted by the digital delivery of financial services. It is not a question of if. It is a question of when banks and credit card companies become disrupted by entrants whose business models are not predicated on charging the consumers excessive fees. It's quite simple: if you look at banking revenue from interest, it's been cut in half in the last twenty years. In response, banks have nearly tripled their revenue from fees. This is not sustainable."

And yet he sold Clarity Money to a bank.

"Goldman sees a massive disruption coming in financial services. And they are in a singularly powerful position. They have an incredible balance sheet and a deep understanding of financial systems. And they have no real legacy consumer business to cannibalize."

Goldman acquired Clarity Money to become a centerpiece of its new consumer bank, called Marcus by Goldman Sachs. As a new partner at Goldman, Adam is instrumental in helping to realize the vision of this new consumer bank, which he says is built around an ethos of no fees, full transparency, and a genuine interest in helping customers improve their financial lives.

"If you find yourself in a situation where you need to borrow $10,000, we're going to be there to help you. But we're also going to be there to help you pay it down, because we want you to pay it down. We do this with the belief that if we do a good job for you, you will trust Marcus to help you over the course of your financial journey."

If the inevitable future of banking means reduced fees and AI-guided consumer advocacy, then maybe the golden age of banking is over and the golden age of the consumer is just beginning.

4 RISE OF THE MACHINES

ROBO-ADVISORS AND INCLUSIVE INVESTING

I t's widely believed that the financial crisis of 2008 was the worst economic crisis since the Great Depression.

By some measures, it was worse.

In 2008, the stock market collapse erased a historic $6.9 trillion worth of shareholder wealth. That same year, homeowners in the United States saw $3.3 trillion of home equity vanish. Together, that's a loss of a staggering $10.2 trillion—one-fifth of the entire world's GDP.[1] The damage continued into the following year: by 2009, the value of houses in America's cities had fallen by a third, the Dow had been cut in half, and the unemployment rate had doubled to 10 percent.

It's hard to find anyone who wasn't hurt by the Great Recession.

But, if you take a closer look, you'll see that not everyone was hurt equally. Typical Americans—Americans of median income—lost 28.4 percent of their net worth between 2007 and 2009. During that same time, the richest 5 percent lost less than half of that percentage: 12.8 percent. In the years that followed, this disparity grew wider. According to a study by the Russell Sage Foundation, by 2013, the net worth of the typical American had gone down by more than a third, while during that same span, the richest 5 percent saw their net worth *increase* by 14 percent.[2]

The biggest reason for this is the stock market. By mid-2013, most stock market indices had rebounded to prerecession levels and kept rising. Meanwhile, housing prices and jobs have been much slower to recover. The "typical Americans" in the scenario above had most of their wealth tied up in their houses, not in the stock market,[3] and with the value of their houses gone, there was little money left to invest. The economic recovery of the past decade has disproportionately benefited the "investor class," the people who had their money in the stock market.

If more people could invest, then more people's lives would be improved by the gains in the market.

In 2008, at the start of the financial crisis, twenty-eight-year-old Jon Stein set out to make that happen.

JON DIDN'T PLAN to get into the investment industry. "I had an aversion, honestly, to financial services. I thought it was kind of a gross industry." What he wanted, as he started college, was to be a journalist. "I figured, 'I have a skill in writing and I can write technically, and I can tell stories that others maybe wouldn't tell. That'd be fun and good for society.'"

FOLLOW A NEED, NOT A PASSION
"I had an aversion, honestly, to financial services. I thought it was kind of a gross industry."

There was one problem. "I didn't love writing as much as I thought I did." He still wanted to do good for society, though, and considered becoming a doctor. "I loved the science, and I loved the satisfaction of helping people, and it sounded like a good life. I didn't like blood."

By the time he graduated, Jon still wasn't sure about his vocation—but he knew he needed a job. In 2003, he started as an entry-level consultant at First Manhattan Consulting Group. It happened to be in financial services. "I wanted something that would teach me about business and make me work really hard and test my limits," he said. "I didn't realize that it would set the direction for the rest of my career!"

The consulting job gave Jon a crash course in banks and brokers and taught him a lot about how the finance industry worked. But he could tell he was different from the people he was working with. "I was a bit of an outsider—like I'd been let in to understand how they worked, but I wasn't one of them. I didn't think the same way."

JON STEIN, "THE DEMOCRATIZER"

As a consultant, being an outsider can help: it's a chance to bring fresh perspectives into an organization. In college, Jon had studied a lot of behavioral economics, and here he saw a chance to put that knowledge into use. If the people in the finance industry could get a better handle on the psychology of their customers, he reasoned, they could really innovate and provide whole new levels of service. "I wanted to rethink the system. I wanted to fix something more holistically."

His clients weren't interested. "When I did propose an out-of-the-box thought, I was oftentimes shut down." A partner at his firm even took him aside, saying, "There are certain industries that make money off of people, and then there are other industries that make money off of money. We make money off of money. So, focus on the balance sheet and let's not worry so much about the customers."

"I don't mean to criticize," Jon said recently. "I just wanted something different. I wanted real innovation—and I realized that wasn't going to come from the incumbents, because they have no incentive to change. They've got the system working for them, and they've optimized it within the current regulatory environment."

But from his view, outside of the system, he saw something that these financial institutions couldn't see: that by leveraging new technologies and focusing on customer behaviors instead of balance sheets, it would be possible to reach new groups of people who were largely left out of the world of investment.

"I wanted a customer-aligned financial service," Jon said. "That didn't exist."

To understand why it didn't exist, it helps to consider how the world of investment worked at the beginning of the twenty-first century.

Outside of pension funds, investment has always been a rich man's game, and partly the reason for this is obvious: you need to have money to invest. One-third of America lives in or near poverty, and 40 percent of Americans say they do not have enough savings to cover a $400 emergency.[4] When people can't afford their basic bills and they have to make hard decisions just to cover each month's rent, it's easy to see why they aren't putting money into a retirement account.

But compared to people in other developed countries, Americans—even Americans of modest wealth—are especially bad about saving and investing their money. There are substantial reasons for this (including policies that allow easy withdrawals from retirement accounts and a culture that encourages conspicuous consumption)—but among those reasons is the simple reality that it's not easy to invest.

Let's say you have a little extra money. You know that the responsible, grown-up thing to do is not spend every penny you make, so you plan to set aside some and save it. The mattress and the piggy bank are both historically tried-and-true ways to save money. But—apart from the fact that your piggy bank can get stolen and your mattress can get burned up in a house fire—whenever you set aside a stash of cash, you're losing money. The Fed's fiscal policies aim to keep the US economy at a steady rate of 2 percent inflation, and for the most part, they do a good job of hitting that target—which means that, every year, the hoard of cash you hide in your mattress is losing 2 percent of its spending power.

As a result, people with some extra money lying around are advised to take that money to their banks and put it into savings accounts, where it's not just protected against theft and fire but also earns some interest. Saving is a kind of investing (remember George Bailey), but it's a very indirect kind of investing: you give your money to the bank, the bank uses it to make potentially lucrative investments, and then the bank pays you a very small portion of the profit.

Operative word: *small*. In the wake of the 2008 financial crisis, the Fed has kept interest rates very low, bringing the rate of return on savings accounts down to just above zero—not even close to keeping pace with that 2 percent rate of inflation. This means that even the people who are conscientious enough to put their money into savings accounts see that money's value shrink a little bit each year.

Which is why most serious investors find other places to put their money: they are looking for an investment with a rate of return that is higher than inflation. Traditionally, if you're looking for a higher rate of return, you might invest in the stock market.

So, how do you do that?

In olden times, you would call—or telegram—your broker and say you wanted to buy shares of stock. But how would you pick the stock? When the New York Stock Exchange first opened for business in 1792, there were just five securities available for trade, so an investor's choices were relatively simple. Today the NYSE has more than 2,800 companies listed, and the decision-making is a little more complicated.

Making money off of stocks—correctly gauging when a company is under-valued or overvalued and then acting on that decision before other people do—is hard. Predicting the rising and falling fortunes of a company that's big enough to be listed on a major stock exchange requires self-education and a lot of ongoing expenditure of time: to make good decisions, you need up-to-date and in-depth knowledge about the company, its rivals, and all of the companies in its international supply chain. The company's stock might be affected by fluctuations of currency and commodity markets, changing laws and policies around the world, breaking news and larger macroeconomic trends, and even by the weather. If you do wind up with information that seems promising, you'll need to act before everyone else: you'll have to "beat the market." But you're racing against global companies with legions of high-paid market analysts whose job is to be better at researching the value of securities than you are. So how are you going to beat the market?

Finally, investing in stock is risky: if you sink your savings into a bad company or at an unlucky time, you could wind up ruined. You might've been better off not investing at all.

To help cut down on this risk, the finance industry invented a number of products to save investors from having to pick individual stocks: mutual funds, index funds, and exchange-traded funds all spread your investment out across a range of different securities—so that instead of buying one hundred shares of IBM, you wind up buying, for example, a small piece from a hundred different companies. Then, if one company goes bad, it won't tank the entire investment.

You would think that these funds should make it much easier for individual investors to get involved in the market, but there are so many funds to choose from—nearly ten thousand mutual funds in the United States alone, each one set up a little differently, each with its own fees and benefits and risks and tax ramifications—and the differences between the different funds can be hard or impossible for a novice to discern.

It's overwhelming, partly by design.

And it's hard to get good, unbiased advice.

Investors who pick their own funds without guidance from an industry professional don't fare well: where the S&P 500 grew 10.35 percent over a thirty-year period, during that same time, the average self-directed equity mutual fund investor earned 3.7 percent[5]—only slightly better than keeping the money in a mattress.

Because of all this complexity, the people who can afford to do it will hire consultants to help them manage their wealth. A good wealth manager acts as both concierge and consigliere: assessing clients' goals over long spans of time; making informed decisions about how to arrive at those goals; and selecting which assets to buy, in what proportions—how many stocks or bonds or mutual funds or index funds or ETFs (or how much cryptocurrency)—and which funds. Wealth managers also consider tax implications of different accounts and withdrawals. When circumstances in the markets change, they adjust and rebalance their clients' portfolios to shield them from excess risk and keep things on track.[6]

This attention and expertise is expensive. Private wealth managers charge an "annual management fee" equal to 100 basis points—1 percent—on the value of the assets they manage.[7] One percent may not sound like much, but it adds up: for an initial portfolio of $500,000, the fee would only be $5,000—but compounded over a thirty-year period, the amount paid out to the wealth manager would be somewhere around $750,000.

And this is regardless of whether or not the investments wind up earning the client any money.

Since wealth managers' incomes depend entirely on this percentage of their clients' investments (the "assets under management"), most wealth managers work only with "high-net-worth individuals" and require minimum investments—customarily $100,000 on the very low end. Anything less is chump change and not worth the effort. (For contrast to the "low" end, the minimum investment for Goldman Sachs Private Wealth Management is $10 million.)

So, for anyone who wanted to benefit from the stock market, those were the options: try your luck on your own, against the odds—or wait until you had an extra $100,000 lying around to turn over to a wealth manager.

Yet Jon Stein knew something from his time as a consultant that many people in the mid-2000s didn't know: these high-end services that wealth managers were offering to their clients were largely automated. The same way that travel agents were the first people to use software to book air travel, wealth managers were using software, internally, to help them handle many aspects of their job.

Jon also knew something else: many wealth managers weren't even outperforming the market!

What were people getting for their 1 percent fee?

What if some version of the software that the wealth managers were using could be offered to the broader public? If the processes of asset allocation, rebalancing, and tax-harvesting could be automated, then it could be scaled—and this would open up investing to whole new sets of people. A private wealth manager might be limited to fifty or a hundred or two hundred clients, but software, if it was well built, could handle investments for thousands, for millions. And there would be no need for sky-high investment minimums, either, because the software would work just as well for $1 as it did for $1 million.[8]

If Jon could create this, it would rethink the whole system. It would fix something holistically.

It would democratize investment.

PASSIVE INVESTING

WHEN PEOPLE TALK about the great innovations of financial technology, not many think to list Bogle's Folly. But if it weren't for John Bogle and his invention in 1975, robo advisors wouldn't be possible.

John C. Bogle was the founder and CEO of the Vanguard Group, one of the largest investment management companies in the world. Vanguard's biggest line of business comes from mutual funds.

Mutual funds predate John Bogle—the first modern mutual fund was created in 1924—but they caught on in earnest with modern capital markets in the '80s and '90s. The idea behind a mutual fund is this: rather than you personally investing in a stock or other asset, you put your money into a pool with other investors, and that pool of money—the mutual fund—is used to buy a collection of assets. Your investment is diversified: if one asset fails, you're still protected against a complete loss. Mutual funds have become an enormously popular investment vehicle: roughly $40 trillion of global wealth is currently tied up in mutual funds.

The assets inside a mutual vary from fund to fund—and this is where John Bogle came in.

Actively managing the assets inside any particular mutual fund is a lot of work: fund managers could spend all their time researching and rebalancing, trading and incurring fees, to try and maximize the return on their funds. What Bogle saw was that, even after all that work, many funds still didn't outperform the S&P 500. So, he wondered, what if there were a fund that followed the S&P 500 exactly—a fund made up of the exact stocks of those five hundred companies and nothing else? Then, by definition, the fund would increase in value in direct proportion with the S&P index and would always do as well as that index—but it would require almost no ongoing management.

This was the start of "passive investments," and on December 31, 1975, Bogle put the idea into practice with the launch of the First Index

JOHN BOGLE, "THE PASSIVIST"

Investment Trust, the world's first index mutual fund (or just "index fund," for short).

Bogle's contemporaries thought it was a terrible idea. Why in the world would anyone aim just to keep pace with the market instead of trying to outperform it? The idea was "un-American," they said, a "cop-out," a "search for mediocrity." One competitor wrote, "Who wants to be operated on by an average surgeon, be advised by an average lawyer, or be an average registered representative, or do anything no better or worse than average?"[9] Though Bogle had been hoping to raise $150 million in initial investments for his fund, he got only $11 million, and the fund earned the nickname "Bogle's Folly."

It took years—and a stock market turnaround—before Bogle was proven right. His competitors derided his fund's "average" returns—but over the long run, "average" turned out to be pretty good. In fact, average turned out to be more profitable than active management, which is too often based on the emotional, reactive, and inconsistent decisions of the wealth managers. Who wants to be operated on by an emotional, reactive, and inconsistent surgeon? No one. Then factor in the higher costs for active management, and the advantages of passive index funds become even clearer.

The Vanguard 500 Index Fund, as the fund was later renamed, is now the world's largest mutual fund, with over $292 billion in assets, and index funds are now considered a core holding in any long-term investment account. Since 2006, active investors have moved $1.2 trillion out of active mutual funds while even more money—$1.4 trillion—has flowed into passive index funds.[10]

Passive wealth management and index funds are at the center of what makes an app like Betterment possible.

Jon decided he wanted to build something that used technology to help everyday people make good investments. Beyond that, he had no idea where to begin. "I wasn't sure what type of company I was trying to build. I had the name, 'Betterment.' I knew that we wanted to make things in financial services better. But I didn't know if this thing [I was making] was a bank, or a mutual fund, or a broker, or an investment advisor. In fact, at the time I wanted

[Betterment] to be none of those. I wanted [it] to be something wholly new and different."

He did what any self-respecting journalism-turned-pre-med grad who wanted to get into financial software would do: he read forty books on the regulatory landscape of the securities industry, enrolled in an MBA program, and worked to get a Chartered Financial Analyst certification. "Oh," he said, "and I taught myself to code."

His study taught him something important: people are not especially good investors. They react emotionally and that leads them to make irrational decisions in the market. People who move their money around on impulse fail to reap the benefits of long-term gains, and they get additionally penalized by wasted time, extra taxes, and transaction fees. They are almost always better off if they get out of their own way—if they set their goals, invest in index funds, and passively let their money do the work for them.

This became the investment philosophy behind Betterment.

Now all Jon had to do was build it.

He spent all of 2007 working around the clock. "The time I was in business school, I was coding nights and weekends and over the summer in between my first and second year. Instead of getting an internship like literally everyone else in my class, I just worked on my business. I built the front end of the site, so I had a thing to start to show people. Then I started building some of the back-end trading systems. At that time, embarrassingly, I really just thought I was going to build this whole thing myself. I wanted this product, and I was going to build it and bring it to market."

But by his second year of business school, reality started to sink in. It would be good for him to have a team. He went out to lunch with an old poker buddy, a lawyer named Eli Broverman, and described the idea to him. The next week, Eli went to Jon's house, took the forty books on regulatory law, and joined Betterment.

Jon's roommate, Sean Owen, also joined the team. Jon described Sean: "He was a software engineer at Google, 1600 SAT, 800 GMAT, CS at Harvard, and he is a great engineer—incredible, even." He thought, "If I can get Sean excited about this thing, then it's a good idea."

Among the things that Sean brought to Betterment was a methodology. By 2008, computer programmers were practicing a new technique of lightweight software development called "Agile." The agile methodology advocates incremental, iterative development: the team works together to set simple achievable goals, builds to them, and then regroups to plan the next incremental iteration. These small steps forward give developers the ability to adapt and adjust before going too far down any particular path, and the frequent check-ins ("scrums") give them opportunities to help each other and learn from each other's mistakes.

Agile methodology was first articulated in 2001 and became more popular as the decade progressed. It had a big impact on the development of fintech, because building apps in simple, short bursts gave the growing startups an ability to react to emerging trends and customer needs much faster than any giant software team at any legacy bank could.

Agile definitely affected the development of Betterment. "Sean had this view that you want to build the simplest app, build it once, build the things in the critical path, and then add on to it." Simple became a guiding principle—or at least making sure that the experience for the user always felt simple, even if what was going on under the hood wasn't.

"I had this idea of what I wanted to build, which at the time was really rudimentary: it was the investing efficiency of Vanguard"—a leading wealth management company—"coupled with the ease of user experience of ING Direct"—an online bank known for its clean, easy-to-use website. "The union of those two ideas materialized in this slider, a simple slider, whether you wanted more in bonds or more in stocks. Then, with a time horizon, you could project out expected returns, a good case with the bad case—simple communicating with the customer."

Just because the interface looked simple didn't mean the underlying code was. If anything, it was the opposite. "It was a ton of work," Jon said. "And it took years. We essentially knew the product that we wanted to build in 2008, and we started working on it at that time—but we didn't have everything we needed until 2010."

And it was next to impossible to get funding. Investors didn't know what to make of Betterment. Nothing like it existed in 2008. Fintech wasn't even a word yet, let alone a buzzword among venture capitalists. Mint.com had just released, but it was nothing more than a curiosity. Who would make financial decisions, especially long-term investment decisions—from their mobile phones? Jon's business background wasn't reassuring either. "I didn't have any prior startup or tech company experience to show, so who was going to trust me? I was just some consultant with crazy ideas about investing."

At one point, things got so lean at Betterment that Jon not only had to ask his employees to take a pay cut—he also asked them to buy equity in the company. He needed them to pay in so there would be more cash flow.

Remarkably, they did. "Everyone believed in what we were doing," he recalled.

The market crash had an impact too. "A lot of people at that time said, 'Don't do this. This is a terrible time to start a financial services company. What are you thinking?' And they were certainly the majority." The Dow had taken a beating for a straight year and a half after the collapse of Lehman, and people had had their wealth wiped out, with one in ten Americans out of work—a less than ideal time to ask consumers to think about creating investment portfolios.

But in some ways, the financial crisis made it the perfect time to launch Betterment. "There was the loss of faith, a loss of trust with the big incumbents," Jon said. "That led a lot of people to look for alternatives." Banks had failed in a spectacular way: even after the government handed the banks nearly a trillion dollars in rescue funds, 165 banks went bankrupt and required the FDIC to intervene so customers wouldn't lose their money.[11] Trust in banks was at an all-time low—falling, according to Gallup, from over 50 percent to 18.1 percent by 2010.[12]

But while trust in banks was falling, people were only deepening their relationships with tech companies. By February 2010, Facebook had four hundred million users, there were one hundred million iPhones worldwide, and the misgivings people once had about sharing personal information with tech companies were falling away. The banks had nearly ruined us, the thinking went, but the tech companies would save us.

So why not trust a fintech app?

Jon said the financial crisis led him to a similar change in his own thinking. "I always looked at Wall Street with this sense of reverence and awe. 'Wow, those people are supersmart!' I still think they're supersmart, but I realized these are just people who are fallible like me and make mistakes like me." This realization gave him the confidence to keep going. "I can do as well at this as anybody, so I might as well try."

In 2010, Betterment was selected from a pool of five hundred applicants to launch its product onstage at the TechCrunch Disrupt conference in New

York, a three-day gathering of software companies and investors. It would be a great opportunity to show off the product not just to the people at the conference but also to the audience of twenty thousand or so who would livestream the event—more publicity than Jon and his team could afford to buy.

The trouble was, they weren't ready.

"It was really down to the wire. We were still testing basic functionality." A couple of weeks before they went live, the team discovered that some of their withdrawals weren't going through. People could put money into Betterment just fine, but the app wouldn't be very popular if no one could get their money out. The team scrambled for weeks to fix and test and resolve the issue.

Then there was regulation to contend with. Remember those forty legal books that Jon and Eli had read? Well, the Dodd-Frank Act—a new regulatory overhaul in the wake of the financial crisis—was about to go into law, and there were many new books to learn and follow.

Staying in compliance with all of these regulations would be a crucial part of making Betterment successful. But in the days leading up to TechCrunch, the company still hadn't received the approvals they needed from FINRA, the Financial Industry Regulatory Authority, which oversees the broker-dealer industry. "We got the final regulatory approval to go live on Friday, and we were set to launch on Monday," Jon remembered. "It was that close to not happening."

It did happen. In June 2010, Betterment not only went public, it also took home an award from the TechCrunch conference as the "Biggest New York Disruptor." Over that first day, the company drew four hundred new customers and the attention of some early investors, and people began putting money in Betterment's accounts. "I remember that first million dollars and thinking, *Wow, a million dollars!*" Jon said.

By the end of the year, Betterment had $10 million under management.

"We celebrated. We couldn't believe it. It seemed like an impossible thing that that many people would trust us. I thought they were crazy, honestly."

TRUST IN TECH
"It seemed like an impossible thing that that many people would trust us. I thought they were crazy, honestly."

Now $10 million worth of deposits is an average day at Betterment. It has four hundred thousand users and somewhere in the neighborhood of $16 billion under management. And Betterment continues to grow—partly because, instead of the 1 percent fee charged by private wealth managers, it offers users many of the same rewards for just 0.25 percent, with no minimum deposit.

"We earn the average customer who is saving for retirement around 40 percent more than they would earn if they managed their money on their own or through some competitive service," Jon said. "Nobody else is doing that for people. We're unique in the amount of value we create."

Since Betterment's launch, a whole industry of competitors—popularly called "robo advisors"—has followed. There are now more than two hundred different robo advisors to choose from, and collectively they hold $980 billion in assets under management.[13] Even more notable than that: the average investment account handled by these robo advisors is around $21,000 per person—significantly lower than the minimums required by private wealth managers. This means robo advisors really are succeeding in reaching a whole different class of investors.

But small startups aren't the only ones building robo advisors. Learning a lesson from Betterment's success, industry incumbents BlackRock, Vanguard, Schwab, and Fidelity all launched their own lower-fee services powered by similar technology, including lower minimum investments to appeal to a broader base of customers.

Jon thinks they're still getting it wrong. "When I read the bank decks these days, I see things like 'Robo is a potential disruptive, competitive threat,' and 'Banks should have a robo.' I don't even know what a robo is. I think it's so silly."

According to Jon, Betterment's success isn't about technology. "It's not about 'having a robo.' It's about actually doing the right thing for your customers and being customer-centric." Banks, he said, still operate in terms of products instead of customers—and those products are generally designed to take advantage of a customer's behavior and optimize against a customer's best interest. "I just don't feel like that's the right way to build a valuable institution in the modern age. I think you have to be more customer-centric at the core."

USERS FIRST
"It's not about 'having a robo.' It's about actually doing the right thing for your customers and being customer-centric."

It's something the banking insiders might never be able to see.

Betterment's platform has continued to evolve as it has grown. "There are multiple algorithms and systems that we've built over the years to take input from customers. It's a constant iterative process. We're looking at how our customers engage, how they trial with us, whether or not we helped them achieve their goals, and we use information about how they're performing to then inform our next cycle of development."

Even so, Betterment's biggest challenges may still be ahead. Its premise, and the premise behind all of the robo advisors that have followed, is that "passive investing"—investing in index funds that follow the broad trends of the market and holding on to those funds—is more lucrative in the long run than "active investing"—trading quickly and frequently based on research, reaction, and hunches.

The data would seem to agree: very few actively managed portfolios beat their passive benchmarks, especially once taxes and fees are taken into account. And this has been true for Betterment too.

But Betterment was built during the nadir of the economic crisis and launched during the first year of the recovery. Since then, the market has been on a long and mostly steady climb upward: the Dow today is fourfold what it was at its low point in 2009. When market gains are this constant, of course the passive index funds offer great returns. Making money is easy when everything is going up.

However, this decade-long bull market is almost without historic precedent—and economists agree, it can't last forever.

So, what happens to passive investing during a downturn?

Will the robos be sophisticated enough to protect investors from losing their wealth in a crashing market? Will they continue to outperform? Or will a downturn reveal the true value of active management: human expertise and judgment during a time when there will be more losers than winners?

No one can know, but the first peek of an answer came on June 24, 2016, and it wasn't entirely encouraging. The day after the British electorate voted, by a narrow margin, to leave the European Union, global markets went into a panic that wiped away $2 trillion of wealth overnight. That day (like every day), index funds followed the market—they plunged too.

The concept of passive investing depends on a long, slow game: it asks people to buy and hold, and to quell their emotional impulses and ride out temporary downturns. Over a long enough time frame, the thinking goes, the market will recover, and so will the index funds that make up the investor's portfolio.

But quelling emotional impulses during a *panic* is easier said than done. Polls and bookmakers had predicted that the Brexit vote would end in a decision to "remain," and on the day of, markets had reacted to this prediction by soaring—so, later that night, when the tallied votes showed "leave" as the winner, market-watchers knew the next day was going to bring a harsh correction.

"As our team monitored this activity overnight," Betterment said in a statement to its users that next morning, "it became apparent that the U.S. market open would be extremely volatile—in other words, a poor environment for long-term investors."[14] Faced with a likely panic that the company felt wasn't good for its customers, Betterment made a controversial decision: it halted trading for the first three hours that the market was open. Traders would neither sell off their holdings during the temporary panic nor buy the assets that other people were selling until the market had a chance to stabilize and the value of things could be better ascertained.

Jon cited famed investor Warren Buffett in defense of his decision to stay out of the volatility: "The stock market is a device for transferring money from the impatient to the patient."

The effect of Betterment's decision to halt trading would have been invisible to the average Betterment investor: because of the nature of the app, its users are shielded from the specifics of the trades that go on behind the scenes. If anything, the company prefers that its users not worry too much about day-to-day changes.

But the decision shone a light on a fact that had been previously hidden in the shadows: these robo advisors are not entirely robotic. There are still humans making decisions about when to intervene and override the algorithms, when they think it's in their customers' best interest. That might comfort some users, because it could potentially save investment portfolios from disaster—but it also reintroduces some of the problems that the software was designed to avoid: emotional overreactions and arbitrary judgments.

Being a "robo" was never Jon's goal. His goal was to offer smart and affordable management of people's money. Algorithms and AI are a crucial part of that. "With the amount of complexity involved in actually allocating capital and actually reading a company's financial statement, it would be ridiculous to think that any individual who is busy with family, job, etcetera should be doing that activity today—so we have robofied many steps of that."

But human judgment will always be a part of it too.

While the higher-end investment firms are racing to catch up to Betterment's automation, Betterment has expanded to include more human judgment in its offerings. For higher fees and with a $100,000 minimum balance, customers can now opt for a "premium" service that, on the face of it, is hard to distinguish from the high-end wealth management that the company was trying to supplant. It includes unlimited access to certified professionals for guidance with the financial planning that is hard to automate: decision-making about buying a home, having a child, or when to retire. And though the company started simple, it continues to iterate, agile-style, to offer 401(k)s, IRAs, trust accounts, and more.

"Over the years our advice has become more and more sophisticated, and the types of services that we provide have broadened out," Jon said. "But the core idea—that people will make better decisions if they have better information and advice, and we can help people live better by helping their money work harder for them—that mission has never changed."

WALTER CRUTTENDEN

WHEN WALTER CRUTTENDEN'S son Jeffrey graduated from college, Walter decided to give him a graduation present. "Let's form a company."

Walter had some experience at starting companies: he was founder and CEO of Roth Capital, a firm that invests in emerging-growth companies, and he also ran the investment banking arm of E*Trade, which funded small-cap businesses and took them to their IPOs.

Walter has four sons, and he has started a company with each one of them, finding an intersection point between their interests and his own. His third son, Jeff, was a math major at Lewis & Clark. "He's a real intellectual," Walter said, "and in 2011, 2012, he was just crazy about all the new apps coming out." Jeff loved mobile apps and had an intuitive sense of how they should work. "Jeff would say things like, 'Man, that color sucks. The buttons are in the wrong place.' And he was right."

The two of them decided to build an app that would help young people—people Jeff's age—to create their first investment account. "Most studies show that, on average, people start investing somewhere during their mid-to-high thirties. We wanted to lop ten years off of that, because ten years can make a huge difference." The investment banker and his math major son both understood that even small sums of money add up quickly over a decade of compounding interest.

But how could they get millennials to invest? For the most part, people just out of college didn't have a lot of extra money, and Merrill Lynch, Morgan Stanley, and Goldman Sachs weren't interested in a twenty-two-year-old's loose change: these companies often required their investment clients to have a portfolio of $100,000 or more.

Loose change.

This was how the light bulb went off for the father/son duo.

"We were talking about Moore's Law," Walter explained, "the idea that computer power is doubling and its cost is falling by half every year—and we thought about the effects this might have on the banking industry. For one thing, it was causing the cost of transfer payments to drop. Wiring money used to cost thirty dollars, but now it's down to a penny and a half."

With costs coming down, they realized that it was now financially feasible to create investment accounts out of literal loose change. And they had an idea to get people to do it. "Round-ups," Walter said. "Whenever someone makes a purchase on their credit or debit card, we round up and deposit the difference into an investment account."

WALTER CRUTTENDEN, "THE CULTIVATOR"

So, if a person used a debit card to buy a coffee for $2.75, the card would be charged an even $3.00, and the $0.25 would get invested. Without any further action or decision required, the user would be making regular "microinvestments," setting tiny, almost invisible sums of money aside—money that would begin earning compound interest. The investor never needed to give it a single thought. This was "passive investing," taken to its logical and literal extreme.

Using Walter's knowledge of business and Jeff's instincts for apps, the two quickly built their idea into a reality. "We got a lot of really good engineers to help figure out the best way to do this. We did hook up with Yodlee and Plaid, which gave us such a cool and easy way to link to the banks. Jeff kept redesigning it and redesigning it—to the point that I got really frustrated," Walter admitted. "You know what, though? It ended up being one of the coolest apps."

They also needed a name—something catchy that millennials could remember and understand.

"I have a little ranch down in Escondido," Walter said. "Jeff and I were walking along and picking up acorns—and we realized that'd be a great name. They grow into big, old oak trees."

Acorns was launched in August of 2014 and now has over five million users. The average age of its investor? Just over thirty years old.

5 BANKING THE UNBANKED

PREPAID CARDS, NEOBANKS, AND BAAS

The improvements of the past decade's fintech have already radically re-shaped—and digitized—the ways we interact with our money. Payment platforms like Braintree and PayPal have made it easier than ever to shop. Yodlee and other banking APIs allow us to move money seamlessly between our accounts, and personal finance managers like Mint and Clarity Money mean that we can see what goes into and out of those accounts with new transparency and ease. When we're short on money, online lenders like LendingClub or Kabbage can transfer money into our bank within days or hours. And online investment tools like Betterment and Acorns give us sim-ple, efficient ways of growing the money in our accounts over time.

Fintech has "debundled" the banks: taken the unwieldy collection of prod-ucts that banks offer their customers and peeled them away, one by one, trans-forming them into lightweight, customer-friendly apps that each provide just one service, but better.

Along the way, the fintechs have opened up financial services to more peo-ple than ever.

But, in order to enjoy these services, fintech's customers still need banks. Online payment is quick and seamless—as long as you have a credit or debit card. A digital loan is fast and painless, as long as there is a bank to receive the loan. And there is no way to begin growing your retirement savings through Betterment if you can't transfer money into your account: the app doesn't accept cash.

Beneath their friendly, branded skins, these fintech apps all require their users to connect their accounts, at some point or another, to a bank.

So what happens, as more of our transactions go digital, to the people who don't have access to a bank? How can they keep from being left behind?

This was the problem that Steve Streit was trying to solve.

"You can't shove cash through a hard drive, right?" Steve said.

WHEN OLD MODELS NO LONGER WORK
"You can't shove cash through a hard drive, right?"

For people who live in big American cities and already move money back and forth with their smartphones, it's easy not to realize: there are a lot of people in America without a bank.

According to an FDIC report from 2017, 8.4 million American households are "unbanked": they live without access to a bank account or credit card. An additional 24.2 million are what is called "underbanked": they might have a checking or savings account but receive the majority of their financial needs from what are known as "alternative financial services"—check-cashing stores, payday lenders, pawnshops, and the like.

That's more than one in four American households, total.

The unbanked and underbanked are disproportionately nonwhite—black and Latino households are more than twice as likely to be unbanked as their white counterparts—and they are disproportionately rural: in counties with fewer than 100,000 people, the percentage of unbanked households gets as high as 33 percent. They tend to have less education than the "fully banked"— only 14.5 percent of underbanked families in 2015 had a member with a college degree—and they tend to be poor. In fact, half of all unbanked households had a bank account once, but no longer do because, they say, they no longer have enough money to keep in an account.[1]

Some of these people opt out of banking by choice, but the vast majority of the people who don't have bank accounts would like to and can't—either because they have too little money to open an account, because the bank has rejected them,[2] or because there isn't a bank close enough for them to use.

The Great Recession swelled the ranks of the unbanked, and not just because bank customers were overdrawing their accounts during times of financial difficulty. The banks themselves were in a time of financial difficulty. In the historically low-interest environment that followed the financial crisis, the banks weren't able to make as much money off of their investment holdings, and found that the next best way for them to generate revenue was to increase their fees—so increase them they did. Overdraft fees rose more than 50 percent from where they were in 2000, and the average ATM fee has gone up for fourteen years running, now between four and five dollars per withdrawal.[3] "Noninterest income," as the banks euphemistically call the revenue from these fees, accounts for a significant part of a bank's balance sheet—at large regional banks, sometimes as much as 40 percent.

These fees alone have been enough to drive the most marginalized people out of the banking system.

But banks did something else, too, during the financial crisis, to help them make up for their lost investment revenue: they started closing bank branches. Since 2008, banks in the United States have shut down nearly nine thousand branch locations. Branches with the least traffic, the fewest customers, and the smallest holdings were the ones most likely to close, and that means many of these closures happened in small rural areas—places that might only have been served by one or two banks to begin with. As a result of the closures, the financial crisis created eighty-six new "banking deserts"—areas that don't have any bank at all within ten miles of population centers.[4,5]

Living without a nearby bank is expensive. If you need cash, you might have to drive an hour or more to your bank's closest ATM, or, if that's not an option, you can use an out-of-network machine that will gouge you with fees. On payday, you might face a similar dilemma, having to decide if it's costlier to deliver your check to your bank or pay the exorbitant fee charged by the local check-cashing store.[6]

Living without any bank account at all is even more costly. Instead of writing checks, you'll pay a dollar or more on each money order. If you need a loan, your options are payday lenders, pawnshops, and loan sharks. Banks are required to comply with usury laws that put a high-end limit on interest charges—but in many jurisdictions, nontraditional lenders aren't covered by these laws.[7]

"Unbanked consumers spend approximately 2.5 to 3 percent of a government benefits check and between 4 percent and 5 percent of a payroll check just to cash them,"[8] reported the Federal Reserve in 2010. Multiplying this out over a year and adding the cost of six money orders per month, a household making $20,000 would pay $1,200 a year in fees for the "privilege" of being unbanked. "Anyone who has ever struggled with poverty," wrote James Baldwin, "knows how extremely expensive it is to be poor."

When more of our economy was more cash-based, the differences between the banked and the unbanked weren't so extreme. But as the internet became more important in our lives, so did online shopping—and online shopping requires some kind of digital cash.

WHEN STEVE STREIT started, he wasn't thinking about the unbanked. He was thinking about music.

"I was in the radio business. My specialty was inventing music formats for, typically, families—moms with school-aged kids. In those days, it was Billy Joel, Phil Collins, Whitney Houston, Mariah Carey. You know, that kind of music."

The radio needed a way to market the music. "We were trying to come up with something that communicated that it wasn't hard rock like Led Zeppelin, but it wasn't easy-listening music like Barbra Streisand." They were having trouble coming up with a phrase that worked for everyone.

Then Steve had an idea. "Guys," he said. "Soft rock."

That's right: before he became a fintech entrepreneur, Steve Streit was the guy who invented soft rock.

"I created a campaign that said, 'Soft rock, never too hard, never sleepy. The music that everyone can agree on. Soft rock.' It became an immediate hit because it made older people feel young and younger people not feel so old, and the mix of music was more upbeat with Madonna and more contemporary artists at that time but never played the easy-listening staples of the day, the Streisands and Barry Manilows, and never played anything hard or edgy or screaming with electric guitar. Then we had the soft rock stations that popped up all over the place."

He spotted a trend and he ran with it. That's what Steve does.

He stayed in the radio industry for many years, while the industry went through a long phase of mergers and acquisitions, and in 1999, Clear Channel bought up the company where he worked. They offered him a compensation package and showed him the door.

"I had kids and a house, and I was panicked," he remembered, "so I went across the street to American Express Advisors. 'I was just given this package,'"

STEVE STREIT, "THE SOFT ROCKER"

he told them, "'but I don't know what any of it means. Can you help me?' And the woman who was randomly assigned as my advisor said, 'Well, Steve, you're a millionaire.'"

Over his decades of work at the radio station, he had been quietly accruing stock options, which, thanks to the acquisition by Clear Channel, now added up to, well, more money than he would have guessed. A good bit more.

He was suddenly in the unfamiliar position of being a millionaire who needed to figure out what to do with the rest of his life.

He wound up sitting down with some friends who were music executives at GO.com, Disney's recently launched internet portal, so they could show off some of their new technology. "Listen," they told him. "One day there's going to be high-speed internet."

In 1999, people didn't yet have broadband in their homes. Millions were using the internet, but if they wanted to connect outside of an office or a university, they mainly did it with a dial-up modem, using services like AOL and Prodigy. At their best, these modems offered connection speeds of fifty-six kilobytes per second—so, assuming your connection didn't stall or drop, you could download a one-megabyte file in just under twenty seconds.[9]

Steve's friends at GO.com showed him a glimpse of the future, a future where everyone had high-speed internet in their homes—a future they imagined would be full of new opportunities for them to showcase Disney products, services, toys, and music through their website.

Once Steve got home from the meeting, he considered this future, and he had an epiphany that was even bigger than "soft rock":

"People are going to buy things online," he realized. Not just on Amazon (which launched in 1994) and eBay (which launched in 1995), and not just on big websites like Disney.com—but everywhere. "I thought, kids will be the first adopters of that technology when it arrives. College campuses will likely be the first adopters of high-speed, always-on internet, and if that happens, young people are going to need a way to buy online."

But, because of the way the credit industry works, young people have a hard time getting credit cards: they usually don't have a predictable income, and they don't have enough accumulated credit history—so they have no FICO Scores. Without an accurate way to gauge risk, the banks weren't going to offer young people credit.

And without a credit card, young people—the people most likely to start shopping online—wouldn't be able to do it.

"We should invent a credit card for kids," Steve thought.

He didn't know yet how this would work or even what it would be, but the idea excited him. He turned on his computer, created a new file that he called "Million Dollar Idea," and wrote down one word: *I-GEN*. He would create a credit card for the internet generation.

"That's how it started," Steve said. "It was just me in my bedroom."

In the end, Steve's "million-dollar idea" wound up being a kind of debit card, not a credit card. When Steve started approaching possible retailers about selling the I-GEN, they didn't quite understand the concept of the card. "They were called 'host-based stored-value cards,' and nobody knew what the heck that was." So he came up with a catchier name.

"'Prepaid.' Because back then prepaid phone cards from Sprint and MCI were very big. 'It's a prepaid Mastercard,' I said. 'When your money runs out, you're done. No overdraft fees.' And people immediately said, 'Oh, I get it.'"

Eventually, he convinced Rite Aid to sell the product. They launched a pilot program in eighty Rite Aid stores around the greater Washington, DC, area.

There was one big problem. "We weren't selling any cards," Steve said. "None. Zero. Every day I would call Rite Aid to see if we made a sale, and every day they'd say, 'No, no sales today.'"

By then, Steve had spent all of the money from his Clear Channel stock to get the I-GEN up and running, and he was living off of his credit cards. "Entrepreneurship—everyone talks about how romantic and exciting it is, and it can be," he said. "But when you have kids in school, and you used to have money but you don't now because you're not working, and every month you know you're not going to be able to pay your mortgage . . . I can't describe the anxiety and the stress. It was anything but romantic."

He couldn't take it anymore. For psychological reasons, for superstitious reasons, he needed a sale. He called a friend in the DC area and asked, "Will you do me a favor? Would you please drive to Rite Aid and buy a card?"

"Will you pay me back?" the friend asked.

His friend did buy an I-GEN card[10]—and soon, other people were buying them too. But they weren't the people Steve had originally imagined. "I thought the audience for this product would be suburban white teenagers whose [parents] would not want them to use their Amex cards. I couldn't have been more wrong."

I-GEN had a call center,[11] and whenever Steve had the chance, he would get on the phone with the people who called in and ask them why they had decided to buy the card. Their answers surprised him. "I have bad credit," one caller told him. Another said, "I don't feel welcome in a bank; they don't want me there." A third caller made it even more clear: "Banks don't like black folk."

Call after call, Steve started to hear similar stories: "The fees are too high." "They all make you do minimum balances." "I need to shop but I can't get a credit card."

"And it occurred to me," Steve said. "We had a great product. But I had the wrong market."

Without realizing it, Steve had designed a product that could help the unbanked.

"That was the first time that I was aware that there are people who want to have a bank, but can't." The card filled a need for anyone who couldn't get a traditional credit card and for anyone who didn't want to carry around a lot of cash but who, for whatever reason, couldn't or wouldn't be able to put it in a bank.

In 2001, soon after the launch of the I-GEN card, Steve pivoted the company away from the teen audience he originally had in mind. He rebranded the company "Green Dot" and aimed his product at the unbanked. "We changed our packaging—we made it more adult and more respectful," he said, "without ever saying that we're here to help 'low-income Americans.' But everyone got it. They understood it, and very quickly we became a very respected product."

In the wake of the financial crisis—when credit cards got more expensive and many people lost their credit—use of prepaid cards took off. By 2009, people had loaded a collective $30 billion onto their prepaid cards; by 2012, that amount had more than doubled to $65 billion.

Over time, Green Dot added more features to their prepaid cards. The original card was meant to be disposable: they weren't personalized (the name on the card read "Valued Customer"), and they couldn't be refilled. But before long, the company was selling personalized cards through its website. These cards were meant to be kept, and their balance could be reloaded at the same retail outlets that sold the cards. This effectively gave Green Dot customers a checking account where they could store their money, without needing a relationship with a bank. These personalized accounts could even be used for direct-depositing paychecks, and the balances were insured by the FDIC.

"There's a riddle we used to use," Steve recounted. "'How many unbanked customers does Green Dot have?' The answer is zero. None."

Yet, despite the riddle's claim, using a Green Dot card isn't the same as having a bank. For starters, Green Dot's personalized accounts aren't cheap: anyone with a balance under $1,000 pays a monthly charge of $9.95, and there's a $5.95 service fee each time the account holder wants to top up the card.

Also, the card is a debit card, not a credit card—and that means the users of prepaid cards can never spend more than they have. This can be a good thing: prepaid cardholders never have to pay overdraft fees, for instance, because it's impossible for them to overdraft.[12] They also don't have to worry about overusing the card and falling into a spiral of household debt.[13]

But during the times between paychecks, when a person needs money to cover a shortfall, prepaid cards are no help. Nor does a prepaid card offer its holder a clear path back to a traditional bank: because it's not a credit card, it does nothing to help build or repair its holder's credit history.[14]

The Green Dot card isn't just for people with poor credit, though. It also serves those living in communities without a bank (the aforementioned "banking deserts").

This demographic inspired Steve Streit's second big revelation.[15]

What if having no access to a bank wasn't actually a problem? he asked. Couldn't most people's banking needs be done online, without ever visiting a branch?

In 2007, Steve watched as Apple launched the iPhone. To a lot of people at the time, the iPhone was little more than Apple's latest overpriced toy. Its screen was small, its internet was impossibly hard to access. Most businesspeople at the time had a BlackBerry, and it was hard for them to imagine that the iPhone might ever become a tool for any kind of serious business.

But Steve thought about how rapidly we had gone from dial-up internet to broadband, from slow and clunky desktop computers to portable quick laptops taking up the tables in every café. He knew about Moore's Law, the principle that computers will double in power every two years. And he knew in his gut that it was only a matter of time before we would all be doing, well, everything, on our mobile phones.

"I just knew that mobile banking would be a big deal, and I went to my board of directors and said, 'Guys, we need to invest a ton of money in mobile banking.'" They struggled to see what he was seeing. "I remember I had one board member in those days who asked, "So you want to have Winnebagos travel into neighborhoods, so people can get access to banking? Like ice cream trucks?"

"No, no, no," Steve told him. "I mean they'll do their banking from their mobile phones."

The man took a moment to process this, then asked, "So people use their phones to reserve a time to meet us at the truck?"

Luckily, another one of his board members was the renowned Sir Michael Moritz, a partner at Sequoia Capital, the $1.4 trillion venture capital firm that backed Apple, Google, Oracle, and PayPal. "So he knew a thing or two about technology," Steve said dryly. Moritz agreed with Steve's insight about the future of mobile banking, and with Moritz's encouragement, the board backed Steve's new plan: to turn Green Dot into a bank that would have no branches.

In 2008, there were over seven thousand banks in the United States—but that didn't mean that creating a new bank was easy, not by any stretch. The process of getting a bank charter is complicated and expensive. In the United States, it requires navigating the rules and regulations of three different federal regulatory bodies—the Federal Reserve Board (the Fed), the Federal Deposit Insurance Corporation (the FDIC), and the Office of the Comptroller of the Currency (the OCC). In addition, each state also has its own laws and regulatory bodies, and any bank operating at the national level needs to stay in compliance with all of them. A bank must meet capital requirements, reporting requirements, privacy requirements, anti-terrorism and anti–money laundering requirements, and even community reinvestment requirements.

The reason for all of this oversight—ostensibly—is to protect the consumer and the community from dangerous or predatory banking practices, and on the face of it, this is a good thing. But the burden of all of this compliance means that filing for a bank charter requires armies of lawyers, whole libraries of paperwork, and years of time—and all of that expense has the (at least somewhat intended) side effect of benefiting the incumbent banks—most of all the five giants: JPMorgan Chase, Bank of America, Citigroup, Wells Fargo, and Goldman Sachs.

The requirements of regulation act as a kind of moat around the banking industry, making it hard for outsiders to get in.

Moats, of course, work both ways: the regulatory moat that surrounds the banks is also a big part of why they are so slow to adapt to new market conditions. Any change that a bank wants to make has to be reviewed and approved by layers of regulators. Then the change must be integrated into the bank's large and often unwieldy infrastructure. Fintechs, on the other hand—small, agile, and unburdened by legacy infrastructure—are much freer to do what they please.

When fintechs began to consider what it would mean for them to cross the moat—to create a new kind of bank—different companies came up with different solutions. But most of them started with the same premise that Steve did: technology had evolved to a point that they should be able to offer core banking services like checking, savings, and debit cards without building physical bank branches. A new, twenty-first-century bank might be able to exist entirely online: its customers could view their accounts, make payments, transfer money, set up direct deposit, even upload images of physical checks.

An online bank could be everywhere at once, simultaneously serving people in big cities and also in rural banking deserts.[16] There would be no need to build physical branches in particular locations, no need to pay rent or hire tellers or choose which neighborhoods to serve and which ones to leave behind. Rather than build ATMs, these online-only banks could negotiate partnerships with existing ATM networks.

And the money that the online banks would save on these traditional bank expenses meant that they would be able to offer their customers a higher rate of return on their savings accounts than would a traditional bank.

The idea of these branchless banks was so new that no one knew what to call them.[17] To some, they were "direct banks," because the customers were able to handle their own transactions directly, online. To others, they were "challenger banks," because they challenged the incumbent banks both with their innovative customer-centric experience (and high-yield savings accounts) and also by their very existence. Still others called them "neobanks"—a term that caught on at least in part because it sounds so futuristic, cyberpunk, and cool.

Whatever they were called, they each had to solve the problem of regulation: they had to get to the other side of the moat and get a bank charter, or they would never be allowed to operate. There are a lot of different ways to structure a bank, and each has advantages and disadvantages. Every nascent "neobank" was looking for a solution that would give them the lowest capital requirements, the most flexibility, and the quickest path to market. But each solution was time-consuming and costly. Once a path was chosen, it would require years of commitment to see it through.

And it was all uncharted. No one had created an online bank from scratch before, so there was no good way to predict which models would work and which ones wouldn't.

Green Dot first approached the regulators about getting a bank license in 2008. At first, they didn't take the pitch seriously. "Here was a guy," Steve said of himself, "who had never worked at a bank, with a product that was largely unknown to regulators. And there had not been a new bank charter issued in a very long time."

"It was incredibly difficult."

So, Steve and his board decided to try another tactic: buying a bank.

This, too, would have to be approved by regulators, but at least it grounded their negotiation in something that the regulators were better able to understand: after all, Green Dot wouldn't be the first company to acquire a bank. In one famous and notorious example, in 1989, Ford Motor Company bought a small California bank called Associates First Capital Corporation as a relatively quick path to getting a banking license. Ford's ownership of the bank gave the company the regulatory structure it needed to offer financing directly to customers, without needing a third-party bank to issue the loan.

Green Dot's business was, of course, very different from Ford's, but the underlying goal was similar: like Ford, Green Dot wanted to acquire a bank in order to add more banking services to its current stack of products. So, the Ford acquisition provided the Fed with a possible model for how to structure Green Dot's regulatory requirements.

But the Ford comparison also offered a cautionary tale, because after Ford acquired Associates First, the bank wound up getting into serious financial trouble—and at that point, Ford, as the parent company, held enormous legal liability. Was this a risk that Green Dot really wanted to take?

It was. In February 2010, Green Dot entered into an agreement to buy the small, Utah-based Bonneville Bank, less for its one branch location in Provo and more for its precious banking license. But, for the sale to go through, first it would have to be approved by the Board of Governors of the Federal Reserve.

Getting this approval took almost two years, but at the end of November 2011, the Fed agreed to let Green Dot take over the Bonneville Bank and become a bank holding company. This gave the company new privileges but also imposed stringent new capital requirements that only banks, and not tech companies, face—including a mandate to keep at least 15 percent of all of its holdings in the form of liquid assets.[18]

CHALLENGER BANKS IN THE UK

IN THE YEARS since the financial crisis, the United States has seen only a handful of neobanks open for business: BankSimple (now renamed, more simply, "Simple"), Moven, Aspiration, and Chime are the few that managed to get and stay on their feet and make their way into the marketplace.

Meanwhile, in the European Union, where regulatory requirements are simpler, more than a dozen neobanks have sprung up: Aldermore (2009), Metro Bank (2010), Shawbrook Bank (2011), Starling Bank (2014), Atom Bank (2015), Revolut (2015), Monzo (2015), OakNorth (2015), Tandem (2015), N26 (2016), ClearBank (2017), and Tide (2017).

Perhaps partly because these UK-based neobanks are more loosely regulated, Steve Streit takes some umbrage when people call Green Dot a neobank. "We're a real bank with real banking products," he said, "and we're directly regulated by bank regulators in the same way that Chase and B of A is regulated. There's nothing 'neo' about Green Dot, except the fact that we've chosen to design our products for different target audiences and distribute them in unique ways."

Almost four years after Steve first had the idea, Green Dot could finally begin its initiative to offer mobile banking to people around the country.

Green Dot's mobile bank, branded as "GoBank," launched to the public in mid-2014, boasting no-fee checking accounts, mobile check deposits, a network of forty thousand fee-free ATMs, and the ability to send payments or transfer money with other banks instantly through a smartphone app.

Because of Green Dot's long history with the underbanked, GoBank's accounts also included features designed specifically for their benefit: overdrafting the accounts wasn't allowed, and this meant no one would ever get stuck in a cycle of overdraft fees. And new accounts were opened without running a credit check or consulting ChexSystems—so people who had been de-risked from other banks were still welcome to become a member at GoBank.

Finally, Green Dot leveraged their relationship with retailers to provide a distinctly non-mobile feature to their new mobile bank: members could make cash deposits into their accounts from any Walmart store.

The bank and its feature-rich mobile app instantly earned critical acclaim and was a gold category winner at the 2013 PYMNTS.com Innovator Awards.

What it did not get, out of the gate, were a lot of new members. "We didn't sell a lot of accounts, frankly, early on," Steve said. "But we showed the world that Green Dot knew how to build cutting-edge banking technology. And that, at the time, was very important for our morale, for the future survival of the company. It allowed me to credibly say Green Dot is a technology company."

The technology didn't just show the world that mobile banking was possible. It did something else too—something Steve hadn't initially expected. To build the mobile banking app, the Green Dot team had essentially distilled all of their banking services into what programmers call an "abstraction layer": they had built APIs to perform each one of the various banking services and then made all of those APIs available to the GoBank app.

Now that the APIs were built, Steve realized that Green Dot's banking services could be made available to any app, not just the company's own. If another company wanted to offer banking services to its customers but didn't want to go through the years-long struggle of getting its own banking license, Green Dot was now in a position to be able to power those services. If a company wanted to create custom-branded bank accounts for its employees and use them for payroll, Green Dot could now do that. If companies wanted to offer their own branded credit cards but didn't want to build the infrastructure to manage the cards themselves, Green Dot could offer this. Anything that Green Dot was doing for its own GoBank could also be licensed to, and re-branded for, any other company.

By creating a mobile bank, Steve had also steered his company toward something else: a "white label" bank, a generic bundle of services that could be repackaged for anyone.

As a line of business, white-label banking—"banking as a service," or BaaS—would become even more important to Green Dot than its GoBank brand would. Within a few short years, the company became the behind-the-scenes white-label bank for Uber, Walmart, and Intuit's TurboTax.

But as an idea, banking as a service is even more disruptive. For years, the biggest bank brands—Chase, Citigroup, Bank of America—have been inseparably synonymous with the services they provide. The concept of white-label banking forces people to consider that these two things—the brand and the service—can be distinguished from one another: a white-label bank can act as pure infrastructure to provide banking services for any brand.

Once this idea is introduced, it begs the question: What is a bank? Is it the brand, or is it the bundle of services? Once we can get banking services from any brand, people begin to wonder, what is it exactly that the brand of Chase or Citibank or Bank of America has to offer? Why does it even matter where I do my banking?

Bill Gates famously said, in 1994, that "banking is necessary, banks are not." He was already imagining a future where banking services could be offered through an abstraction layer and delivered to any brand. It's taken many years for technology to catch up to what he envisioned.

But we are finally here.

6 BORDER CROSSINGS

REINVENTING THE WORLD OF REMITTANCE

Ismail Ahmed had just been awarded a scholarship to the University of London when the war arrived at his hometown of Hargeisa, Somaliland.

Hargeisa, the largest city in Somaliland, was the home of the Somali National Movement, an anti-communist group dedicated to overthrowing Somalia's dictator, President Mohamed Siad Barre—so the city was also the dictator's biggest target.

Siad Barre had been the only Somali president that Ismail had ever known: a major general in the Somali army, he had come into power during a 1969 coup and enjoyed brief popularity until he began a costly war with Ethiopia and started pursuing policies of brutal persecution against many of Somalia's minority clans—including the members of the Isaaq clan, who make up the population of Somalia's northwest, the region of Somaliland.

When Siad Barre brought war to Hargeisa, he brought it hard, bombing the city so thoroughly that it became known as "the Dresden of Africa." By the end of the bombing campaign, only 5 percent of Hargeisa buildings were left standing, and nearly all of its three million inhabitants were refugees.

Ismail had a visa and a plane ticket to London, but the airport in Hargeisa had been taken over by fighter jets, and the entire region was overrun with

Somali armed forces under Siad Barre's command—soldiers who would have killed Ismail on sight because of his Isaaq heritage.

Outside the city wasn't any better: an armored division called "The Isaaq Exterminators" rolled through Somaliland's desert in tanks, targeting any spot where they thought people might go looking for water, and murdering them there. The brutal campaign, by the time it was done, resulted in as many

ISMAIL AHMED, "THE REFUGEE"

as two hundred thousand civilian deaths and was being called the "Hargeisa Holocaust."[1]

On what was easily the luckiest day of his life, Ismail was picked up by a stranger driving a dump truck out of Hargeisa. "The guy who helped me took a big risk. I acted as a worker helping him, while he hid my passport in the truck."

At the border to the neighboring country of Djibouti, Ismail was able to use his student visa to gain legal entry and escape the Somali Civil War—though he was still a long way from London and had no money to get there.

Almost the entire population of Hargeisa was in flight, scattering to any nearby region that would harbor them and with no good way to stay in touch with one another. Ismail's family, like many of Somaliland's refugees, wound up in Ethiopia—and when they couldn't find Ismail in any of the refugee camps there, they assumed he had been killed. It was only through word of mouth that the family discovered that all of its far-flung members had survived the attacks. When the family learned that Ismail was stuck in Djibouti without any way to continue on to London, his brother-in-law in Saudi Arabia wired him money for a plane ticket, and Ismail was finally able to get to school—and safety.

Remittance—the practice of sending money to another country—is something that the vast majority of contemporary Americans have not experienced firsthand. But go back a generation or two or three or five, and sooner or later, you'll likely find the story of a family member who migrated to the United States to try to make money and then remitted some of that money to the people back home.

Somaliland is no stranger to this cycle of migration and remittance. In the 1970s and 1980s, while the Siad Barre regime was inflicting economic instability and civil war throughout the Horn of Africa, just across the Red Sea, the oil-rich nations of Saudi Arabia, United Arab Emirates, Kuwait, and Qatar were booming. Tens of thousands of men migrated from Somaliland to work in the oil fields and in the other industries that sprang up around the new accumulation of Middle Eastern oil wealth. The jobs were often undesirable, but way more lucrative than anything they could have found back home. "It was like a gold rush for us," Ismail remembered. "Whether you were a clerk or a construction worker, if you crossed the Red Sea, you could make a lot of money."

The migrants who worked these overseas jobs then sent money to their families back home, in staggering amounts: since the 1970s, remittance has accounted for up to 40 percent of Somaliland's GDP, and after the bombing and the civil war, remittances from refugees rebuilt the Hargeisa economy.

Wherever there has been migration, there has been some system for moving money back across the distance. The practice is as old as time itself.[2] And, of course, for as long as people have been moving money, moving money has been complicated: it is slow, cumbersome, and dangerous.

In the eighth century, to get around some of the dangers inherent in moving money, merchants along the Silk Road invented a money transfer system called *hawala*—a system that is still used today in South Asia, the Middle East, and the Horn of Africa, where Ismail Ahmed was born.

Hawala allows people to transfer value without needing to physically transfer money. It works through a network of brokers: If a person in Egypt wants to send one hundred dollars to a person in India, the first person visits the Egyptian *hawala* broker and pays the one hundred dollars. The broker makes a note of the transaction in a ledger and sends word to a corresponding *hawala* broker in India. The Indian broker then contacts the intended recipient and pays the money out of the broker's own pocket—even though the Indian broker never received a payment from the Egyptian broker. Instead of transferring cash, the two brokers simply update their respective ledgers to reflect that the one owes the other one hundred dollars.

Then, at some future point when someone wants to move money in the other direction, the two *hawala* brokers have the opportunity to settle their accounts.

The system works on trust, without the use of promissory notes, on the premise that all of these debts will be sorted out eventually. But sometimes "eventually" can take a long, long time: *hawala* has been in place for more than a millennium, and brokerages and their ledgers of debts are passed down through families for generations.

The twentieth century brought changes to the *hawala* network, and not just because of the advent of telecommunications: governments throughout the developing world began regulating foreign currency and implemented exchange rate controls that made the moving of money across international borders more difficult and more expensive.

So, by 1988, when Ismail's brother-in-law was sending money for Ismail's plane ticket, the practice of *hawala* had become more complex. To transfer one hundred dollars from Saudi Arabia to Djibouti (where Ismail was marooned as a refugee), Ismail's brother-in-law would have had to give the money to a Saudi trader. The trader would have used the money to buy goods—usually food, clothing, or construction material—and would have shipped the goods to an importer in Djibouti. The importer then had to sell these goods in order for the recipient—in this case, Ismail—to receive the one hundred dollars. The practice of exchanging goods allowed the *hawala* brokers to get around the currency laws, because they weren't strictly dealing in currency. The sender—in our example, Ismail's brother-in-law—was effectively financing a short-term business loan, and in exchange, the recipient—Ismail—would receive the full value of the original currency.

But it would often take months to complete the transaction—and indeed, Ismail was stranded in Djibouti for a whole season before his brother-in-law's money arrived and he was able to buy his plane ticket.

Over recent decades, changes in the world economy have worked to undermine the *hawala* system. First, the economic boom in the Middle East slowed down, and migrants from Africa and India instead began seeking opportunities in the West—outside of the network of *hawala* brokers.

Second, policies of "economic liberalization" meant that Western corporations were setting up shop in Africa and the rest of the developing world—and they demanded ways of transferring money that left a clearer and more auditable paper trail. *Hawala*, which had always relied on trust and which now also depended on buying and selling goods—transferring value, rather than transferring cash—left almost no paper trail.

Finally, because the *hawala* network lacked a paper trail, it had become a powerful tool for terrorists and money launderers, and in the name of anti-terrorism, the West shut a lot of this "value transfer system" down.

That left migrants with only one good way to remit their money overseas: wire transfers.

In the West, for a century and a half, the main way to transfer money has been to "wire" it.

Wiring money was invented in 1851 by the New York and Mississippi Valley Printing Telegraph Company, which changed its name soon after to a name that better reflected the company's goal of creating a telegraph network that spanned America from coast to coast: the Western Union Telegraph Company.

It came to be known, more simply, as "Western Union."

The company achieved its goal of sending the first transcontinental telegraph in 1861, and in the years that followed, the company grew so fast that its name became synonymous with the very act of sending a telegraph: people would "Western Union" messages to one another.

Western Union spent several decades at the forefront of technological innovation, in no small part because of one of its Morse code operators, a young man named Thomas Edison. It was while working at Western Union that Edison designed one of his most iconic inventions: the glass-domed stock ticker, which received share prices over telegraph lines and printed them out, one character per second, onto a long paper strip that came to be known as "ticker tape."[3] The stock ticker was an early and transformative "fintech" that greatly increased the speed at which people traded stocks, and the "ticker symbols" that were invented to accommodate the narrow strips of ticker paper are still in use today.

In 1871, Western Union found another way to put its telegraph lines to use: money transfer. For the first time in history, people could walk into a telegraph office in Boston and "wire" money to San Francisco. The process used by Western Union wasn't unlike the process used by *hawala* brokers: the Boston office would take the customer's money and telegraph an encoded message to the corresponding office in San Francisco, and then the San Francisco office would pay the recipient out of its own till. The main difference between *hawala* and wiring was that the telegraph allowed the two offices to update their respective ledgers almost instantly.

There were two main limitations to wire transfers, though. The first was technological: the system could only be used in places that had telegraph lines—and telegraph lines were expensive and somewhat fragile. Abraham Lincoln tried to discourage the company from investing in transcontinental lines, even though he saw the obvious value in having them: "I think it is a wild scheme. It will be next to impossible to get your poles and materials distributed on the plains," he advised Western Union's chief executive, "and as fast as you complete the line, the Indians will cut it down."

Laying telegraph cables across oceans was even more difficult and costly.[4]

The second thing that made wire transfers complicated was cash. Though the process of sending the request was almost instant, the agent on the receiving end needed to have cash on hand to distribute to the recipient, and this required Western Union to keep significant sums of money at telegraph offices all over the country, and eventually, all over the world. And as we've seen from so many Hollywood stagecoach heists and train robberies, the transporting of cash is a risky business.

Eventually, the telephone replaced the telegraph as people's main way of communicating, and the business of money transfer became Western Union's most reliable source of income.[5] Western Union expanded its network around the world, and though the telegraph lines have been replaced by radio and internet, Western Union is, to this day, the market leader in money transfer service, with 525,000 agent locations across more than 200 countries.[6]

But maintaining this global network is expensive. Western Union's agent locations spread to all corners of the globe, and each location requires real estate, employees, and cash. Currencies vary and their value fluctuates, and different regions and countries are governed by differing regulations. In the farthest-flung branches, electricity and even safety aren't assured, and regardless of location, the physical moving of money remains dangerous as ever.

To cover these costs and mitigate their risks, Western Union charges steep fees to its remittance customers.

Ismail Ahmed was about to discover exactly how steep.

When Ismail arrived in London, he found himself, for the first time in his life, on the opposite side of the remittance process: now he was sending money home. As soon as he received his scholarship payment and paid his school fees, he decided to send most of the remaining money back to his family. Finding a money transfer service that could remit the money to Ethiopia wasn't easy; the closest one he found was a three-hour commute from where he lived in the outskirts of London.

And it wasn't cheap, either. For the service of transferring the money to Africa, the agent tacked on a fee of 10 percent: a literal tithe.

Since there was nothing else he could do, Ismail paid the fee.

But Ismail's school had miscommunicated the true cost of his program. Though he had budgeted for his estimated expenses, he quickly found that his university teaching job wouldn't cover his cost of living, let alone pay him enough to keep sending money back to his family. So he took a second job, picking strawberries, and worked whenever he could. Before long, every waking hour of every day, he was either working or studying.

Now the three-hour commute to the money transfer agent was more time than he could spare. Between the high service fee and his cost of traveling back and forth, he was losing closer to 30 percent of the value of the money he was trying to send home.

Time is money: in a practical sense, these fees meant Ismail had to work 30 percent more and sleep or study 30 percent less to make up the money he was losing with each money transfer.

His efforts to send the money paled in comparison to what his family had to do to receive it. The money transfer agent in Ethiopia was in its capital, Addis Ababa—but his family was in a refugee camp one hundred kilometers away. Going back and forth to pick up Ismail's money took them two or three days each time.

And there would never be any guarantee that the money would arrive.

Ismail was doing everything he could to help his family in their time of desperate need—but the process that was in place for remitting money was making it prohibitively difficult and expensive. The people who needed money the most were also the ones who faced the greatest challenges in getting it. The system was broken.

Since he was a student of business and economics, he decided to study the remittance industry and fix it.

By the time he graduated, he was *Doctor* Ismail Ahmed, with a PhD in economics and a job in the United Nations Development Programme. His role was to help the money transfer companies in Africa implement new practices to come into compliance with post–September 11 money laundering laws—to help ensure that the money wasn't being transferred to terrorists.

From what he already knew about the remittance industry, he expected this to be a challenging job—but he soon discovered something he hadn't expected: the biggest challenge of all came from the UN itself. While working with the UNDP, Ismail discovered evidence of widespread corruption and fraud inside the UN's remittance program in Somalia.

He collected a dossier of evidence to give to the UN's Office of Internal Oversight Services so they could investigate. But his supervisor told him not to send it.

"My boss said if I submitted the dossier, I would never be able to work in remittances again, and I took that threat very seriously." By now, remittances were his main field of expertise, and there was no better place in the world from which he could work to improve the remittance industry than from his current office at the UN.

He submitted the report anyway.

"I lost my job to uncover the fraud."

His boss made good on his threat: Ismail was transferred to Dubai, where his contract expired, and he was blacklisted from other jobs in the remittance industry, despite his expertise. Meanwhile, the inquiry he had launched at the UN went nowhere, stalled for years and passed from office to office, until a nonprofit whistle-blower advocate group called the Government Accountability Project took up Ismail's case.

Under pressure from the group, the United Nations Ethics Committee finally reviewed the case, and on December 11, 2009, they found Ismail's original allegations of fraud to be correct. The Ethics Committee also ruled that he had been a victim of retaliation—in violation of the UN's own guidelines for whistle-blower protection—and they awarded him £200,000 as compensation.

He used the money to create WorldRemit.

If you were trying to rebuild the remittance industry from the ground up in 2010, how would you do it?

This was the question that Ismail and his new company faced.

The biggest problem was cash.

Having the sender deposit hard currency in one place and having a receiver pick up currency somewhere else had never been easy. But in 1871, when Western Union started doing it, it at least made a kind of sense—because there was no good alternative.

What about in the twenty-first century?

Digitization, mobile phones, credit cards, online payments—all of these technologies were making it so that cash might no longer be a necessary part of the money transfer process.

If the process of remittance could be digitized, then there would no longer be a need for money transfer agents to keep buildings and piles of currency and security guards at hundreds of thousands of locations around the world. There would be no need for money transfer agents period—and there would be no need for the enormous fee structure that had been the norm in the remittance industry for Ismail's whole lifetime.

WorldRemit set out to create a digital platform for remittance.

Designing a way for migrants to *send* money digitally wasn't hard. The majority of migrants who were sending money were doing so from highly developed nations that already had a reliable infrastructure designed around digital.

Though not every migrant has a bank account, most do—as many as 97 percent in Europe—so WorldRemit could send those people's funds electronically from a bank, debit card, prepaid card, or credit card.

WorldRemit's system for submitting money digitally varied a bit from nation to nation: in some countries, it was easiest to plug directly into bank data; in others, it was a better solution to accept payments from debit and credit cards. But for each nation, the WorldRemit team tried to find the simplest way for customers to send money without using cash.

On the receiving side, things were a lot trickier. The people who receive remittance money tend to be in developing nations—places where people may not reliably have internet access or smartphones or bank accounts. So much of the cost of traditional remittance had always come from the fact that, in these places, there haven't been good alternatives to cash. You can't wire money to a person's bank if your recipient doesn't have a bank. You can't send it to a smartphone if there is no smartphone.

So, even if WorldRemit managed to remove cash from the sender's side of the transaction, this didn't ameliorate the much bigger problems—or costs—on the recipient's side. A typical recipient of a money transfer would still have to travel to a centralized location, usually the nation's capital or some other city where a money transfer agent was located, and this was often miles or days away. The costs and risks of this sort of travel were nearly unbearable.

If Ismail couldn't find a way to remove cash from the receiving side of the remittance transaction—if he couldn't find a better alternative for people who mostly didn't have bank accounts and mostly didn't have smartphones—then he would not be able to drastically improve the remittance industry in the way that he hoped.

Luckily, he did find a better alternative. It is called M-Pesa.

BEFORE THERE WAS Venmo, before there was Zelle, before there was even an iPhone, there was already a service that allowed people to send money back and forth using their mobile devices, and it was created in Kenya in 2007.

M-Pesa was the product of a partnership between Vodafone in the UK and Safaricom, a mobile network operator based in Nairobi. M-Pesa was designed to solve a specific problem: it helped the people of Kenya, many of whom did not have bank accounts or easy access to them, receive and pay back loans.

"Vodafone participated in a proposal that was set out by DFID [the Department for International Development, a government agency in the UK tasked with administering overseas aid] about trying to deepen the financial penetration into the unbanked community," explained Michael Joseph, former Safaricom CEO and founder of the M-Pesa program. "A guy called Nick Hughes in Vodafone came up with this idea of using the mobile phone for disbursement and repayment of microfinance loans, and they asked Safaricom, fortunately, if we could trial it here in Kenya."

The idea was to allow customers to store money on their cell-phone accounts. Using the phone's SMS service, plus a PIN number, money could be transferred in and out; a customer could pay bills without visiting a bank branch or even having a bank account. People could add money to their accounts the same way they added pay-as-you-go minutes to their cell phones—by visiting any participating vendor.

M-Pesa (*pesa* is the Swahili word for "money," and the *m* stood for "mobile") didn't even require a smartphone. It could run on any mobile device with SMS capability—and that meant that, even in 2007, nearly half the population of Kenya would be able to access the service.

Basic Nokia mobile phones had been turned into devices for branchless banking.

But during Safaricom's first trial of the service, the company quickly noticed that microfinance repayments were not the main way people were using M-Pesa. Instead, they were using it to send money back and forth to one another—and especially from the cities and towns, where many of the jobs were, into Kenya's more remote rural areas.

Seeing an opportunity, Safaricom went back to the drawing board and reconceived M-Pesa around this central idea: sending money home.

"It required a tremendous amount of investment and a tremendous amount of risk," Joseph said of his company's pivot. "We knew that it would only work if the people who were receiving the money from the towns actually had someplace where they could do a cash-out." That meant Safaricom had to establish a network of agents throughout the remote regions of Kenya, places where people could go to exchange the money in their M-Pesa accounts for hard currency when they needed it.

Even after making this investment and building out the infrastructure, the Safaricom team still didn't know if people would choose to use the service.

Their business plan told them that they needed 350,000 users by the end of their first year if they wanted to be viable—but Joseph felt that number was way too low. If M-Pesa didn't catch on and go viral throughout all of Kenya, it wouldn't survive. "We had to have a ubiquitous distribution network. We had to have a good strong brand. It had to be standout in the community. The product had to work all the time."

"If you don't get a million customers," he told his staff, "I'm going to fire you." He was being somewhat tongue-in-cheek.

Somewhat.

They officially launched M-Pesa in March of 2007, and by December of that year, they had 1.2 million customers. Joseph's staff weren't just keeping their jobs; they were keeping very, very busy.

During the next years, M-Pesa captured more and more of Kenya's money transfer business, and M-Pesa users grew into the millions, then tens of millions. By 2010, M-Pesa had expanded into Tanzania, Afghanistan, and South Africa and had become the most successful mobile-phone-based financial service in the developing world, providing banking services to people who otherwise had no access to them and helping to lift the poorest people out of poverty.[7]

Crucially, Joseph doesn't think that a bank could have launched the service. "A bank will normally need to make this profitable in the first six-to-nine months, because they would want to see a return on the investment," he explained. "A mobile phone operator doesn't need to make money from M-Pesa. It's nice if they do, but they don't need to, because the benefit for them is the stickiness and loyalty of the customer." Anyone who wants to use the service and its cut-rate money transfer fees has to be a subscriber on Safaricom's mobile network—and this has earned the company two-thirds of the Kenyan market. It has continued to expand throughout Africa, Asia, and Eastern Europe, and now has thirty million users.

UBIQUITY FIRST, REVENUE LATER

"A mobile phone operator doesn't need
to make money from M-Pesa. It's nice if
they do, but they don't need to, because
the benefit for them is the stickiness
and loyalty of the customer."

M-Pesa was one of the first, and largest, of a quickly growing "mobile money" industry that offers financial services to people using basic cell phones and local carrier networks instead of bank accounts. In the wake of M-Pesa's success, other telcos have created their own "mobile wallets"—MTN in Uganda, EcoCash in Zimbabwe, Tigo in Tanzania—and, by 2020, it is expected that there will be five hundred million mobile subscribers across Africa.[8]

This was exactly the sort of technology Ismail Ahmed needed to achieve his vision for WorldRemit.

But just because he had found what he was looking for didn't mean that the telcos were eager to partner with him.

"In the early days, because of MoneyGram and Western Union, a lot of the telcos were quite skeptical about whether we could convince migrants to switch from the traditional methods to mobile," Ismail remembered. "And the banks on the receiving side were very, very skeptical."

He would have to convince them that his business was a viable alternative to Western Union—and he knew he couldn't do this without proving WorldRemit could handle a large volume of transactions.

"We got licenses in more than thirty countries—around thirty-five countries—within two years. [That level of] growth is quite unheard of in our industry." Navigating compliance rules for just one nation is challenging, but doing this concurrently for almost three dozen nations was largely considered impossible—and would have been, if it hadn't been for the twenty years of expertise Ismail had gained in the remittance industry. "We wanted to show our partners that we can deliver the volume, we can deliver the traction. If we had only stayed in the UK alone or Europe alone, we wouldn't have been able to deliver."

But this required WorldRemit to burn through a lot of money up front. "I didn't take money from VCs for the first three or four years." He didn't want investors looking over his shoulder, asking him why he was wasting money on expansion. "I only 'wasted' money from our angel investors," he said with a laugh. "We were building. We wanted to make sure what we were building would work. It was only late in 2013, after we started sending money to mobile money accounts—particularly in Africa—when we started talking to VCs."

KNOWING WHEN—AND HOW—TO GROW

"I didn't take money from VCs for the first three or four years. . . . We were building. We wanted to make sure what we were building would work."

What WorldRemit was building were software interfaces—the "rails"— that they needed to connect the banks on the sender's side and the mobile money accounts on the receiver's side. Once these rails were in place, people could use WorldRemit to send money instantly between any of the partner institutions, at a fraction of the cost demanded by Western Union.

It did work—and investors noticed. In March 2014, WorldRemit received a $40 million series A investment from Accel Partners, an early backer of Facebook, and in 2015, $100 million of series B funding followed, led by TCV.

But the real proof of the platform's success has come from its users. WorldRemit has been named the fastest growing technology company in the UK, and it currently handles 1.1 million payments per month. The company estimates that 10 million people will be using the service by 2020—and why wouldn't they? WorldRemit's money transfer fees average between 2 and 3 percent— compared to fees upward of 10 percent from its traditional competitors.

And its users on the receiving side of the transfer save substantially too— even more than on the sending side. Digitization—the removal of cash from the transfer—doesn't just save money on the transaction itself; it also means that the recipient is spared a potentially dangerous and time-consuming trek to retrieve the payment from a money transfer agent in a faraway city. Instead, the money arrives directly onto a personal phone in less than three minutes.[9]

When people talk about "disruptive technologies," it is because those technologies make it hard for us to remember or imagine what life was like before them. Psychologists call this "hedonic adaptation": the things that shock us and suddenly change our circumstances and our behaviors quickly become normal and taken for granted.

WorldRemit is one such technology. Once people see that money can be transferred internationally, so quickly and at a fraction of the traditional cost, it becomes impossible not to wonder: Why are those other companies charging so much? What is it I'm paying for, exactly?

Traditional money transfer services like Western Union now have to try and catch up to the new narrative. Their old way of doing things, the only way they knew how to do things—the risky, time-consuming, and costly way—is in danger of becoming obsolete, and they are scrambling to digitize, reduce their overhead, and reduce their fees.

But most of all, they are scrambling to prove that they are still relevant in an era when cash is less relevant, when money transfers can be done from our mobile phones, and when the value of banks themselves is starting to be called into question.

What is it we're paying for, exactly?

7 MYSTERY MONEY

THE RISE OF CRYPTOCURRENCY

Charlie Shrem stands five feet, five inches tall, and half of it is eyebrows. The other half is pure hustle.

Charlie has always been a hustler. He needed to be. By the time he was in high school in Brooklyn, Charlie knew he wasn't going to get ahead on his grades ("I wasn't the brightest crayon in the box") or his social skills ("I would hang out in internet relay chat rooms . . . where all socially awkward people would hang out").

What Charlie had was guts, and if he was going to make it in the world, that was how.

He was already running a little business in Flatbush helping people with their computers and printers when his cousin, who worked in the electronics space, approached him with an idea for how to move electronic products that were collecting dust in company warehouses.

"We'd go to these electronics companies and we'd say, 'You have a thousand digital cameras? Don't sell them, don't do anything with them. Hold a thousand pieces for me.'"

Charlie was a high school student; he didn't have enough money to buy a thousand cameras.

But he did have guts.

"We started a website, DailyCheckout.com." Daily Checkout was a "daily deal" site: each day, the site featured a single consumer electronics item and offered to sell it at a discount. Every morning, Charlie updated the site, and the orders came pouring in. Before the day was out, he had a full bank account.

Then, Charlie would go back to the electronics companies and negotiate a bulk-rate discount to buy what he needed. "Whatever we sold, we'd buy from

CHARLIE SHREM, "THE HUSTLER"

these guys and then reship it to the customers. We'd basically try to make a one- or two-dollar profit."

The most important part of Daily Checkout's business plan was that they never needed to hold their own inventory: they secured their sales first, without spending a dime, and only then purchased whatever they needed to complete their orders. The customers loved it because they were getting quality electronics at a discount, and the electronics companies loved it, too, because it helped them move their inventory. "A lot of these companies would just ship to our customers directly for us."

For an eighteen-year-old's first business, Daily Checkout was a great success. "The company just kind of ran itself. We were shipping six hundred to fifteen hundred boxes a day. It was pretty great. It paid the bills, it was fun, we had a good time."

And it paid Charlie's way through college.

College was also helping Charlie to thread together some of his separate interests: money and people-watching. "I love studying people. I'm the type of person that would sit in a café and just watch people and watch reactions." But he never tried to understand those reactions in a more systematized way—never tried to identify the principles behind those reactions—until college. "I had a really good economics professor, and he taught me the concept of socioeconomics," Charlie said. "Essentially, it's seeing how human behavior affects our day-to-day world when it comes to money and value and all these different properties of how we act."

The study of economics helped a lot of things click for Charlie, and it became a bit of an obsession. It opened up his mind to new ways of thinking. "I didn't know what 'Austrian economics' was. I didn't know what the Mises Institute was. I just knew what we use today: capitalism with Keynes and that whole thing."

"Capitalism with Keynes"—Keynesian economics—has been the bedrock of fiscal policy-making in the developed world for most of the past century. Named for the British Depression-era economist John Maynard Keynes, Keynesian economics says that financial systems are volatile by nature, and if they are left uncontrolled, they will always be subject to the practices of the "decadent and selfish" and will swing between booms and dangerous recessions and depressions. Since these swings inflict great harm on society, Keynes suggested that governments and central banks should make efforts to mitigate this volatility by using regulation and currency manipulation to guide the economy—by injecting or removing cash to affect inflation, for example, or by using tariffs to control the flow of international trade.

Though Keynes's ideas weren't popular when he first published them in 1936, they have since caught on to the point that every developed nation in the world practices them to some extent or another. "We're all Keynesians now," Nobel economist Milton Friedman once said, and the phrase was later echoed even by archconservatives like Richard Nixon and Margaret Thatcher.

But the ideas behind Keynesian economics didn't resonate with Charlie. He had no particular reason to trust the government or the central banks to do what was best for people. Regulations favored middlemen, and, he said, "I don't like middlemen. Whatever it pertains to, I don't like middlemen."

What Charlie liked was a free market. That's what he saw in front of him every day: buyers and sellers who were able to assign the value of things based on what they agreed those things were worth, without government regulation putting any thumbs on the scale. That was how his website Daily Checkout worked, and, to his mind, it was how the economy worked more generally—at least until outside forces gamed it for the benefit of some people over others.

This is why Charlie was so reassured, during his college years, when his friends in the internet relay chat rooms introduced him to the Austrian school of economics.

The Austrian school is essentially the opposite of Keynesian economics. Led by economist Ludwig von Mises and his associates, Austrian economics argues that any time a government intervenes in the free economy, intervention invariably winds up favoring one group over others; and this isn't just unfair—it's actually an infringement on people's liberty. The only solution that's truly fair, Austrian economists would say, is one where everyone is treated equally, and that means a free market. The best thing a government can do for an economy is to be "laissez-faire"—to do nothing at all.

Charlie loved this. Once he started studying the Austrian School, there was no stopping him, and he spent more and more time on his IRC channels, chatting passionately with faraway strangers in Norway and England about the dangers of government regulation and currency manipulation.

That's when one of them sent Charlie his first bitcoin.

• • •

BITCOIN CAN BE a little hard to understand.

"The early days of Bitcoin, no one really knew what it was," Charlie said. "The search term didn't even exist on Google. There was no website or anything yet; there was just a white paper."

That's right. The world's first cryptocurrency started as a white paper.

SATOSHI NAKAMOTO, "THE INVISIBLE MAN"

On October 31, 2008—six weeks after the collapse of Lehman Brothers and four days before the presidential election of Barack Obama—a man no one had ever heard of, named Satoshi Nakamoto, released a nine-page proposal entitled "Bitcoin: A Peer-to-Peer Electronic Cash System" to a small mailing list of cryptography experts.

In the paper, Nakamoto theorized about a new digital currency, one that could be designed to work without the need for intermediaries, governments, or central banks. "A purely peer-to-peer version of electronic cash," the paper begins, "would allow online payments to be sent directly from one party to another without going through a financial institution."[1]

The idea of "electronic cash" wasn't new to this cryptography mailing list. The group was made up of privacy advocates and computer coders who called themselves "cypherpunks," a mash-up of "cipher" (a code) and "cyberpunk" (a sci-fi genre about computer hackers in a high-tech dystopian future); among the list's members were some of the foremost cryptography experts in the world.

Why would a group of cryptography experts care about something like electronic cash?

What brought the cypherpunks together, and what they mostly discussed on their mailing list, was their shared belief that privacy-enhancing technologies like software encryption aren't just prudent; they are essential for freedom inside a technological society. "Privacy is not secrecy," says the opening paragraph of the *Cypherpunk Manifesto*, drafted by one of the group's early members, Eric Hughes, in 1993. "A private matter is something one doesn't want the whole world to know, but a secret matter is something one doesn't want anybody to know. Privacy is the power to selectively reveal oneself to the world."

This—the power to sometimes choose discretion and anonymity—is a power that we have almost entirely lost in our new electronic age. Cameras track our movements, facial recognition software reveals our identities, and our banks and credit card companies have long records of our entire purchase histories. "When I purchase a magazine at a store and hand cash to the clerk," the *Manifesto* continues, "there is no need to know who I am." But in an electronic transaction like a credit card purchase, a person's transaction and identity are linked—and that history can be bought and sold by anyone who has access to it. "I have no privacy. I cannot here selectively reveal myself; I must always reveal myself."[2]

So the cypherpunks had long been curious about ways to develop electronic cash payments that could preserve personal anonymity in transactions, on the premise that our liberty requires that we have an option for privacy.

But to design such a system, there were a few problems the cypherpunks needed to solve. First, they needed to be able to create a digital file that couldn't be easily counterfeited. Digital files are, by default, easy to copy—so any form of electronic cash would have to involve a system that made each denomination of its currency somehow unique, and therefore hard or impossible to counterfeit.

Second, electronic cash would need a way to specify ownership—whose money is whose—while also protecting a person's real identity. This problem in itself isn't new to cryptography and isn't especially difficult. It can be solved with what is called "asymmetric cryptography," where each person has a digital signature made up of two parts: a "public key" that can be shared and distributed with anyone and a separate linked "private key" known only to the owner. Information can be encrypted by anyone (using the public key) and turned into encoded data that can be safely transmitted. But it can only be decrypted and read by the holder of the private key.

But the bigger problem surrounding these keys is: Who should verify their authenticity? Who is the keeper of that software? How do we trust any particular agent with that oversight—when even the best-intentioned agents might be subpoenaed or hacked?

And this oversight problem doesn't just apply to the digital signatures that show who owns a piece of electronic cash; it also applies to any transfer of that cash. When someone wants to spend money or send it to someone else, how will everyone know that this money has moved? In a real cash system, it's easy to see when value passes from one person to another because we can see who is left holding the cash. There's no danger that someone will be able to spend the same twenty-dollar bill in two places. But with digital currency, there is no visible cash, and that means there needs to be an accounting mechanism in place to prevent a person from spending money more than once—what the cypherpunks referred to as the "double-spending problem."

Credit card companies and banks solve this double-spending problem by keeping a ledger of transactions—and that is why, every time you make a credit card purchase, the merchant swipes your card and waits for approval: the issuer of the card is verifying that you actually own the money that you want to spend. They check their ledger to see if the money is available, and if it is, they approve the transaction and update the ledger to reflect your new balance.

But the cypherpunks wanted a solution that could do all of this record-keeping without reliance on a "trusted third party" to maintain the ledger—because, they argued, no single third party could be sufficiently trusted.

In fact, the issue of trust was the biggest motive for creating a new currency in the first place.

Money as it works today relies completely on trust. The only reason that the dollars we pass back and forth hold value is because we all agree that they hold value—and we agree on this because we trust the underlying system, in this case, the Federal Reserve Bank and the United States government.

Historically, this trust came from the "gold standard," the decision by the US government to tie the value of the dollar directly to the value of gold at a fixed rate of $20.67 per ounce. Anyone holding a dollar bill knew what it was actually worth and was legally permitted, at any time, to exchange the dollar for gold at this rate. Everyone could trust the value of the dollar because it was defined and unchanging, in relation to gold. And, as long as there was a gold standard and people could redeem their money for gold, the government only had one way to increase the amount of cash in the economy: acquire more gold.

But during the Great Depression, this became a problem: the government was facing growing unemployment and snowballing deflation, and it needed to inject more money into the system—but couldn't, because the number of dollars in circulation was tethered to a gold standard. In 1933, Congress and the Roosevelt administration ordered people to exchange their gold for cash and then reset the gold standard, from $20.67 to $35.00 an ounce—immediately inflating the system with more cash.

It is widely agreed that this move—a textbook case of Keynesian economics—was instrumental in getting America out of its depression.

But what about trust?

What about people whose wealth, in dollars, had just been suddenly devalued by a government that was supposed to be acting in their interest?

If the federal government can reset the value of the dollar overnight, then how can anyone trust that the dollar is a reliable or predictable place to store one's wealth?

Since removing the gold standard, the value of the dollar has fluctuated not according to the value of gold but instead according to the market's trust in the value of the United States as a whole.[3] And federal monetary policies are constantly gaming the system to increase or decrease the number of dollars in circulation in an effort to smooth out potential upsets to the markets. The Fed's policy aims to keep inflation at a rate around 2 percent—meaning that someone holding wealth in dollars will lose 2 percent of that wealth per year—because this inflation rate belies a gradually expanding economy.

So far, the market's trust in the value of the United States has managed to hold. But you don't have to look very far back in history to find examples of times when this sort of trust has faltered, leaving people—and whole societies—ruined. Probably the most notorious example comes from Weimar Germany, where the currency devalued so extremely that people found its best use was to burn it in their stoves to keep warm. But this same sudden devaluing also happened in Greece and Hungary after World War II, in Yugoslavia after the fall of the Soviet Union, and in Zimbabwe in 2008, where inflation reached a mind-boggling 79 billion percent.

As soon as the trust in the underlying state fell apart, the value of the state's currency vanished in an instant.

SO, ONE ADDITIONAL problem that many cypherpunks wanted to solve with electronic cash was a more solid system of trust: they wanted a currency that wasn't dependent on a single state and couldn't be artificially manipulated by any third party. "Real trusted third parties, whether central banks or private note issuers," wrote cypherpunk Nick Szabo, "have always been tempted to overextend and overinflate, although occasionally the reverse happens. They are also vulnerable to government takeover."[4]

• • •

OPEN SOURCING
"Real trusted third parties, whether central banks or private note issuers, have always been tempted to overextend and overinflate, although occasionally the reverse happens. They are also vulnerable to government takeover."

The issue of trust wasn't a problem that could be solved with an algorithm, either. "Any algorithm," Szabo continued, "like the gold standard of old, is likely to be modified in a 'crisis': a trusted third party cannot make a strong credible commitment to keep running the same algorithm."

Therefore, to be truly reliable, whatever system of electronic cash cypherpunks could invent needed not just to solve the encryption problems, counterfeit vulnerabilities, and the problem of double-spending—it also needed to solve the problem of possible manipulation of any third party, *including the issuer of the currency*. The only currency that could truly be trusted was one that could not be manipulated—so, a currency that operated according to transparent rules, the value of which would always and only be determined by the free market.

The cypherpunks had been working for years to come up with solutions to these issues. As far back as 1998, one of the group's members, Wei Dai, proposed something called b-money, which tried to solve the double-spending problem by suggesting that every user of the b-money currency would maintain personal, separate ledgers of all b-money transactions. This way, if anyone tried to double-spend, the rest of the ledgers on the network would be able to detect the discrepancy.

In 2005, Nick Szabo proposed a solution to digital currency's counterfeiting problems by borrowing an idea first introduced to the group by Adam Back as a way of preventing email spam, which Back called a "proof-of-work" system. To prevent the indiscriminate creation of digital files, each file could be required to include this proof of work—basically, the answer to a math problem that is difficult and time-consuming for a computer to complete, but one that, once complete, would be dead simple for other computers to verify. The proof-of-work system would make the cost of counterfeiting a digital file relatively high (in terms of time and computing power) but would also make the likelihood of getting away with counterfeiting close to zero, because the counterfeiter's proof of work could be fact-checked easily by the rest of the network.

NICK SZABO, "THE CYPHERPUNK"

But none of these proposed solutions for electronic cash adequately solved for all of its problems—until Bitcoin.

The Bitcoin white paper addressed everything that the cypherpunks had been working on for decades. Though the paper was only nine pages long, it revealed a deep understanding of cryptography, economics, computer science, and all of the prior work that the cypherpunks had done over the years to solve the problems of digital cash.

The paper didn't just understand the cypherpunks' earlier proposals; it improved on all of them.

Who was Satoshi Nakamoto? Where had he come from?

And could Bitcoin actually work?

Regarding the first two questions, there was precious little information. Except for a vague bio he had written for himself ("37, Male, Japan"),[5] no one could find a record of a person with such a name with the expertise that would have been required to write the Bitcoin white paper.[6] The paper's author—clearly an expert in privacy-enhancing technology—had gone to great pains to make sure that any posts to the mailing list couldn't be traced to reveal the author's true identity; it seemed implausible that a person so intent on protecting his privacy would publish the white paper under a given name.

Plenty of the group's members had their own guesses about the author's real identity. There weren't all that many people in the world with the appropriate expertise.[7] But every time a name was floated, that person denied being Nakamoto, and the debate raged on.

Meanwhile, Nakamoto himself (herself? themselves?) was far more interested in discussing the content of the paper than the details of Nakamoto's identity. Nakamoto worked with other members of the cypherpunk mailing list—including many of the people who had been cited in the paper and had helped to take some of the earlier steps toward solving the problems of electronic cash.

Then, on January 3, 2009, Nakamoto launched the Bitcoin network, making all of the ideas of the white paper a reality.

At the core of Bitcoin's solution is the "distributed ledger"—something called a "blockchain." Every time a bitcoin is created or traded, this transaction gets recorded in the database in what is called a "block," and that block gets appended to the end of all the other blocks to create a "chain." The blockchain is a ledger of all of Bitcoin's transactions.

But there is no one, single, definitive copy of this ledger. Instead, identical copies of it are distributed all over the network, so it can't be lost and can't be manipulated. Tampering with one copy of the ledger—say, to try and mint counterfeit bitcoins or complete an unverified transfer from one owner to another—won't work: this one anomalous ledger won't match the other ledgers on the network, so it will get overruled and overwritten by the others.

A lot of the technology in Bitcoin is dedicated to ensuring that every new entry in its blockchain ledger is authentic. Using asymmetric cryptography, every transaction is associated with a unique digital signature, displayed to the public as each user's public key, but users' true identities are protected by private keys and stored in their "wallets" (the software that holds their bitcoins).

The system adds a new block every ten minutes, which contains all of the Bitcoin transactions since the prior block. To verify the authenticity of each block, the system relies on its peer-to-peer network to complete a complicated cryptographic math problem, and it attaches the answer to this math problem to the new block as a "proof of work"—ensuring that each new block is hard to build, but easy, once it's been built, to verify.

Solving these math problems requires an enormous amount of computer processing power, and to reward people on the network for the use of their computers (and all that attendant electricity), users who complete the proof-of-work computations receive new bitcoins.[8] This process—the race to do these cryptographic math problems in exchange for new coins—is called "mining," and it is the only way that the system is able to generate new coins.

In the beginning, when Bitcoin was new and the blockchain was just a small record of transactions, miners were able to solve the math problems relatively easily, introducing a lot of currency quickly into the system.[9] This is why, in the weeks and months that followed the launch of Bitcoin, a relatively small number of enthusiasts wound up with sudden, large stockpiles of what they assumed to be mostly worthless and unspendable currency,[10] which they gifted back and forth to one another by the thousands, just for fun. Nakamoto himself mined an estimated one million bitcoins during the network's first year.

Then, on December 12, 2010, Nakamoto vanished.

That's when things really got interesting.

Charlie Shrem loved Bitcoin. "I realized that Bitcoin was actually taking all of that Austrian economic theory and putting it into practice. It was a pure market, supply and demand, inflation, all of that. That was super fascinating for me."

PUTTING IDEOLOGY INTO PRACTICE

"I realized that Bitcoin was actually taking all of that Austrian economic theory and putting it into practice. It was a pure market, supply and demand, inflation, all of that. That was super fascinating for me."

Charlie decided to sell his Daily Checkout site and go all in on Bitcoin.

The trouble was, in those early days, there wasn't a good way to go all in on Bitcoin. "In those days, if you wanted to buy bitcoin, which was trading at like fifty cents or a dollar, you'd have to go to one of these pseudo-currency exchanges on the internet and wire money to some shady bank account in Japan." The whole process was slow, clumsy, inconvenient, and potentially rife with fraud.

Charlie believed in the idea of Bitcoin and he knew it had real potential—but not if it was this hard for people to get. He went (as he often did) to internet forums and got into long discussions about economics and cryptocurrency, but especially about the buying and trading of bitcoin.

It was on one of these forums that he met Gareth Nelson, who had an idea to "make buying bitcoin faster." Charlie reached out to him, and the two of them traded notes. A few months later, in September of 2011, the two of them launched a company called BitInstant, with Charlie as the public-facing CEO and the autistic Nelson working behind the scenes as the CTO.

They funded the company with $1,000 of Charlie's plus a $10,000 loan from his mom.

"The premise of the company," Charlie said, "was to essentially allow people to buy small amounts of bitcoin, $300 to $400 worth." BitInstant teamed up with retail stores across America to give people a place where they could go to trade their cash for bitcoin. "We had partners with various payment processors that had physical locations in CVS, Walmart, Duane Reade, Walgreens, 7-Eleven."

The business worked like this: People would go to BitInstant's website to place an order for bitcoin. They would enter their Bitcoin wallet's ID—their public key—so the bitcoin could be transferred to them. But they wouldn't pay for the order on the website with a credit card, because that would defeat a lot of the point of bitcoin in the first place, the anonymity of cash. Instead, they would print a receipt and bring it to one of these retail outlets where BitInstant had a footprint. They would pay the cashier, and within twenty minutes, Charlie's company would transfer bitcoin into their Bitcoin wallet.

In a way, BitInstant wasn't so different from Daily Checkout:[11] Charlie didn't hold inventory, at least not much, at least not for long. He would receive customer orders, tally them up, order a whole sum of bitcoin from one of the larger "pseudo-currency" exchanges where he had an account, and collect a small transaction fee from his customers for each of the sales.

But the way the business model worked, he did need "float"—enough money on hand to cover these orders short-term, until he received payment from the retail outlets who had collected the cash.

"If you were buying bitcoin," he explained, "let's say at a 7-Eleven, I was using a payment processor like SoftPay. You'd walk into 7-Eleven and you'd say to the teller, 'I want to pay my bill,' and then they'd take your money. And at the end of the week, SoftPay is settling with me minus whatever their fee is. But I need to give the customer the bitcoin within twenty minutes. So, I need double. Whatever my volume was, I needed to double the amount of money in order to process transactions." He needed enough capital to buy the bitcoin his customers had ordered from his exchange and also needed to deliver that amount to the customers—even though he wouldn't be reimbursed for, on average, another six business days.

For a remarkably long time, the $10,000 from his mom was enough to cover this float from week to week. "As long as we could get that $10,000 back within a six-day period, we were okay."

This somewhat precarious business model worked well enough for BitInstant to get off the ground. But then, something happened: Bitcoin started to grow. Thanks to coverage in mainstream media outlets like *Time* and *Gawker*, awareness of the cryptocurrency was spreading beyond the handful of enthusiastic computer geeks who helped get it started. As these newcomers began buying the currency, its value—which started the year at thirty cents per coin—soared to over thirty dollars by midyear.

But even its early adopters were a bit at a loss to explain exactly what Bitcoin was or how it worked: it was a bizarro asset that everyone said might double or triple in value overnight, but you couldn't see it and you couldn't touch it. BitInstant, in contrast, was something everyone could understand. It was tangible. You could walk into a store and buy that bizarro asset, and get a piece of paper that said you owned it. "There was no other retail way to buy bitcoin," Charlie recalled. "When you could walk into a Walmart and buy bitcoin, people were all over that."

BitInstant took off. Within a few months, the company had a footprint of almost a million locations in the United States.

"Overnight, our volume exploded," Charlie said. "Growth was unbelievable. Our first month we did like $30,000 the whole month, and our second month we did like $60,000, and then it went to $100,000, and then it was doubling every month."

This growth meant that the bitcoin orders he was placing to the currency exchanges every day were getting much larger—and every day, he needed more cash to cover his float. "We realized by like day forty-five, we weren't going to have enough money to cover everything. And then we worked out credit agreements with our liquidity provider, and then we borrowed money from people at stupid rates. I almost [had] to shut down BitInstant, until I went on this internet TV show and told everyone who was watching, 'I need money, like, now!'"

He got a Skype message that night from a man he had never met named Roger Ver, asking, "How much do you need?"

Ver, a Silicon Valley native and radical libertarian who did jail time for selling explosives on eBay before relocating to Japan, became BitInstant's first outside investor. "Before we even got the paperwork done, he was wiring me like $120,000."

That was enough to keep BitInstant in business.

As the company grew, so did Charlie's celebrity. There weren't a lot of people in the Bitcoin community back then, and there certainly weren't a lot of people who were as tenacious and outspoken as Charlie. His face, and his enthusiasm, became synonymous with the strange new currency, and Charlie was a ubiquitous presence on the message boards where the Bitcoin community hashed out the details, debates, and decision-making of their nascent industry. In September of 2012, roughly a year after BitInstant's launch, Charlie and a handful of other cryptocurrency proponents created the Bitcoin Foundation, to "accelerate the global growth of Bitcoin through standardization, protection, and promotion of the open source protocol."

It was through his newfound celebrity that Charlie attracted his next angel investors—a pair of six-foot, five-inch Olympic athletes who were themselves something of a celebrity power couple. Cameron and Tyler Winklevoss had become household names (the "Winklevii") thanks to the 2010 David Fincher movie, *The Social Network*. Cameron and Tyler famously claimed to have been instrumental in the creation of Facebook and sued Mark Zuckerberg for co-ownership. By the end of that suit, the twins had received a reported $500 million in cash and stock.

Now they were looking for a place to invest it.

IF YOU'RE A venture capitalist, finding a startup company willing to take your investment money usually isn't that much of a problem, especially in the tech sector. But when Cameron and Tyler approached companies about investing, they kept getting turned down.

The trouble was, they had waged war with Mark Zuckerberg, and since every startup in Silicon Valley staked its hopes on eventually selling to a tech giant, no one was willing to risk getting on Zuckerberg's bad side. Word had spread through the Valley that Facebook would never acquire a company that had the Winklevoss twins attached as investors. The twins found their money was radioactive—no one on the West Coast wanted to touch it.

So, they flew east to discuss possible investment opportunities with the CEO of a Bitcoin company that had been getting a lot of press coverage. What they discovered when they got there was Charlie Shrem, a twenty-two-year-old who kept three bongs on his desk.

But whatever Charlie's shortcomings, he knew about Bitcoin, and he knew how to talk about it intelligently and passionately. "Charlie has been in the space for a very long time," Cameron said, "and he has an impeccable reputation among Bitcoiners. He knows everyone in the space and everyone in the space knows him. . . . One of the most exciting things about people who are into Bitcoin is that they're a really passionate community, and Charlie is a passionate entrepreneur. He would be in that category of someone who lives, breathes, and sleeps Bitcoin."[12]

Despite the bongs on Charlie Shrem's desk, the Winklevoss twins decided they trusted him to carry Bitcoin into a rich future, and them along with it. By the time they were all done talking, Charlie had convinced them to go big into

Bitcoin and turned them into true believers: they spent $1.4 million to acquire 200,000 bitcoins—making them the owners of about 1 percent of all of the coins in circulation. They also agreed to fund BitInstant with $1.5 million in capital in exchange for a 2 percent stake in the company.

What persuaded them, believe it or not, was Charlie's business acumen. "The entrepreneurs in the space are very impressive," Tyler said, "but it takes really two areas of expertise: One is technology, and the second is understanding

CAMERON AND TYLER WINKLEVOSS, "THE TWINS"

money services and regulation and all those things that are important for sustainability. Most entrepreneurs and companies we see in the space have the tech down, and they're super strong there, but in terms of being buttoned up and looking like an average bank, it's hard to couple both of them together. We think that BitInstant and Charlie do a fantastic job of doing both."[13]

"Looking like an average bank" wasn't something many people thought about Charlie and his company. "We had this real estate agent we hired to find us a new office," Charlie remembered, "and he's like, 'What do you guys do?' And we couldn't explain it to him. But we were telling him, 'We need an armed security guard, we need hazed glass walls so no one can see inside when they come off the elevator. For licensing requirements, we need our own floor.' . . . He's like, 'So, I don't understand. You're a bunch of kids.' We actually hired a guy who was just this fifty-year-old dude. . . . His job was to go to the banks and go to the insurance companies. It helped, because a bank wasn't opening an account for a twenty-year-old."

Charlie became one of the first Bitcoin millionaires. The price of currency soared, and the volume of trades at BitInstant went from a few hundred per day to a few thousand. Charlie's wealth rose along with it. He moved out of his parents' basement, bought a nightclub, and threw parties every night. He was featured on the cover of *Businessweek*. He started wearing a gold ring inscribed with the private key to his Bitcoin wallet—a piece of jewelry that earned him the nickname "four-finger Charlie," because people were sure someday a thief would cut the key to the wallet right off of him.

"It got to my head a little bit," he admitted, "that whole lifestyle."

Bitcoin had been, since its inception, a bit of a Wild West entity and had always attracted a certain breed of digital cowboy. A lot of this was tied up in the cryptocurrency's design: it had no central authority, and its only rules were the ones coded into its software. This also meant that the use of bitcoin required some amount of technical acumen, which made it a plaything of a growing online hacker community.

Of course, the wildest thing about bitcoin was that it could be traded back and forth in complete anonymity—and the trouble with anonymity is its adjacency to trouble. Cryptocurrency appealed to "crypto-anarchists" for philosophical reasons—the deeply held belief in the right to privacy. But Bitcoin had much more practical, hands-on appeal to anyone who needed to conduct an online transaction in secret—and that set of people included, in no small numbers, drug dealers, weapons smugglers, and black marketeers. Bitcoin was a great way to buy and sell illegal things online.

Three years after the launch of Bitcoin, in February 2011, a staunch and maybe radicalized libertarian who went by the name "Dread Pirate Roberts" launched a shopping website, called Silk Road, on the premise that "people should have the right to buy and sell whatever they wanted, so long as they weren't hurting anyone else."[14] To preserve its users' anonymity, the Silk Road marketplace could only be accessed through the Tor browser, an encrypted web browser that anonymizes its users' network identity; and shopping transactions could only be completed using bitcoin.

Whatever idealistic intentions the "Dread Pirate" had for the site, Silk Road quickly became known as a place to buy drugs: narcotics made up 70 percent of Silk Road's inventory. And though the site's terms of service specifically forbade the sale of child pornography, weapons, or anything meant to "harm or defraud," Silk Road also listed for sale stainless-steel nunchucks (0.4182 BTC), a fake US passport (0.2646 BTC), and a guide on how to hack ATM machines (0.5652 BTC).[15]

Since Silk Road was, in 2011, one of the few online vendors that accepted bitcoin, the reputation of the darknet site also stained the reputation of the currency—and led law enforcement to start scrutinizing both. In 2012, the FBI drafted a report that itemized all the ways that Bitcoin had succeeded in making their job of crime prevention much, much harder.[16]

Regulators and courts were starting to notice Bitcoin too. By 2013, the currency's price was going atmospheric: it began the year at $13.30 and ended at $770.00, and even dubious investors were starting to buy. A series of hacks and frauds on cryptocurrency exchange sites meant consumers were starting to look for some kind of government oversight and protection.

But how were they going to regulate a currency that was designed, in part, to be impervious to regulation?

Was it even a currency, really? There are two functions that currencies fulfill. One is that you can buy things with them and the other is that they act as a store of value. Cash is useful because you can spend it and because you can hoard it.

But bitcoin wasn't something that a person could easily spend. No one could go to the supermarket and use bitcoin to buy a loaf of bread. Partly this was because it hadn't been widely adopted by merchants, and this was something that might change over time. But partly it was because the value of bitcoin was fluctuating so wildly that it wasn't practical to use: in early 2011, bitcoin was worth a dollar, by mid-June it was about thirty-two dollars, and by November, it was down to two dollars.[17] What you spend on a loaf of bread today might buy you a Lamborghini tomorrow—so it's much safer to buy your bread with a more stable currency.

Bitcoin's instability also made it a poor place to store value: it was too unpredictable. If you converted all your dollars into bitcoin to hide in your proverbial (and digital) mattress, you'd have no assurance that your wealth would be there when you went looking for it in six months or six years or sixty. Historically, when a currency is that volatile, people move their wealth out of it and into commodities that are more assured to keep their value, like gold or oil or even sugar.

But, in 2012 and 2013, when the people of Cyprus were faced with a financial crisis—the EU essentially raided people's private savings accounts in order to collect on bank and government debt—many Cypriots flocked to Bitcoin as a *safer* place to put their money, and one that the EU banks couldn't access. The Cypriot financial crisis affirmed that Bitcoin was a viable currency and also proved its founding premise: that you can't trust government- or bank-issued fiat currency, because there is no such thing as a "trusted third party."[18]

For all of its strangeness, it was becoming clear that more and more people—and institutions—were treating Bitcoin as a legitimate currency, and the government began to follow suit. In 2013, a federal judge ruled that Bitcoin is in fact a currency, and that it needed to be treated as such by the Texas-based Bitcoin Savings and Trust that the SEC had accused of misappropriating funds. The following week, the New York State Department of Financial Services issued subpoenas to twenty-two different Bitcoin-related companies so the department could evaluate the companies' roles in various illicit activities and try to come up with a regulatory framework.

"Illicit activities" was the main driver behind the government's push to regulate Bitcoin. The currency undermined many of the rules that had been put in place after September 11, 2001, to crack down on terrorism and money laundering, and the intelligence agencies weren't going to let that happen without a fight. In October, the FBI shut down Silk Road and decided to make an example out of its creator, who was revealed to be a twenty-nine-year-old named Ross Ulbricht. After his conviction for money laundering, computer hacking, and conspiracy to traffic narcotics, the nonviolent, first-time-offending "Dread Pirate" was condemned to two consecutive life sentences plus forty years, with no chance for parole.

The government also tightened up its regulation of the bitcoin exchanges, ruling that they needed to be licensed as "money transmitters"—a costly process that also required ongoing oversight. The government maintained that this regulation was necessary in order to keep tabs on money laundering—but to the Bitcoin community, it had more than a whiff of corporatocracy. "The money transmitter laws were started by the payments roundtable," explained Charlie, "essentially the big Western Union–, PayPal-, MoneyGram-type companies. There's a whole rumor that they actually helped push those laws into existence because they're the only ones that can afford to get [licensed]."

But the government wasn't going to back down. In June, the New York State Department of Financial Services sent BitInstant a warning letter, demanding that it comply with the regulations that govern a money transmission business.

Charlie was not just BitInstant's CEO; he was also its chief compliance officer—so he looked into the licensing process. "In order for you to get a money transmitter license in all fifty states, you're looking at $15–$20 million between legal fees and bonding. So, it's virtually impossible, unless you raise a crazy amount of money."

BitInstant couldn't do that. In July, Charlie shut the service down.

"It was really heartbreaking. It sucked."

It also wasn't fair, he complained. "PayPal, they never had a money transmitter business license, but they were so big that when it was time for them to get a license, the government just fined them and helped them get the license, and they never shut down. They operated illegally for a while, and they just were legal overnight. We didn't have that luxury."

But if Charlie thought that shutting down BitInstant would be the end of his troubles, he couldn't have been more wrong. On his way back from a Bitcoin conference in Amsterdam, he was greeted at the airport by fifteen government agents—a joint task force of the FBI, IRS, DEA, and the NYPD.

"They walked up to me and handed me an arrest warrant."

He was being charged with conspiracy to commit money laundering, failure to file a suspicious-activity report, and operating as an unlicensed money transmitter—charges that all stemmed from BitInstant's relationship with a client they knew as "BTCKing," who bought $1 million worth of bitcoin from Charlie in order to resell it, at a markup, to users of Silk Road.

BitInstant was an exchange that operated like any other bank or currency exchange service—so why was he being held liable for what his customers were doing with their money? Roger Ver, Charlie's first investor after his mom, came to his defense. "Even if absolutely everything the government is alleging is true, Charlie has done nothing that's morally wrong."[19]

But in the end, Charlie wound up agreeing with his accusers. According to the law, any money transmitter is required to report potentially illegal activity back to the government—and Charlie didn't. "I am guilty of the crime. I knew that he was reselling bitcoins to other people who were then going on Silk Road."

He resigned from his vice chair position of the Bitcoin Foundation and, at age twenty-five, was sentenced to two years of prison.

His first day in prison was "a blur," but one thing he does remember: waiting on a money transfer from Western Union, the company that had lobbied for the money transmitter licensing that had landed Charlie in prison, the company that represented, in many ways, exactly what Bitcoin was trying to undo.[20]

The experience of prison made him circumspect. "You won't find people in prison that are like, 'I'm innocent, I didn't do it.' People don't do that. If you're in there, you're guilty. You did your crime, you're moving on, you're admitting to it, you're doing your time, becoming a better person, and you're moving on with your life."

Charlie has done okay at "moving on" with his life: since being released from prison, he has, somehow, acquired a $2 million house in Florida, two Maseratis, two powerboats, and a handful of other real estate investments, and he's had a thriving career as a cryptocurrency consultant.

Two other people who have "moved on" since the days of BitInstant are Cameron and Tyler Winklevoss. At the time of Charlie's arrest, the Winklevoss twins claimed to be "passive investors" in the company, without any involvement in its day-to-day operations, and they denied any knowledge of Charlie's interactions with "BTCKing" or Silk Road.

Cameron and Tyler remain deeply committed to—and invested in—cryptocurrency. When the government's new, expensive licensing requirements put many of the cryptocurrency exchanges like BitInstant out of business, the twins saw it as an opportunity, because, unlike most of those exchanges, the two of them were sitting on a Facebook fortune and could afford to pay the up-front cost of the licenses.

"When there's a gold rush," the saying goes, "sell picks and shovels."

In October of 2015, the twins launched a new cryptocurrency exchange called "Gemini" (get it?)—and their compliance with licensing requirements is their biggest selling point, proudly displayed right in the company's tagline: "The Regulated Cryptocurrency Exchange." Gemini is also the first cryptocurrency exchange to be insured by the FDIC.

Though Gemini has mostly targeted institutional investors—Wall Street traders looking to include crypto in their portfolios—in 2019 the company unveiled an ad campaign around New York City, postering the city with declamations like "Crypto Without Chaos" and "The Revolution Needs Rules." Gemini's head of marketing told the *Wall Street Journal*, "We believe that investors coming into cryptocurrency deserve the exact same protections as investors in more traditional markets, adhering to the same standards, practices, regulations and compliance protocols."[21]

But Gemini's embrace of regulation runs counter to the ideals of many in the cryptocurrency community, who think it undermines the reason that these currencies were created in the first place; Gemini has succeeded where BitInstant failed mainly because the Winklevoss twins had enough money to jump through all the government's regulatory hoops. That is not a system that favors everyone equally. It is not, the Bitcoin enthusiasts argue, what Satoshi Nakamoto would have wanted.

"Bitcoin," wrote Charlie in a recent essay to the cryptocurrency community, "is the awakened sleeping giant, because it has fundamentally and forever changed money and, more importantly, money's seat of power. For me, this is the most important aspect of Bitcoin and cryptocurrency: its role in propagating power to the greatest number of people possible. What Satoshi did when he democratized money was hand every individual alive—and generations to come—vast personal liberty."[22]

While this fight rages between the cypherpunk-spirited crypto-anarchists, on the one hand, and the people who would prefer to legitimize cryptocurrency with regulation, on the other, Nakamoto's real legacy is turning out to be something else altogether—because it turns out that the real innovation in the Bitcoin white paper wasn't Bitcoin.

It was the blockchain.

And some people believe that this is what will really fundamentally and forever change our world.

8 DISTRIBUTING & DECENTRALIZING

THE BLOCKCHAIN

Vitalik Buterin was seventeen when his father first told him about Bitcoin. Vitalik was an unusual kid. He was six when his parents left Kolomna, Russia, an ancient city seventy miles southeast of Moscow, and immigrated to Toronto. When they settled there, Vitalik's father, Dmitry, remembers his son working hard on something he called the Encyclopedia of Bunnies. "Basically, he came up with this whole universe that is populated by bunnies, but it's all governed by very strict formulas. . . . It was all full of math and charts and calculations."[1]

In third grade, Vitalik got plucked out of his mainstream classes and put into a special program for the "gifted." He had also started playing with computers. "I would program video games that I would then play myself until I got bored, then I would program more."[2] When he was fourteen, he started attending the Abelard School, a private high school with a teaching style founded in the Socratic method.

"I was never particularly inspired by the traditional education system," Vitalik said, "never really seeing a reason why I should put time and effort toward my homework rather than earning an extra level on World of Warcraft."[3] But Abelard changed him. "Something about the environment, whether it was the level of dedication and focus on intellectual inquiry, the closer connection between students and teachers or the level of depth at which the material was taught, made me want to learn, and to focus on learning as my primary goal."[4]

Vitalik was already something of a math and computer whiz by 2011, when his father introduced him to Bitcoin. Vitalik thought the idea was "interesting," but he didn't understand how a currency that had no intrinsic value

VITALIK BUTERIN, "THE BOY WONDER"

could catch on. But his curiosity was piqued; he learned everything he could about the cryptocurrency and wondered how to get his hands on some bitcoin of his own. He couldn't afford to buy it, and the process of mining bitcoin had already been taken over by wealthy individuals and small companies running giant computer networks with souped-up video cards, racing to earn every new coin.

"I started poking through the Bitcoin forums," he remembered. "I eventually found the guy who would pay me in Bitcoin to write articles for a blog that he was working on."[5] He earned five bitcoin per article, and meanwhile built up a reputation inside the Bitcoin community—so quickly, in fact, that a few months later he was invited to become a cofounder and head writer of *Bitcoin* magazine.

Though he was beginning a full course load at the University of Waterloo and a part-time job as a research assistant in cryptography, he agreed to take on the role at *Bitcoin* magazine. Somehow, he juggled all of it, and over the next year, he became proficient both at writing about Bitcoin and also writing code for the technology that makes it all run: the blockchain.

It was in that role that he was flown out to "Bitcoin 2013," a convention in San Jose hosted by the Bitcoin Foundation. The convention's keynote speakers were the largest holders of bitcoin in the world: Cameron and Tyler Winklevoss.

"That moment really crystallized it for me," Vitalik remembered. "It really convinced me that, hey, this thing's real and it's worth taking a risk and jumping into."[6] He wanted to take a leave of absence from school and instead travel the world to meet other developers in the Bitcoin community, to learn everything he could.

His father was all for it. "I told him, 'You know what? If you stay, you will have a very nice, guaranteed job at Apple, Google, whatever. You'll make $100,000, probably more. . . . If you drop out, it will be different, more challenging in life. But you will learn so much more than you learn in university.'"[7] So Vitalik traveled to Israel, Amsterdam, London, Las Vegas, San Francisco— anywhere that would give him a chance to work on people's cryptocurrency projects while writing for *Bitcoin* magazine.

The more work he did, the more an idea kept nagging at him, and he worked at it through most of the year.

Then, in November of 2013, at the age of twenty, he published the "Ethereum White Paper."

"When Satoshi Nakamoto first set the Bitcoin blockchain into motion in January 2009," the paper begins, "he was simultaneously introducing two radical and untested concepts. The first is the 'bitcoin,' a decentralized peer-to-peer online currency that maintains a value without any backing, intrinsic value or central issuer." But, the paper points out, somewhat lost in the hype around the currency, "there is also another, equally important, part to Satoshi's grand experiment: the concept of a proof of work-based blockchain."[8]

Blockchain, the technology that makes Bitcoin possible, allowed for the creation of a new decentralized form of money. But what if money was just the beginning?

What if blockchain was also capable of decentralizing other functions of our society, removing the need for intermediaries and "trusted third parties" up and down many sectors? What if, in addition to being used to record the transfer of bitcoin, the blockchain were used to record the transfer of stocks, real estate deeds, and any other asset?

Blockchain is a ledger that can be updated securely and instantly, and it's immutable: once it's updated, it can't be tampered with. What if it were used to record votes? What if a blockchain could be used to replace or improve *every* transaction that depends on a trusted third party?

Vitalik wasn't the first one, since the creation of Bitcoin, to consider broader uses for the blockchain. Members of the Bitcoin community had been looking for ways to expand its functionality and leverage blockchain for purposes other than just the creation and transfer of bitcoin.

The trouble was, the programming language that Nakamoto had created to power Bitcoin was an intentionally simple one, a basic scripting language that was designed to do one thing: evaluate and update blocks of the chain. The language is what computer scientists refer to as "Turing incomplete," meaning it is incapable of complicated computational logic. This design—Turing incompleteness—was to prevent people from writing over-complicated or malicious code that would bog down the processing power of the vast peer-to-peer network.

But this also meant that anyone trying to get extra functionality out of the blockchain was using, essentially, hacks. This is what Vitalik saw while he traveled around the world working on different blockchain projects. "I discovered that they were doing this sort of Swiss Army knife approach of supporting 15 different features and doing it in a very limited way."[9]

Vitalik's white paper reimagines the blockchain—not as a tool for creating a decentralized currency but rather as a tool for creating decentralized applications of any kind (and Bitcoin is just one such application).

To achieve this, he needed to take the ideas from the original implementation of Bitcoin but build on them in a substantial way, first of all by replacing Bitcoin's modest scripting language with a more robust, "Turing-complete" programming language he called Solidity. In Nakamoto's version of Bitcoin, each block is a record of transactions—essentially a set of instructions to transfer value from one person to another: delete an amount of bitcoin from one user and add an amount of bitcoin to another user.

But Vitalik and others in the Bitcoin community understood that the block wasn't just a record of a currency transfer; it was a set of instructions to the computer.

With Ethereum, he was proposing to allow these instructions to become more complicated by adding conditional "if/then" rules to the code: *if* a certain requirement is met, *then* some amount of currency gets added to the account as a payment. The Ethereum white paper described how this computational logic—the series of instructions that paired certain conditions ("if") with certain actions ("then")—could be assembled into what Vitalik calls "smart contracts."

"Vending machines are kind of a smart contract," explained Buterin. "There's a set of rules implemented in physical hardware that say, 'When you put a dollar in, some bottle or drink comes out.'"[10]

Smart contracts had first been conceived in 1997 by Nick Szabo, a cryptographer who was involved in Bitcoin from its earliest days. If the terms of the contract were defined in computer code, he suggested, and were executed by the computer instead of human intermediaries, then the contract wouldn't depend on the trust of a third party to enforce it. The code itself would enforce the contract.

But code lives on computers, and computers have owners—third parties—who might tamper with, or just plain lose, the contract. In 1997, Szabo's dream of a truly trustless smart contract was out of technical reach.

So, what about a smart contract that runs on a blockchain?

This was the central idea of Ethereum: smart contracts that execute on all of the distributed computers running the blockchain, a kind of "world computer" without a centralized authority and where no single party could manipulate the code of the smart contract, because that manipulation would be overruled by the other computers on the blockchain.

"The Ethereum protocol," Vitalik wrote in the white paper, "was originally conceived as an upgraded version of a cryptocurrency, providing advanced features such as on-blockchain escrow, withdrawal limits, financial contracts, gambling markets and the like."

But smart contracts could do much more than just transfer value, like the blocks of the original Bitcoin. Since the contracts are made up of Turing-complete code running on a computer (on many computers), they could be assembled to do things—to do, more or less, anything that code can do. "The Ethereum protocol moves far beyond just currency. Protocols and decentralized applications around decentralized file storage, decentralized computation and decentralized prediction markets, among dozens of other such concepts, have the potential to substantially increase the efficiency of the computational industry."[11]

But the possibilities for Ethereum weren't limited to just "dozens" of concepts. This was an open-ended platform. Ethereum could be used to develop any number of decentralized applications—computer programs that could run anywhere on the network and wouldn't require any human intervention. "We believe," the paper concludes, "that it is extremely well-suited to serving as a foundational layer for a very large number of both financial and non-financial protocols in the years to come."

Vitalik released the paper two months before the cryptocurrency community would be meeting for a conference in Miami. He had no idea how his paper would be received. "My first thought was, okay this thing is too good to be true and I'm going to have five professional cryptographers raining down on me and telling me how stupid I am for not seeing a bunch of very obvious flaws. . . . Two weeks later I was extremely surprised that none of that happened."[12]

In fact, the opposite happened: some of the best developers in the crypto space reached out to him to say they wanted to help him build it. In January, a half dozen of them, flush with the new wealth they'd acquired from Bitcoin, rented a house in Miami and began the hard work of figuring out how to turn Vitalik's idea into a reality. Then, in late January, the soft-spoken, lisping

Vitalik stepped onstage at the North American Bitcoin Conference to present their ideas. He received a standing ovation.

The team continued developing the project remotely—like the technology itself, the developers working on Ethereum were "decentralized": a Brit, an Israeli, a few Canadians, a Romanian—but they met up again six months later in Switzerland. By then, Vitalik had become something of a celebrity, and not just in the crypto community. He had just been awarded a Thiel Fellowship, the strange $100,000 prize given out by PayPal creator Peter Thiel to talented college students who promise to drop out of school. "We hope the 2014 Thiel Fellows inspire people of all ages as they demonstrate that intellectual curiosity, grit and determination are more important than credentials for improving civilization," read the announcement of the award, throwing Buterin and Ethereum into the mainstream media spotlight.

A year later, after vigorous development and testing, Vitalik and his co-creators launched Ethereum to the public, with a clearly stated goal: "Decentralizing everything."

The best way to understand the promise of Ethereum and its decentralized applications is to consider some of the "centralized" applications they aim to replace.

"Uber is an app for ridesharing," explained Michael Casey, senior advisor to the MIT Media Labs Digital Currency Initiative. "If you're a driver, sign up with Uber, the company. And then as a passenger, I sign up with Uber, the company. And Uber, the company, intermediates between the driver and the passenger. It delivers us both this service. We exchange value with each other, but it's all intermediated through Uber. Everything, all the data, all of the management of that system, runs internally."

Web 2.0—the web that arose from the intersection of social media, APIs, and mobile phones—has allowed people to connect to one another in ways that used to be impossible: Kickstarter lets us fund each other's projects, Uber lets us ride in each other's cars, Airbnb lets us stay in each other's homes, Dropbox gives us a way to store files on other people's computers, Upwork connects freelancers with employers.

But each of these services is run by a middleman—a middleman who makes the rules and often charges a fee. Kickstarter keeps 5 percent of all of our donations. Uber collects 25 percent of each fare. Airbnb charges service fees to both its hosts (3 percent) and its guests (up to 20 percent).

Ethereum provides a way for developers to offer these same services directly, without an intermediary, by using a blockchain. This is why some people refer to the platform as "Web 3.0."

"We're creating protocols that nobody controls," continued Casey. "Rather than have some central authority dictating the rules around which all of those transactions take place, there's a decentralized network of many, many computers all coming to a consensus around the authenticity of those transactions."

And developers are already working to build these decentralized, Web 3.0 alternatives ("dapps"): a dapp called Golem is an Ethereum-based version of Airbnb. One called WeiFund offers crowdfunding. Ethlance uses a blockchain network to offer a decentralized version of Upwork. Gnosis offers a purely peer-to-peer prediction market, where people can guess and bet on the outcome of future events. Radix is a zero-fee currency exchange.

"Rather than having to trust, say, a bank to intermediate between us or somebody else, we'll actually let this computer system do it. Any computer in that network is now going to do so, and it will be recognized as having done so without breaching the terms because there's a consensus network that makes it so. So, now we have the capacity to automate so much of what happens in the world."

Advocates of this decentralized blockchain technology imagine using it to innovate overhaul supply chains, cybersecurity, the insurance claims process, betting, escrow—anything that depends on the model of a trusted third party for leadership or authentications, straight up through the most fundamental parts of our society: voting and even government itself.

But far and away the biggest use of Ethereum has been to create even more new cryptocurrencies. Since the platform launched, more than 1,600 new cryptocurrencies have been introduced into circulation.

Why? Why does the world need so many cryptocurrencies, when it's still not clear that it needs even the first one?

Bitcoin is not blockchain, and blockchain is not Bitcoin. However, there was a reason that Nakamoto created the one in conjunction with the other: incentive. A peer-to-peer network needs a critical mass of computers to run effectively, and this is especially true for a blockchain, where the validity of the transactions are being verified by the network: if 51 percent of the computers on the network say that a transaction is good, then it is good. That means Bitcoin needs the majority of the computers on the network to operate honestly—in the best interest of the network, rather than in their own interests.

The currency, bitcoin, was Nakamoto's solution to the "tragedy of the commons": the tragedy, specifically, that there will always be thieves in commons. It was designed as a way to incentivize people to participate in the network, operating under the assumption that if people who are validating the blockchain (the "miners") are rewarded periodically with bitcoins, more computers will be incentivized to join, and any single bad actor or consortium will have trouble dominating the network. (If you imagine a very small blockchain network made up of just three computers—one owned by you and the other two run by people who want to rob you—you quickly see why you would want more people on the network. If the thieves control two-thirds of the network, they can validate any transaction they want.)

The tragedy of the commons didn't go away with Vitalik's version of the blockchain, and his initial proposed solution was similar: the validators on the Ethereum network earn a token called Ether.

But Ether is more nuanced than bitcoin, because while a person might hoard Ether as an asset in the hopes that it will increase in value, it has a more practical use too: anyone who wants to run an app on Ethereum's "virtual machine" rents processor power from the network—and this computing power can only be purchased with Ether. The easiest way to get Ether is to earn it by validating the transactions on Ethereum's blockchain. This built-in incentive system keeps the whole engine running: the incentive for validating the blockchain in the Ethereum network is that you earn the tokens you need to use dapps on the network; and your use of dapps on the network is your incentive to act in the network's best interest.

"What these tokens are trying to do is incentivize common behaviors around a common interest," Casey said, "trying to resolve the tragedy of the commons so that a group of people with a common interest can now act together and know that each is doing so because they'll be rewarded with this token for doing the right thing."

The reason there's been such an explosion of new cryptocurrencies since the launch of Ethereum is that many dapps have adopted this same incentive system, where users of the dapp must earn tokens by validating the dapp's transactions, and then, in turn, they can spend these tokens inside the dapp.

For example, there is a dapp called Storj that offers Ethereum-based, decentralized cloud-based file storage. That is, Storj works like Dropbox—a remote place to store your digital files—except without Dropbox acting as an intermediary. If you want to store your files on Storj, you have to buy storage space using a token called Storjcoin. How do you earn Storjcoin? By offering up storage space on the network.

These tokens have also become a new way of funding startup companies. When Storj was first getting started, rather than seek financing from angel investors or venture capitalists, its developers auctioned off tokens in what is called an "ICO"—an initial coin offering, a round of completely decentralized fundraising. During this ICO, Storj raised $500,000 from a wide community of supporters without becoming beholden to any single investor. In 2018, various ICOs raised a collective $21 billion,[13] through a decentralized avenue of financing that wasn't available before blockchain and Ethereum.

But that wasn't the only benefit of Storj's ICO. It also put tokens into circulation, and more specifically into the hands of potential users who now had the resources they needed to begin using the Storj software. The ICO provided Storj both with funding and with the fuel needed to power the system.

But the use of tokens both for fundraising and for fuel is not without its problems. "There's a complete disjuncture, as far as I'm concerned," Casey said, "between the ICO as an investment vehicle that bypasses venture capitalists and as a commodity that is used to manage this particular decentralized application's interests. If everybody is in there trying to scramble and chase prices higher with bubble trading, then how is the token going to fulfill what it's supposed to do, which is to be a fluid medium of exchange?"

What good is fuel if people want to sit on it as a precious commodity, while you need it to power the engine?

Bitcoin, it's important to remember, was created at the height of the 2008 financial crisis. Nakamoto's white paper came out in October 2008, the same month that Congress passed the $700 billion Troubled Asset Relief Program that bailed out the banks. The code in the first block of Bitcoin's blockchain, mined by Nakamoto on January 3, 2009, was embedded with a headline from that day's *London Times*: "Chancellor on Brink of Second Bailout for Banks"—a gratuitous Easter egg that Bitcoin's mostly libertarian community largely understood as a criticism of the banks and the government's handling of the crisis.

The Bitcoin white paper wasn't just suggesting a way that we *could* operate without banks. It was also suggesting that we *should*. In the wake of 2008, the reasons for us to distrust our "trusted third parties" were more apparent than ever.

The banks had done a horrible job managing their risk, they had obfuscated the nature of that risk behind complicated and inscrutable derivative products, and, when it all exploded, the government stepped in, injected new fiat currency into the system, and passed the risk from the banks over to the taxpayers. The rallying cries of Occupy Wall Street, which began in September 2011, wound up becoming the rallying cries of the crypto community—and eventually wound up getting stitched into the ideology behind Ethereum: "Decentralize everything." They said "decentralize everything," but what they meant, most of all, was, "Decentralize finance"—so much so that "DeFi" became its own buzzword to describe the myriad dapps that started to take on every aspect of the financial services industry: dapps to replace commodities exchanges, dapps to replace money market funds, dapps for asset management, dapps to issue and underwrite debt. For every sector of the banking industry, there were people in the DeFi community looking to decentralize and dismantle it.

So it's ironic that, in recent years, the biggest entrants into the blockchain space have been the banks themselves.

BLYTHE MASTERS STARTED working at JPMorgan when she was eighteen years old, as an intern, during a gap year before she started studying economics at Cambridge. Though she went on to receive her degree from the school, it's the bank that she refers to, affectionately, as her "alma mater." To say that she had a successful career during her twenty-seven years at JPMorgan Chase is so much of an understatement that it borders on being inaccurate: she became, at twenty-eight, the youngest woman to achieve the title of managing director in JPMorgan's history, then was named the bank's head of global credit portfolio and credit policy and strategy, then CFO of JPMorgan's investment bank, then head of its global commodities division.

"Blythe has about as much wrapped up in one brain as I've ever encountered in finance," said John McQuown, cofounder of the widely used credit analytics tool KMV.[14]

Perhaps what she's best known for, though, is her role in creating the credit default swap, a financial derivative designed to help insure banks against credit risk. In 2008, when the subprime mortgage market collapsed, the credit default swap wound up playing a starring role in the financial crisis: Lehman

Brothers and AIG found themselves on the losing side of trillions of dollars worth of these insurance products—leading Warren Buffet and then *The Guardian* to describe them as the "financial weapons of mass destruction" that wrecked the economy.

"It wasn't really about derivatives, per se," Blythe clarified. "It was about structured credit, and how to think about credit risk—and derivatives were a big part of that. A group within JPMorgan was able to innovate on a scale

BLYTHE MASTERS, "THE AMBASSADOR"

previously not really imagined, even in investment banks, and that led to a huge shift in the way that people thought about credit risk. They created something not just interesting but that changed the way markets worked in major ways. Enhanced liquidity in credit markets opened markets and led to restructuring, even to mergers and acquisitions, and other things that wouldn't otherwise have happened."

And then, she said, during the run-up to the financial crisis, "other people went on and did some really stupid things."

"Unfortunately," she said, "tools that transfer risk can also increase systemic risk if major counterparties fail to manage their risk exposures properly."[15]

Her first encounter with Bitcoin happened when her ex-husband, Danny Masters, sent her "a trivial amount" of bitcoin. "Honestly I think he sent it just to irritate me"—and to persuade her to finally start paying attention to this cryptocurrency phenomenon that she'd been ignoring.

"I took a look, and I did what I think most people did at the time," she said of her first reaction to the currency. "I dismissed it."[16] No one in the finance industry was taking Bitcoin seriously. "There was criticism of Bitcoin as being problematic from the point of view of its inherent volatility, its potential risk to users because of the lack of infrastructure, and because of the fact that it was being used to perpetuate crimes, essentially. Cryptocurrencies were *personae non grata* of financial services."

But in 2014, Blythe left JPMorgan, and for the first time in almost three decades, she suddenly had time on her hands—"Time and space and sort of mental bandwidth to learn." When she went out at breakfast with an old colleague named Sunil Hirani, he kept going on and on about Bitcoin. "Can't we talk about something more serious?" she asked him.[17] But to Hirani, Bitcoin *was* serious—so serious that he was launching a startup called Digital Asset Holdings that would focus on developing financial technologies using blockchain.

Hirani was no crypto-anarchist. He was a former banker with Deutsche Bank and had gone on to found Creditex Group, one of the first brokerage firms to deal in credit default swaps. He knew banking from the inside—and he believed that blockchain was going to revolutionize the finance industry.

"It led to me having a pretty big 'ah-ha' moment," Blythe remembered, "where I came to appreciate that the technology in play here was inherently interesting in ways that went far beyond the creation of new alternatives to fiat currency. The cryptocurrency use case was just one of an almost infinite number of use cases that could make use of features of the technology."

IMAGINING NEW POSSIBILITIES
"The cryptocurrency use case was just one of an almost infinite number of use cases that could make use of features of the technology."

In fact, knowing what she knew about the banking industry—which was a lot—she was able to see use cases for blockchain that most of the people inside the Bitcoin space couldn't see. "The original Bitcoiners said, 'Okay, the financial intermediaries that let us down are bad, and middlemen generally are bad, and regimes that conduct experiments—potentially enormously inflationary and dangerous experiments—with their money supplies in order to bail out banks are bad. They steal from those of us who save our money because they depress interest rates and they print money, and that's bad. Therefore all of the above should go away.'"

But talking with Hirani, Blythe came to understand that this technology, which had been invented to circumvent the banks and render them obsolete, could in fact be used to make banks better. "The supreme irony was, well, actually the technology that was used to eliminate banks could in fact equally be used to enhance the visibility and transparency and reliability of existing financial actors and infrastructure or replace it with better financial infrastructure." Blockchain was a tool that could allow banks to make and verify trades instantly; it could provide regulators and law enforcement with a ledger that they could audit in real time; and it could remove a lot of waste and risk from the system.

"I spent my whole career thinking about risk, markets, infrastructure, and regulation," Blythe said. "I had seen the financial crisis unfold, and I had seen the credit derivatives market get operationally ahead of itself, which resulted in systemic risk counterparty exposures. I began to believe that distributed ledgers had the capability to tackle that problem."[18]

She became CEO of Digital Asset Holdings in March 2015 and began preaching the gospel of blockchain to the rest of the financial world. "My job was absolutely a sort of evangelical, ambassadorial, marketing role for a good chunk of the beginning year or more."

The financial world wasn't hearing it. Blythe's former boss, JPMorgan CEO Jamie Dimon, repeatedly railed against Bitcoin, calling it a "fraud," a "waste of time," and a "stupid" investment with "no actual value"—and his opinion was shared by most of the banking industry.[19] The currency's volatile valuation and its association with black markets and money laundering scared people off, and blockchain suffered from a taint by association with everything going on in the crypto space.

It was such an uphill battle for Blythe to convince people of the merits of blockchain that Digital Asset largely began to avoid the "b word" altogether, referring to its platform as "distributed ledger technology"—partly to minimize the association with Bitcoin.

But she knew that this technology could help the financial sector address some of the pain points that were getting in the way of its growth: "the large number of intermediaries in the financial value chain, the fragmentation of the associated data, the inability to run processes seamlessly because the data is kept segregated and not reconciled, and the enormous resulting rates of error and inefficiency." Banks also spend enormous time and resources validating the truth of transactions—holding trades in limbo for days or weeks while verifying that the money is really there—and every delay also increases the risk that the trade will fall through.

Once Blythe got people to take blockchain seriously, then she had to answer their next wave of concerns: Would it actually work? Blockchain had never been tested at an enterprise level. Could it scale? Could it offer compliant treatment of privacy? Would it create whole new and unforeseen systemic risks?

Plenty of financial firms were curious about the possibilities offered by blockchain, but none of them were eager to be the first to jump in and test the water.

Then the Australian Securities Exchange said yes.

Banks have been deeply interested in, and invested in, financial technology since long before this past decade's rise of fintech. Of course they have: banks have always been in the business of conducting trades and maximizing value, and they've had deep pockets—so any technological advance that would make these trades safer, faster, and more secure would be worth considering. Coins are a financial technology, designed to keep people from having to cart around gold and salt and sheep wherever they go. Cash is a financial technology, designed to keep people from having to move around coins. Credit cards are a financial technology to save people the trouble of cash. And so on.

During the rise of computers and internet connectivity, the banks were not *not* innovating: they had the capacity to hire the best and brightest minds to help them create technological solutions to their problems—and they did.

But the problems they were trying to solve generally weren't customer-facing problems. Banking's technological innovations were usually aimed at removing internal pain points—particularly, inventing ways to reduce risk and speed up trades.

These two goals—reducing risk and speeding up trades—are interrelated: the longer a trade takes to complete, the greater the risk that the trade will fall through or lose its value, or that the circumstances underfoot will shift and make the trade less advantageous. (Think of Ismail Ahmed, waiting for a month in a foreign city for his brother-in-law's remittance payment to arrive, and all the things that could have befallen him or his money during that time.)

Fifty years ago, if someone were to buy a hundred shares of IBM stock, a bike messenger would pedal across Manhattan with physical "shares" in his knapsack to deliver them to their new owner. These days, the transfer of information is much easier, but even now, banks are surprisingly reliant on fax machines to conduct their trades so they can file away paper copies of the transactions.

Delays are the norm, often because the buyer and the seller need time to verify the truth of the transaction. Does the buyer really have the money? Does the owner really own the thing for sale? The world of finance makes a distinction between the transaction date ("T")—the day that the two parties make the deal—and the settlement date—the day the transfer actually goes through. For decades, the norm for trading stocks has been "T+5"—that is, the parties have five days after their initial agreement to settle their deal, or else the deal becomes void.

Of course, during those five days, the value of that stock might change substantially, and what seemed like a good deal on Monday might look terrible by

Friday. Since this is true in either direction (the stock might go up or might go down), it's in the interest of both parties to bring the settlement of the deal as close as possible to the transaction date.

The Australian Securities Exchange (ASX) is that country's primary exchange for trading stocks, bonds, commodities, and other assets, and it has existed in some form since the mid-1800s. In 1994, ASX launched a settlement system called CHESS for clearing its payments, a world-leading (at the time) system that allowed Australia to begin T+5 settlements. They have been using this system ever since.[20]

In 2015, ASX began looking for replacements for CHESS, and in January 2016, ASX hired Digital Asset "to develop, test and demonstrate to ASX a working prototype of a post-trade platform for the cash equity market using DLT (an example of which is commonly referred to as 'blockchain')."[21]

"Distributed Ledger Technology could provide a once in a generation opportunity to reduce cost, time and complexity in the post-trade environment of Australia's equity market," ASX Managing Director Elmer Funke Kupper said in the company's statement.[22]

By December of the following year, ASX had decided to go forward with a full-fledged version of the project—replacing the existing trading system with a new one based on distributed ledgers.

To address some of the banking industry's concerns about security and scalability, Digital Asset created a solution that is anathema to many in the original Bitcoin space: a "permissioned" blockchain. The original blockchain was designed to be a "permissionless" network, open to anyone. Transactions on the blockchain are secured with encryption, but the network itself is public: no one needs special permission to join. This is meant to be the source of its strength: the more people there are on the network, the harder it is for any single bad actor to gain 51 percent control and threaten the integrity of the system. "ISIS could be running a node within the Ethereum network," said Michael Casey, "and it wouldn't matter to the security proposition."

But enterprise clients balked at the idea of storing their proprietary data on a public network, and the solution that emerged is a permissioned blockchain—a ledger that is distributed only across a private network of known computers. These permissioned blockchains run against the initial idea of Bitcoin because they require that there is some trust between the permissioned parties. But they are emerging as a preferred solution for banking, one that offers the best of both worlds: instantly verified transactions between a con-sortium of trusted parties.

Digital Asset designed a private, permissioned distributed ledger for ASX, and Blythe is confident in the technology.

"What first and foremost needs to happen is that securities need to be able to be cleared and settled within the appropriate time frame, period. Because if that doesn't work, then everything else becomes irrelevant. But what ASX are pursuing is the upside—the potential of creating valuable financial ecosystems where they're much more deeply integrated and providing for a higher quality service to their customers than they're able to do with today's infrastructure.

"I think time will prove ASX to be trailblazers in their industry," Blythe said.

The trail is, in fact, already blazed, and it's getting more crowded by the day. Nasdaq, the London Stock Exchange, and the Japan Exchange Group have all started blockchain-based pilot programs. Meanwhile, a collection of banks launched a company called R3 to explore distributed ledger technology for intrabank transfers, and they quickly added another three hundred partners to their roster.

Jamie Dimon has conceded. "Blockchain is real";[23] his bank is rolling out its very own token, a stablecoin called JPM Coin.

Blockchain, initially created by cypherpunks as a way to disintermediate the banks, has been co-opted and inverted by the intermediaries themselves.

But maybe the greatest innovation of the blockchain is yet to emerge. The technology was meant to decentralize currency—to allow people to transact and trade commodities directly, without middlemen.

"What is the most valuable commodity in the world right now?" Michael Casey asked. "It's data. The biggest value in the world is being derived by those who figure out how to aggregate and analyze data. That's what Amazon, Face-book, Google, are. They are data aggregators. So, data is essentially a currency. Uber is powerful because it holds control of the data. Facebook is powerful because it holds control of the data."

And what is the blockchain except decentralized data?

"If we can imagine a world in which my data is in my control—just as we want my currency to be in my control and everything else—then we are talk-ing truly about a disintermediated thing. We are truly talking about financial disruption."

9 THE EMPIRE STRIKES BACK

FINTECH AND THE BIG BANKS

In 2015, Jamie Dimon wrote to JPMorgan's shareholders. "Silicon Valley is coming," he told them. "They all want to eat our lunch."[1]

It was a dire warning—and it was true.

In the years since 2008, Silicon Valley had been radically reinventing finance, debundling the bank as if stripping it for parts and then rebuilding those parts into newer, prettier, souped-up versions of themselves. Almost no aspect of financial services was left unchallenged. Platforms like PayPal and Venmo enabled people to transfer money back and forth using their smartphones. Braintree and other payment gateways made shopping easier than ever, without touching cash or even a credit card. Peer-to-peer lenders like LendingClub and Kabbage offered better loans, faster, to more people, and at lower rates, giving them a chance to refinance and improve their situations. Because of personal finance managers like Mint and Clarity, and thanks to APIs like the ones designed by Yodlee, people could now see the money coming and going from all of their accounts with new transparency, and they could tap down on unwanted spending and change their habits. Investment apps like Betterment and Robinhood showed that it was possible for all people, not just rich people, to make money off of the markets. White-label banking providers like Green Dot found a way to make their banks' services completely distinct from their brands—so those services could be licensed to any brand at all, relegating the banks to a behind-the-scenes infrastructure role. Blockchain challenged the idea that we need banks to maintain the ledgers of our transactions, and cryptocurrencies challenged the concept of money itself.

The decade had brought a sea change to the ways that people interact with—and think about—all aspects of their financial lives.

And through it all—this ten-year parade of innovation and evolution—what had the banks been doing? Where had they been? How did they let this happen?

The answer to those questions depends on what story you're trying to tell, because there are two conflicting versions of the history of fintech since 2008. In the first version, a band of ragtag misfits from outside the banking industry—insightful, tenacious, irreverent, and most of all agile—were able to see what was going on: how the economic crisis, the rise of the smartphone, and people's changing attitudes about banking and technology all intersected to create a unique opportunity to innovate finance. Meanwhile, the incumbent banks were too lumbering, too myopic, too rigid in their thinking, and too invested in their old business models. They failed to adapt, and now, in the way of dinosaurs and dodos, they are at risk of becoming extinct.

For the most part, this is the version of the story that the fintechs will tell you.

But it's not the only way to tell the story. Another way to understand what's been going on is to consider how the banks have been doing everything right.

In the decade since the financial crisis, they've gotten their houses in order, fixed their balance sheets, freed themselves from unwanted liabilities—and they have waited. They have bided their time, watched the fintech sector emerge, measured its value, assessed the risks, learned at a safe distance from its various mistakes, and now—only now, when they believe that conditions are right and the surviving companies are properly vetted and matured—they're stepping into the field to decide where to partner and where to compete.

Isn't this, after all, exactly what a bank is supposed to do?

So—which version of the story is the right one? Were the banks cautiously hanging back waiting for an opportunity, or did they get caught on their heels and now have to race to catch up?

If you were a bank, which version of the story would you prefer to tell?

Conventional wisdom tells us that banks are full of smart people, they have a lot of buying power, and they are greatly incentivized to outperform any potential rivals. They also spend vast sums of money on developing technologies that they believe will improve their competitive edge.

So, what happened?

Why weren't the banks competing head-to-head with the fintechs from the beginning?

To answer, it helps to look a little further back in time. Economies tend to move in roughly ten-year cycles. A decade prior to the collapse of Lehman Brothers, the world's economy was coming to the end of the dot-com bubble. When that bubble burst in 2000, the fortunes of the tech companies collapsed, and so did people's faith in Silicon Valley. The companies that survived the crash needed to retrench, cut costs, lick wounds, and find their way back to profitability.

They were, according to the model offered by Gartner's "Hype Cycle," deep in the "Trough of Disillusionment" and struggling to survive long enough to begin climbing the "Slope of Enlightenment."[2]

They were, in other words, in no spirit for expanding or innovating.

When the dot-com money evaporated, many of the smart, creative people who might have gone to jobs in Silicon Valley went, instead, to Wall Street, and began innovating there.

They just weren't innovating for consumers.

The Wall Street jobs that people wanted, the ones that paid the most, weren't on the deposit side of the banking business; they were in trading and investment. This is where banks attracted their best talent, and it is where they focused their innovation. They sunk their creativity, brain power, and dollars into algorithmic trading that could execute large-scale trades at computer speeds, competing with other banks to come up with the lowest-latency software—trimming fractions of a second off of a trade to get there first.

Also, they innovated by creating new financial products. It can be easy to forget that financial products are inventions, and, in some manner of speaking, they are technological innovations: even the simplest financial instruments, stocks and bonds, use knowledge about math and economics to build a product that can act as a store of value.

In the first decade of the new century, the creators of these products—people like Blythe Masters—used their ingenuity to invent increasingly lucrative derivatives, like the credit default swap, to offer banks new ways of managing their liquidity and risk. The effect of these new products transformed Wall Street—and flooded it with new wealth.

When Wall Street talked about "innovation" in the early 2000s, this is what they meant.

Then, in a moment—a yearslong bearish moment—*innovation* became a dirty word: it was synonymous with disaster. The banks—much like the tech companies a decade earlier—were facing gigantic systemic problems. They were scrambling to cut costs, meet new regulatory requirements, and rebuild their demolished market caps. They weren't thinking about innovation; they were thinking about their own survival.

In this climate, the smart, creative people who had been, for the past decade, chasing big paychecks on Wall Street now saw that their best opportunities for applying their skills were elsewhere—mainly, in Silicon Valley. They got out of banking.

The tide had turned again.

Particularly in those first years after the crisis, banks were in no position to innovate—but during those early years, there also wasn't any compelling pressure coming from the fintechs. They were too small, too new, too trivial. The dollar amounts of the loans originated by LendingClub or the assets under management by Betterment were, for tech startups, on a scale that meant the difference between a company's life and death. But from the banks' perspective, this was pocket change.

As the years wore on, though, the fintechs grew more market share, and banks started to notice.

First, the fintechs had scaled up to a point that they were beginning to present a material threat to some of the banks' lines of business. For years, the startups had been pursuing the Silicon Valley strategy of "ubiquity first, revenue later"—building up their user base as quickly as possible, even if it meant operating at a loss, on the premise that eventually the sheer volume of users would provide the path to revenue. This was the strategy that led Venmo to absorb the cost of every financial transaction, losing money every time someone passed money with the app, in order to build out its social network—and the strategy paid off, because the social network was the thing that made Venmo valuable to Braintree and PayPal.

When Braintree acquired Venmo, the app had three thousand users—a trivial number that presented no particular threat to the banks. But that network grew by orders of magnitude when it was plugged into Braintree, and then grew exponentially again when it became integrated with PayPal. Suddenly this "trivial" network was too big for banks to ignore. The app, which seemed to come out of nowhere, was suddenly everywhere, and the banks found themselves in a position of scrambling to catch up.

Other fintechs followed similar trajectories, growing slowly until an economy of scale led them to grow, very suddenly, into ubiquity. Because fintechs mostly focus on smaller dollar amounts than the big banks, scale matters. A wealth manager who only deals with high-net-worth individuals may consider everyone else "lobby trash," but as wealth consolidates among fewer and fewer people, the wealth manager's potential client base keeps shrinking. Meanwhile, the fintechs have earned the loyalty of all the "lobby trash." When three hundred or three thousand individuals withdraw their savings from their bank and move their money into Betterment or Acorns or Chime, the amount is an insignificant percentage of a bank's holdings; the bank doesn't notice or especially care. But as the app's users grow and the numbers become three *hundred thousand* people, the activity is suddenly more significant—it still doesn't result in enough lost revenue to threaten the bank, exactly, but it's certainly enough to get the bank's notice.[3]

Of course, by that time, it may already be too late for the bank to draw customers back.

Yes, the banks have been losing customers to the fintechs, and sometimes in enough numbers to present a material threat. But they have been losing something else too—and it presents a much bigger danger.

They have been losing control of the narrative.

Before the financial crisis, a bank was a trusted institution without compare. Banks had their ups and downs and their share of scandals and crises (the savings and loan crisis of the late '80s and early '90s was another low swing of the ten-year cyclic economic pendulum). Nonetheless, the bank was a monolithic institution at the unquestioned center of our financial lives: if you wanted to open a savings account, write a check, get a credit card, apply for a mortgage or a business loan or a car loan, buy foreign currency, or set up an investment account, the bank wasn't just the first place you'd think to go; in many cases, it was the only place you could go.

Making your first deposit in the bank was a rite of passage into adulthood long enshrined in our culture and immortalized by Mr. Dawes, the old banker at the Fidelity Fiduciary Bank in *Mary Poppins*, who happily tells the children, "You'll achieve that sense of conquest as your affluence expands!" Never mind that the kids didn't take his advice.[4]

In the wake of the crisis and with the fintechs gaining more and more mindshare, a wedge drove itself deeper and deeper into this supremacy, crumbling it in ways large and small.

Fintechs' debundling of the bank—peeling off select banking services like lending or payments or investments and offering them up as stand-alone apps—called into question the notion that these services ever needed to be bundled in the first place. Banks have long been the "Swiss Army knives" of consumer finance: they offer a tool for every occasion. In some ways, it's convenient to have all of those tools offered under one roof: that way, customers always know where to go for any of their banking needs.

It's handy to have a corkscrew and a saw blade in one convenient place. But the fact is, it's rare that anyone needs a corkscrew and a saw at the same time— and the Swiss-Army-knife version offers neither the best corkscrew nor the best saw. Stand-alone, single-purpose tools are better at their one task—and fintech suggested that this idea is as true in banking as it is anywhere else.

The banks were losing control of the narrative in a thousand smaller ways too. Once people saw how easy it was to move money with Venmo, the annoying friction of writing a check became suddenly unbearable. As soon as Robinhood began offering stock trades for free, this introduced the idea that stock trades *could* be free—something that hadn't really occurred to anyone before—and then, upon realizing they *could* be free, customers demanded that they *should* be free. Robinhood pulled back the curtain to reveal that stockbrokers had been charging fees unnecessarily, and as soon as people understood this, they would no longer stand for it. Free is very compelling. Once consumers believe that a service should be free, it's very hard to walk that back and convince them otherwise. Soon, in order to compete with Robinhood and with the idea that it had introduced, the brokers had no choice but to race to zero—even though it meant cutting into their own business model.

App by app and sector by sector, the fintechs tore away at enshrined bank narratives, calling every facet of a bank's value into question. So yes, the fintechs were winning a growing portion of the banks' market share—but greater than that, they were winning people's hearts and minds.

Eventually it became inevitable: the banks would have to respond.
They would have to innovate—or die.

"FOR AMERICANS WHO have dreamed of an exciting retail banking
future experience, HSBC and SoftBank Robotics are bringing that future a
little closer."[5]

PEPPER, "THE ROBOT"

HSBC is the largest bank in Europe and the seventh largest in the world, but it's got a relatively modest footprint in the United States: 229 branches, with the vast majority of them in New York. In June of 2018, the bank added a new staff member to the team at its US flagship on New York's Fifth Avenue: Pepper, a humanoid robot.

"Beginning today, HSBC becomes the first financial institution in the United States to bring SoftBank Robotics' humanoid robot, Pepper, to retail banking."[6]

Pepper is a four-foot robot with big black anime eyes, wildly gesturing hands, a touch-screen tablet for a chest, and a foot—a fin?—that looks like something between a mermaid tail and a vacuum cleaner.

"How may I help you?" Pepper asks as you approach. Pepper talks and has reasonably good speech recognition, though the touch screen on its chest offers more clues about the ways in which Pepper is actually able to help you. Pepper, it turns out, is good at showing you whichever products the bank is currently trying to promote, and can even send more information to you via email or text. Pepper can play you a tutorial on how to use the bank's smartphone app. Pepper can display a locator to help you find nearby ATMs (though, since the robot is inside a bank branch, the nearest ATM is probably right beside you).

Oh. And it can also dance. Pepper loves to dance. "That was fun!" the robot says after finishing. "Would you like to see another?"

But if you want to check your balance, transfer money, apply for a credit card, or take advantage of any of those products it is trying to sell you—if you want to do any, you know, banking—then Pepper will have to call you a bank teller of the human variety.

HSBC's Head of Innovation, Jeremy Balkin, said that the bank brought in Pepper to "revolutionize the retail banking customer experience"[7]—part of a program that the bank is calling the "branch of the future."

"By creating a revolutionary new type of digitally enhanced retail banking experience that uses data intelligence and leading-edge robotics," he said, "HSBC is transforming the everyday task of a branch visit into the extraordinary."[8]

He also freely admitted the limitations of the robot. "For complex personal transactions, if you walk into a bank branch, you want to be in a secure room with the privacy of your own human advisor," he said. "You are not going to be doing that on a robot."[9]

Translation: the centerpiece of the bank's "revolutionary" innovation doesn't actually let you bank.

"Pepper reduces wait times by 75 percent, letting people know, for instance, that they can use the ATM to deposit a check," he explained. "They don't have to wait for a teller."[10]

To be fair, HSBC's investment in technology isn't limited to just Pepper the robot. The company's new CEO, John Flint, just committed $17 billion to new tech investment.

But if Pepper is any indication, then of the many, many things that the bank might have learned from the past decade of fintech—like how to offer always-on mobile, branchless banking, or how to use personalized data to make smart, tailored product recommendations—HSBC seems to have missed all of them. Instead, HSBC has staged what can only be described as innovation theater, a showy song and dance (literally) to give the appearance of being on the cutting edge of technology, without actually changing the substance of the underlying experience.

Each year, banks pour billions into their technology budgets: in 2018, JPMorgan invested $11.4 billion, B of A spent $10 billion, Citigroup spent $8 billion, and, collectively, North American banks spent $104 billion on technology.[11]

But spending isn't the same as innovating.

If banks fail to learn the right lessons from fintech, Silicon Valley will almost certainly come to eat their lunch.

"The writing is on the wall," said Adam Dell. "There's no one in these banks who doesn't know that they're fleecing the consumer and delivering very little value."

And just because they know they're doing it doesn't mean they're going to stop. "The writing's on the wall for crack addicts too," he added. "But they can't put down the crack pipe, because they're addicted." The banks, according to Adam, are addicted to the income they get from overcharging their customers. "The fees that pay for the bonuses for the managing directors at Citi are coming straight out of the pockets of their consumer customers—so the banks' ability to get off of that addictive fee structure is very, very, very tough."

The first step to beating an addiction is admitting that you have a problem.

"There are only two types of banks. . . . There are banks that are screwed. And banks that don't know they are screwed."[12]

INNOVATE OR DIE

"There are only two types of banks. . . . There are banks that are screwed. And banks that don't know they are screwed."

The first will perform innovation theater to distract from their dying business model.

The second will do whatever they can to innovate.

Adam, who has made his career out of anticipating trends and getting there ahead of the curve, joined Goldman Sachs in 2018 because he believed they were doing exactly that.

IN 2014, OMER Ismail's boss tapped him on the shoulder and asked him if he would consider starting a bank.

It was an unusual request—not least of all because Omer and his boss already worked at a bank. And not just any bank, but one of the biggest, most respected banks in the world: Goldman Sachs.

Given Goldman's stature and its life span (it just celebrated its 150th anniversary), it may be surprising to discover that, for most of its years, Goldman Sachs hasn't been a bank at all. It has been an investment bank, which of course has the word "bank" in it but in practice is a very different business from a commercial bank. Investment banks act as middlemen, trading the stocks and bonds of their client companies. Since, generally, these activities have only indirect bearing on consumers and public well-being, investment banks aren't subject to the same scrutiny and consumer protection as commercial banks.

Or, rather, they *weren't*—past tense. In 2008, the world discovered the expensive and expansive ways in which investment banks do, in fact, impact consumers and public well-being. The risky gambling on mortgage derivatives by the investment banks cost a lot of everyday people their retirement savings and their homes.

After Lehman collapsed, the government agreed to step in and save the investment banks—but only on the condition that they change their legal status to "bank holding companies"—a designation usually reserved for companies involved in commercial banking. Becoming a bank holding company would give the investment banks access to TARP money and other emergency loan programs, but it would also mean that they would be subject to the same strict capital requirements and oversight that governed commercial banks.

Goldman (along with Morgan Stanley and Amex) made the switch, if somewhat reluctantly. "While accelerated by market sentiment, our decision

OMER ISMAIL, "THE BANKER"

to be regulated by the Federal Reserve is based on the recognition that such regulation provides its members with full prudential supervision and access to permanent liquidity and funding," Goldman's CEO, Lloyd Blankfein, said in a carefully worded statement at the time.[13]

Like it or not, by the end of 2008, Goldman was a bank.

But that didn't mean it was expected to act like one. In 2008, Goldman was in a very different position from its biggest competitors. JPMorgan, Citigroup, Bank of America, and Wells Fargo were all formidable investment banks—but each one also already had an established business in consumer banking: they had bank branches, infrastructure, brand recognition, and, most importantly, they had customers, whose steady stream of deposits and loan repayments gave the banks reliable reserves of capital.

Goldman, on the other hand, had never had a commercial banking business—it had never been consumer-facing—and the Fed wasn't asking Goldman to start now. The designation of bank holding company was meant to be a quick way for regulators to provide relief and gain oversight during the crisis, but no one was expecting Goldman to suddenly start a new line of business, open up bank branches, and drum up new consumer customers. Goldman was a "bank" only in a strict, formal sense of the word.

"For the first five or six years of the existence of the bank," Omer remembered, "we really talked about the bank kind of in the third person, like 'The Bank.' We thought about it as a legal entity. And there was a necessary legal compliance infrastructure that came with the bank. The first few years there was a decent amount of internal debate about whether or not we would be a bank forever. Will we ever de-bank? These were internal conversations that Goldman was having.

"But we didn't really think about the bank as a strategic avenue or a strategic asset for growth."

Omer had spent his whole career at Goldman. He worked briefly as an investment banker before switching into the organization's merchant banking division. MBD's role at Goldman is private equity business investing—the division seeks out companies that show promise and invests in them, so that when the companies grow, Goldman and its clients can sell their stake and get a return on those investments.

The job requires a smart eye, good instincts, and an ability to accurately gauge what makes a company a good or bad investment. Generally, Goldman's merchant bankers tend to specialize in a particular sector, gaining granular expertise in, say, media, health care, or financial services—and they rely on that expertise to make their judgments about where and where not to invest. But Omer's career was, he said, atypical. "I chose not to specialize in a particular industry, but gravitated toward businesses that were more challenger models, more technology-enabled models, and more growth businesses."

He did well, becoming a managing director of the merchant banking division.

In 2014, Omer and his boss, Rich Friedman, the founder of MBD, started to wonder aloud if there might be more to "The Bank" than just a regulatory designation. Rich asked Omer to take the rest of the year to explore whether or not Goldman Sachs might find some opportunities in consumer commercial banking.

If Goldman was going to be a bank, they might as well try and make the most of it.

But where to begin?

MBD spends all of its time studying companies to see what works and what doesn't—and one thing they had seen clearly over the years was that there were a lot of things about consumer banking that didn't work.

"One of the things that we had been observing . . . was what was happening in the fintech space," Omer said. "We saw how broken the traditional banking system was, how significant the consumer pain points were. And we saw how customers were increasingly willing to engage with digital apps, digital tools, and digital ways of satisfying their banking needs."

Omer realized that Goldman might be uniquely positioned to create the bank of the twenty-first century. The company had a vast balance sheet and a deep understanding of financial systems. But unlike its competitors, Goldman wasn't yoked to any antiquated infrastructure: it didn't have a network of branch locations that required monthly rent, didn't have old core banking software that was hard to use and update, didn't have old org charts powering outmoded business models, didn't have customers who had felt burned or betrayed during the financial crisis. If Goldman got into consumer banking, the company would start with a clean slate, free to build the best model for banking—not as it had been, but as it could be.

Was this something they should do? Consumer banking would be very different from every other business that Goldman Sachs was doing or had ever done. It would mean developing new tools, new processes, new people serving customers in a very different way—a whole new culture.

For it to be worth the trouble, Omer knew that he would need to find a real value proposition: What are the customers' unmet needs? What are Goldman's competitive advantages? And how could a Goldman Sachs consumer bank marry the two in order to do something that no one else was doing?

He had spent years studying the fintech space, and from them, he realized the most important thing he would need to create wasn't technology. It was trust. "Too often in fintech, people get very jazzed up about the technology or get jazzed up about artificial intelligence, or machine learning, or cloud compute, or elastic compute," Omer said. "All of those, in our mind, are enablers that exist to solve customer pain points, to give them value, and to do it in a way that's simple and easy."

SOLVING REAL PROBLEMS
"Too often in fintech, people get very jazzed up about the technology or get jazzed up about artificial intelligence, or machine learning, or cloud compute, or elastic compute. All of those, in our mind, are enablers that exist to solve customer pain points, to give them value, and to do it in a way that's simple and easy."

So what were the pain points?

"We've spoken to over one hundred thousand consumer or prospective consumers about their pain points and what they need," Omer said, "and if there's one word that I can use to describe the average US financial services consumer, it is *overwhelmed*. People feel a complete lack of control over their financial lives and understanding what their choices are."

A new consumer bank by Goldman could change that. "We can create experiences and actual product features that give consumers value, and do it in a way that is simple and transparent."

The value proposition, the thing that Goldman could offer better than anyone, was to apply many years' worth of expertise to help everyday people achieve financial well-being.

Using everything he had learned from the past half decade of fintech, Omer drafted a proposal for a new kind of bank, a bank that was genuinely designed to help people improve their lives. This new bank would have no branches; it would be entirely online. Its interface would be clear and easy to use. There would be no hidden fees. If a customer needed to borrow, the bank would help that customer pay down the debt. If the customer wanted to save, the bank would offer a fair rate of return.[14]

Blankfein and the board approved the endeavor, and Omer's proposal became the blueprint for what would become "Marcus by Goldman Sachs," the company's first venture into consumer banking.

Designing a blueprint is one thing. Building a bank from scratch is something else. And this wouldn't be just any bank. It would be a Goldman Sachs bank.

"If we were doing this as a private equity investment," Omer said, "we would have put four guys in a garage, given them $10 million, and let them try and figure it out." If you're a fintech trying to build a bank from scratch, you get to think agile-style: you start small, learn with each incremental step, make adjustments, and grow.

But if you're Goldman Sachs, starting small isn't an option. The company has many (many, many) advantages over the average fintech startup, but one disadvantage is that Goldman is highly scrutinized. Whatever the company chose to do—right or wrong—would get a lot of media attention. Things needed to get done right.

In April of 2016, Goldman Sachs launched an FDIC-insured, online-only savings account that offered a rate of return 1 percent higher than Goldman's competitors. The minimum deposit to open an account was $1—slightly less than the $10 million Goldman requires of its wealth management clients.

In October of the same year, Marcus by Goldman Sachs began offering personal loans for up to $30,000—competing directly not just with other banks but also with fintechs like LendingClub. True to the ethos of Omer's blueprint, the bank charged no fees on these loans—no origination fee for the borrower, no prepayment fees, not even late fees.

Since then, Goldman has made a series of acquisitions to round out Marcus's offerings, buying a small business lender called Bond Street, a credit card startup called Final, and then, of course, acquiring Clarity Money, Adam Dell's personal finance management software, which Marcus intends to integrate as the centerpiece and dashboard of its customer experience.

In building Marcus, it's as if Goldman looked over the fintech menu of debundled banking services and ordered à la carte—rebundling those services in an improved and streamlined way. If you were trying to design a consumer bank for the twenty-first century, you would be hard-pressed to do better than Marcus. "Our advantage all comes down to being a startup with 150 years' experience," Omer said. "We have all the benefits of being a bank, without any of the legacy."

That's not to say legacy banks aren't trying to compete. Many have started offering more online banking services, like mobile check deposits, to save their customers a trip to the branch. But there's a limit to what they are willing to do to undercut their own business model. "They're not going to offer you 2.25 percent on a savings account that's really easy to open," Omer said of his competitors, "because they don't want to self-cannibalize their checking accounts. And they're not going to offer you an open architectural way to buy other products, like Clarity Money does," because the banks have too much invested in keeping people using the same expensive products that they already have.

Is this the future of fintech? "The banks that don't know they are screwed" will slowly fade into irrelevance, while "the banks that know they are screwed" will buy or copy the best innovations of the fintech startups.

In some ways, this is already happening. The payment app Zelle was designed by a consortium of banks to be a Venmo-killer. Fidelity Investments, one of the largest wealth-management companies in the world, released its own robo advisor, Fidelity Go, which charges a 0.35 percent fee and has no minimum deposit—just like Betterment. Having decried Bitcoin, JPMorgan Chase is developing its own cryptocurrency, JPM Coin, to facilitate money transfers, and, through its Marcus division, Goldman Sachs has lent more than $4 billion.

The list goes on and on.

Blythe Masters hinted that this was inevitable. "It's not just the advent of the technology that enabled the fintechs to make a difference," she said. "It's the fact that the major incumbents were focused elsewhere. There's no in-principle reason why the existing incumbents can't use the same technologies and the same approaches to make their businesses more effective. So, the next phase of the fintech revolution, if you're going to call it that, is going to be the fallout around who wins that race—essentially using the tools of the fintech revolution to make their businesses better and to strengthen the moat around their businesses."

Now that the big banks are finally noticing fintech, that might appear to be an existential threat to the upstart companies who set this revolution in motion—and for some fintechs, it will be. There are more than ten thousand fintech startups around the world: the revolution is almost certainly reaching the peak of its "Hype Cycle"; the lowest-hanging fruits have been plucked, and the VC money is starting to dry up. Some significant number of these companies won't survive the unavoidable coming collapse of the fintech bubble.

But as the VC money vanishes, the money from banks is beginning to pour in—because, for a bank, purchasing or partnering with a fintech is often a better business decision than building a copycat solution from scratch.

For many fintechs, these bank partnerships couldn't be coming at a better time. For years, fintechs have thrived beneath the notice of regulators—but many are now bursting at their legal seams. They've reached a scale that regulators can no longer ignore. If they want to keep growing on their own, then they will need banking licenses, and they will need to submit to regulatory oversight.

Otherwise, they can choose to partner with (or sell to) a company that has experience with regulatory oversight, just spent the past decade learning the most efficient ways to work with regulators, and already has a bank license (aka—a bank).

The right partnership, at the right time, with the right bank, could save a fintech from stagnation—and it could do the same thing for its partner bank.

Jamie Dimon warned that the fintechs were going to eat the banks' lunch, but the way his former colleague Blythe Masters sees it, "the fintechs are making the big institutions better at least as much as they are eating the lunch of the big institutions."

Anyway, according to Blythe, the question of who's winning the battle between the banks and the fintechs misses the real point of what's coming next: "The big institutions are not so much worried about what a Lending Tree or a

SoFi are doing to them. They're worrying about Apple, Amazon, Facebook, and Google. They're worrying about what happens if Apple, Amazon, Facebook, or Google really, really make significant headway into creating their own financial ecosystems that are leveraged off the back of their existing networks."

They have reason to worry. Big Tech is coming, and the bankers—at least the bankers who "know they're screwed"—know it.

Who will learn the best lessons from the past decade's fintech revolution? The innovations in financial services haven't just been a consequence of the iPhone and the App Store, of high-speed downloads and always-online connections. They have also been a consequence of new kinds of thinking—thinking that prioritizes transparency, democratization of access, a frictionless and customer-centric user experience, and an evolving understanding of the role of a brand in that experience. There is no going back. What remains to be seen is, who will lead us forward?

MARGARET KEANE

"I KNOW THIS sounds silly, but this company started on innovation."

Margaret Keane is talking about her $24 billion bank, Synchrony, where she is CEO—and the reason she says it sounds "silly" is that, prior to 2014, Synchrony was part of GE Capital, one of the nation's biggest, oldest, most stalwart financial institutions.

Valuable? Yes. Powerful? Yes. But innovative?

"Think about the Depression," she says. "This company was started out of selling appliances."

Remember the little lab that Thomas Edison opened in Menlo Park, New Jersey, back in 1876? By 1932, that lab had become General Electric, and it had moved beyond telegraph lines to become a power utility, a radio broadcaster, and even an early pioneer in television. But one of the company's main lines of business was electrical appliances. General Electric sold vacuum cleaners, coffee makers, waffle irons, and just about every other kind of household appliance.

Then the Depression came and wiped out one in five American jobs, eliminating, along with it, most of GE's market: even if they wanted to, even if they needed to, people weren't going to be able to buy appliances without money. If people didn't buy appliances, then they would also use less electricity. All of GE's businesses were in serious trouble.

Then, according to Margaret, "someone innovatively said, 'Hey, why don't we finance those appliances?'"

GE created a new business division, GE Capital, to lend people money for the appliances they needed. "They would pay five dollars a

MARGARET KEANE, "THE CONVERT"

week until they paid for the refrigerator or the stove or whatever. That's how people bought appliances back then."

Consumer financing and credit are so commonplace now that it's easy to forget they were technological innovations—technologies invented in order to move money forward and backward in time. "At the time," Margaret said, "it was very innovative."

Margaret—who joined GE Capital in 1996 and worked her way up through its ranks to become CEO of its North American retail finance business in 2011—likes to remind people of Synchrony's origins, because, "if we're going to be a financial services company that's around for another eighty years, then we have to be on the forefront of technological innovation."

The 2008 financial crisis cemented this view for her. "One thing that stunned me in the crisis is how fast it moved." For her company to survive this crisis, and any crisis after that, it would have to learn to move quickly too.

So, she went to Silicon Valley, to study how tech companies worked.

"I'll never forget," she said. "I went to Splunk, which is a large company now, and I was horrified. They had desks all over the place. It looked so messy to me. I immediately wanted to go in like a mom would and straighten up the place."

But she watched how the teams worked together, talked to them about their methodologies, and started to realize that everything about the structure of her team at GE was backward. It was top-down, heavy on rules, low on empowerment. "We weren't harnessing the value of our teams," she said. "We had young kids in cubicles, and we told them they couldn't have headphones. You know what I mean? That's how we operated at GE."

What she saw in Silicon Valley was the opposite. "They work in teams. They work across functions. They are quick to have the kid who's best at speaking do the presentation and to have the engineer do the engineering. They quickly assess skills and just move a lot faster."

She wanted to bring this culture back to GE Capital. "I pulled two guys from IT up from the basement and I said, 'We need to do this. We need to create a whole different way we're doing technology and innovating.'"

This was the beginning of what Synchrony came to call its "Innovation Station."

From the outset, the Innovation Station did things differently than the rest of GE Capital. For starters, it was made up of a cross-functional team—not just technologists, but also people from marketing, credit, compliance. All points of view from inside the company were welcome, were needed, to make the team work.

BEING AGILE

"They work in teams. They work across functions. They are quick to have the kid who's best at speaking do the presentation and to have the engineer do the engineering. They quickly assess skills and just move a lot faster."

Second, the team was tasked with "moonshots"—big goals that weren't mired in the detail-level day-to-day operational concerns of the company. "We were with GE," Margaret said, "so we had this bureaucratic process that limited innovation." Every penny needed to be accounted for and justified in terms of bottom line. "So, one thing we did, which was unheard of at the time: we gave [this team] a budget and said, 'You guys decide how you want to spend the money.' It wasn't like hundreds of millions of dollars, but whatever it was, we told them, 'Here is your budget. Go do it.'"

What they did with their budget was innovate. Synchrony's biggest business is "private label" credit cards: the company provides the back-end banking infrastructure for store-brand credit cards offered by companies including Lowes, Chevron, and Gap—and the Innovation Station team went all in on what they saw would be a key part of their emerging business: mobile. The team prototyped and then developed proprietary technologies to allow shoppers to apply for credit cards, pay bills, and service their accounts, all via their smartphones.

If that doesn't sound especially innovative now, it's largely because of the work Synchrony did to make these technologies prominent.

How was Synchrony able to see what other banks couldn't? To innovate while other banks got left behind?

"It's about silos," Margaret said—the tendency for people within a big enterprise organization to think narrowly on their own tasks and their own departments. Escaping this kind of thinking is especially hard at a bank. "We're highly regulated. We've got people looking at us every five minutes. We want to always check the boxes and cross the t's, which we need to do from a regulatory compliance perspective. But," she said, "to compete today, you need to build companies that have enterprise-wide thinking. And I wouldn't even say we're there. We're getting better and we're improving every day. But we're not really there yet."

THE FUTURE

BIG BROTHER IS WATCHING

Y ou're on your way to a friend's party when your smartphone chirps with a new message. "Can you pick up a few snacks?"

"Sure," you write back.

Without leaving the messenger app, you look to see which nearby grocery stores have gotten good reviews from their customers, and with the click of a button, you hire a rideshare to take you to one. Instead of making small talk with the driver, you use your time in the car to finish a few errands: you pay your electric bill, schedule a dental exam, order some new shoes to be delivered to your home, and even manage to squeeze in a quick video game—all still without leaving that same messenger app.

At the store, your friend starts a video chat so she can look over your shoulder while you shop, and you buy the groceries by scanning barcodes into your phone's camera. You also pick up some alcohol, and since the messenger app is linked to your government ID, it's able to verify your age automatically. The money for the groceries is deducted straight from your bank account—and a moment later, your friend repays you, posting to social media that you are her "#hero." You respond by uploading a selfie from the store. Then, noticing your fitness tracker says you haven't taken many steps yet today, you decide to walk the rest of the distance to your friend's party. She messages you the location and it pops up on your map. "See you in five!" you tell her.

You've done all of this using a single app called WeChat.

WeChat is not hypothetical software dreamt up by futurists for an imaginary sci-fi tomorrowland. The app is real—now, today—and it has more than a billion daily users.

It turns out, to see into the future, you only have to look as far as present-day China.

Tencent, the company that created WeChat, started in 1998 as a chat and microblogging service. Now it is one of the biggest financial companies in the world, processing more than one billion payments per day. It's as if ICQ, the early instant messenger, had overtaken and replaced Mastercard. WeChat isn't a bank; it's a platform that first came to be known for emoji, stickers, and video games. So how did it find itself at the center of commerce in one of the largest economies in the world?

The answer is easy: WeChat has users, lots and lots of users.

WeChat is everywhere in China—it is used by 79 percent of the nation's smartphone owners—but, even more important, WeChat is everywhere that people *shop*. Any place that you want to purchase something, online or off, WeChat can handle the transaction with the frictionless push of a button.

Banks might have money and the infrastructure for moving that money around, but WeChat, apparently, has the more powerful part of the commerce equation: it has the people who want to do the shopping.

In the West, for practical purposes, our experience of the world is now mediated by four companies: Google, Apple, Facebook, and Amazon. The companies that Google's former CEO Eric Schmidt once referred to as the "Gang of Four" and what the rest of the world call, more simply, "Big Tech" now exert outsized influence over, well, just about everything.[1]

How big is Big Tech? Big. Half of all e-commerce in the United States goes through Amazon, Google and Facebook control more than half of all digital ad revenue, and half of the US smartphone market belongs to Apple—a company that makes roughly as much money every day as 2,500 average US households make in a year and three times more per day than ExxonMobil.[2] Collectively, the Big Four tech companies have a valuation of over $2.5 trillion—roughly the GDP of the United Kingdom.

But these numbers, stupefying though they are, still don't describe the real nature of the existential threat that Big Tech poses to the banking industry.

On the face of it, the Big Four would appear to be running very different businesses: Google is where we go when we need to learn something; Facebook is where we go to connect with our friends; Amazon is where we go to shop; and Apple puts phones and apps in our pockets.

What the four companies have in common, though (apart from all that wealth), is that they each have a vast network of loyal users, who come to these platforms when they need something.

This is—WeChat shows us—a powerful combination.

And one that seems to be on an inevitable collision course with the banks.

"I absolutely believe that companies who are platform companies, like Amazon, Apple, Google, are going to offer financial services to their customers," said Adam Dell, "as a way to build mindshare and wallet share and affinity with existing customers. Why wouldn't they?"

Sukhinder Singh, who worked at Amazon before founding Yodlee and then went on to run Google's operations in Asia, agrees. "For good or for bad, nobody is better poised to offer financial services than the Big Four or Five internet companies. They are the entry point to finding something."

WHERE THE CUSTOMERS ARE

"For good or for bad, nobody is better poised to offer financial services than the Big Four or Five internet companies. They are the entry point to finding something."

Like WeChat, the Big Four interact with their customers directly at possible points of sale—so, when the customer decides to make a purchase, what if the tech company didn't use a bank to process its payments but instead decided to do the payment processing itself? Whenever a customer wants to finance a payment using a credit card or a loan, what if, instead of sending that person to a bank or credit card company, the tech company lent to the customer directly?[3]

This leaves the Big Four poised to disrupt lending in a major way—and just on the consumer side. For every purchase that a consumer might want to make on one of these platforms, there is a vendor—and that vendor will have banking needs, too, sometimes looking for a line of credit or a small-business loan.

"If you're a merchant," Singh said, "and Amazon offers you float or lending in order for you to forward and get better supply—which leads to more supply for them, more exclusive supply—are you going to think about it? Sure. It's much easier than going to Bank of America and trying to get a small business loan."

At that point, why do you even need a bank?

The tech companies have a few powerful strategic advantages over the incumbent banks, even beyond their vast pools of loyal users. First, Big Tech has data. Lots and lots of data—and this matters. Margaret Keane explained why: "The reality is, you want to know that things are happening before they happen." During the financial crisis, she said, the banks got caught "flat-footed" because they made business decisions on the assumption that the crisis would play out like similar times in the past: they assumed people might default on credit cards or car loans but would absolutely keep making mortgage payments. In fact, the opposite happened. The banks didn't perceive this difference quickly enough, or react to it quickly enough—and this exacerbated the crisis.

Data, and an understanding of that data, might have saved the economy from collapse in 2008. "So, how do we use data more effectively?" Margaret asked. "Are there signs where we could see behaviors sooner? How quick can you move based on the data that you're seeing?"

If you are a Big Four tech company with a billion customers and a whole division dedicated to processing user data with machine learning, then, presumably, you can see patterns more quickly—and more accurately—than can the big banks.

This gives tech companies an edge in spotting macro trends, but it also helps them at a micro level to make judgments about each of their customers. Google, Facebook, and Amazon have already shown that they're able to deliver ad content and product recommendations based on sophisticated models of a person's online behavior. So why not recommendations for financial products?

But there's another, still bigger, advantage that the tech companies have when it comes to offering financial services:

They don't need to make money off of them.

"Apple decided it didn't care about making any money in music," said Adam Dell. "It just wanted to enable the platform to distribute its hardware." Apple sold music on the cheap in order to move iPods. "It totally changed the music business." According to Adam, there's no reason that the Big Four won't do the same thing with banking. "Amazon, I think, will conclude—already has, probably—that they have no interest in making money in financial services, but they want to enable those capabilities for their customers so as to win more mind and wallet share with consumers."

The Big Four already have profitable business models that work. If they add financial services to their repertoires, it won't be to replace their existing business models; it will be to get people to use their core businesses more.

For example, Adam said: "If you buy your food, your milk, your sugar, your eggs from Amazon and you have a cash shortfall and you have your banking account with them, I'm sure they're happy to float you a $500 low-interest-rate personal loan to smooth out your cash flow, to help you continue to shop. They'll do that with very little regard for making money on it, because—from a loyalty and a customer lock-in standpoint—it's money very well spent."

This is no longer conjecture. The tech companies have already started experimenting with offering financial services. Apple Pay and Google Pay encourage users to make purchases with smartphones instead of credit or debit cards.[4] Amazon Lending is an invite-only B2B line of credit offered to select merchants (invitations sent out, no doubt, based on some algorithmic assessment of the merchants' creditworthiness), offering loans between $1,000 and $800,000.

And Facebook, not to be left behind, just announced its plans to release a cryptocurrency called Libra, which will allow people to make payments and money transfers across any of Facebook's platforms—including Instagram and WhatsApp—and to store their money in a digital wallet, without the need of a bank account.

The potential disruption that Libra could cause to commerce is downright WeChatian—a comparison that's not lost on Mark Zuckerberg.

Is it inevitable, then, that Big Tech will take over the financial services industry?

Maybe.

But if the tech companies hold all of these advantages over the banks, then why haven't they taken over already? Compared to the way that WeChat and its main Chinese competitor, Alibaba, swarmed the marketplace, the tech companies in the West have been comparatively very cautious. Why?

"It's not fun to be regulated," said Margaret Keane. "It's a very different world to be regulated as a bank. And I think they wouldn't like that."

Blythe Masters, who has spent all of her professional life inside the world of finance, notices another trend that's emerging as the economy's ten-year pendulum moves into its next swing: "If you look at what happened from 2009 onward for the next decade, the financial sector went through a regulatory tsunami, an extraordinary amount of pain and restructuring. That pain led to what is, ten years on, a very strong financial services sector, at least in the US. The wave of reregulation is more or less complete. But," she said, "it's just beginning to hit the likes of Google and Facebook."

Government regulation is meant to limit systemic risk. During the time since the financial crisis—a time that saw the release of the iPhone, the explosion of social media, and whole new paradigms for how we interact and transact online—regulators haven't been watching the tech companies; they've been watching the banks. And while the banks have gotten their businesses into better order, the systemic risks posed by Big Tech have grown hard for regulators to ignore.

Blythe has no doubt that regulation is coming for Big Tech. "They have become significant enough actors in global economies that they're going to be held accountable for the unintended consequences of what they're doing." But, she said, "there isn't a regulatory framework anywhere in the world today that adequately contemplates the scope of what the tech companies can do."

As these giant companies lurch forward into the future, they are taking steps into financial services but also taking some care not to crush the banks underfoot. It's better, they've reasoned, to stay focused on their core businesses, to provide their users with the best possible experiences, and to seek out banking partners to handle, behind the scenes, the messiest aspects of running the bank.

Maybe this is the model, going forward.

It's a model that seems to be working—for now.

Until someone disrupts it.

ACKNOWLEDGMENTS

This book is about a lot of fascinating people, all of whom deserve eternal thanks for participating. But as important as the names featured in this book are the friends and colleagues who helped make this book a reality.

First, the team at Vested, particularly my cofounders, Binna Kim and Ishviene Arora, for giving me the space to put this together. Also, Eric Hazard for his input and insights as well as Erica Thompson, Adrienne Robbins, and Ashley Jones for their support around production and promotion.

This book would not be possible without the efforts of my writing partner, Chris DeWan. He is a phenomenal thinker and storyteller and a delight to work with.

Thanks also to Jason Schechter from Bloomberg, whose support over the years has put me in the place to produce a book like this. I could say the same of Milton Ezrati, Vested's chief economist, and Dr. David Cowen, CEO of the Museum of American Finance.

My parents, Jon and Sue, deserve special thanks for simultaneously encouraging my love of the written word and sensibly steering me away from a career in journalism, as does my wife, Erin, for keeping the kids entertained long enough for me to get some writing done.

Finally, thanks to Michael Levin and Jill Marsal, who liked the idea of the book enough to fully back it, and to my editor, Tim Burgard from Harper-Collins, who helped bring it to life.

ABOUT THE AUTHOR

DANIEL P. SIMON is a columnist, speechwriter, entrepreneur, and financial communications expert. He has been part of the Fintech Revolution since its inception, advising some of the biggest brands in the financial industry, including Morgan Stanley, Bloomberg, and American Express.

Daniel's focus on finance and its future led him to become CEO and cofounder of Vested, an integrated communications firm where he and his team partner with top financial and fintech companies.

Daniel is a regular columnist for *Forbes*, *Markets Media*, and *CoinTelegraph*, and he is a commentator on Cheddar TV, FinTech TV, Asset TV, and RT. He is also the CEO of the online news site TalkingBizNews and a cohost on the popular financial podcast *Wall & Broadcast*.

When he's not living and breathing fintech and media, Daniel is spending time with his wife and two daughters, Charlotte and Eleanor, at their home in Brooklyn.

NOTES

PROLOGUE

1. Steve Jobs, "iPhone Keynote 2007," Genius.com, n.d., https://genius.com/Steve
   -jobs-iphone-keynote-2007-annotated.
2. Cal Newport, "Steve Jobs Never Wanted Us to Use Our iPhones Like This," *New
   York Times*, January 25, 2019, https://www.nytimes.com/2019/01/25/opinion
   /sunday/steve-jobs-never-wanted-us-to-use-our-iphones-like-this.html.
3. Lorenzo Franceschi-Bicchierai and Brian Merchant, "The Life, Death, and Legacy
   of iPhone Jailbreaking," *Vice*, June 28, 2017, https://www.vice.com/en_us/article
   /8xa4ka/iphone-jailbreak-life-death-legacy.
4. Reuters, "Key Excerpts from Steve Jobs' Biography," October 24, 2011, https://
   www.reuters.com/article/us-apple-jobs-excerpts/key-excerpts-from-steve-jobs
   -biography-idUKTRE79N6TE20111024.
5. Saul Hansell, "Steve Jobs Girds for the Long iPhone War," *Bits* (blog), *New York
   Times*, September 27, 2007, https://bits.blogs.nytimes.com/2007/09/27/steve
   -jobs-girds-for-the-long-iphone-war/.

CHAPTER ONE

1. Market Pulse, "U.S. E-Commerce Sales (unadjusted)," https://www.marketplace
   pulse.com/stats/us-ecommerce/us-e-commerce-sales-unadjusted-23.

2. M. Szmigiera, "Number of FDIC-Insured Commercial Banks in the United States from 2002 to 2017," Statistica, last updated September 5, 2019, https://www.statista.com/statistics/184536/number-of-fdic-insured-us-commercial-bank-institutions/.

3. Andrew Kortina, "Origins of Venmo," *Kortina.NYC* (blog), June 2, 2014, https://kortina.nyc/essays/origins-of-venmo/.

4. Brodie Beta, "The Top iPhone, iPod Touch & iPad Apps of 2010," GeekBeat, December 15, 2010, https://geekbeat.tv/the-top-iphone-ipod-touch-ipad-apps-of-2010/.

5. Sarah Perez, "Zelle Forecast to Overtake Venmo This Year," TechCrunch, June 15, 2018, https://techcrunch.com/2018/06/15/zelle-forecast-to-overtake-venmo-this-year/.

CHAPTER TWO

1. *It's a Wonderful Life*. Directed by Frank Capra. Hollywood, California: Liberty Films, 1946.

2. How much money a real bank keeps on hand varies from country to country and even from bank to bank, but in the United States, banks generally have a "reserve requirement" (also called a "liquidity ratio") of between 3 and 10 percent. This means banks can invest between 90 and 97 percent of their customers' savings. They keep very little of their customers' savings in cash. The rest of it is "illiquid," tied up in assets like loans. Assuming the ledger is accurate and there's nothing going wrong, the bank should have all of its customers' *wealth*, in some form or another. It just doesn't have it as *cash*.

3. In fact, this was largely what had gotten the banks in trouble in 2008: they lent out too much money to too many strangers and wound up suffering from what was essentially a run on the bank.

4. "Fico History," About Us, FICO, accessed October 8, 2019, https://www.fico.com/en/about-us#our-company.

5. "LendingClub Statistics," LendingClub (website), last updated March 31, 2019, https://www.LendingClub.com/info/demand-and-credit-profile.action.

6. Caroline Howard, "The World's 100 Most Powerful Women in 2017," *Forbes*, November 1, 2017, https://www.forbes.com/sites/carolinehoward/2017/11/01/the-worlds-100-most-powerful-women-in-2017/.

7. "Kabbage," *Forbes*, last updated February 4, 2019, https://www.forbes.com/companies/kabbage/#275782b02b90.

8. Small-business owners, often unable to secure business loans from banks, would instead run their businesses using personal credit—credit cards, home equity loans, and the like. But after the financial crisis, lines of personal credit dried up, and these small-business owners were left with very few options.

9. "Lending Club Review," CreditLoan.com, accessed October 8, 2019, https://www.creditloan.com/personal-loans/lending-club-review/.

10. LendingClub, "LendingClub Reports First Quarter 2016 Results - Chairman & CEO Renaud Laplanche Resigns," press release, May 9, 2016, https://ir .LendingClub.com/File/Index?KeyFile=34233669.

11. LendingClub, "LendingClub Reports First Quarter 2016 Results."

12. Connie Loizos, "After Much Drama, LendingClub Founder Laplanche Gets a Slap on the Wrist by the SEC," TechCrunch, October 1, 2018, https://techcrunch .com/2018/10/01/after-much-drama-lendingclub-founder-renaud-laplanche -get-a-slap-on-the-wrist-by-the-sec/.

CHAPTER THREE

1. M. Szmigiera, "Number of FDIC-Insured Commercial Banks in the United States from 2002 to 2017," Statista, September 30, 2019, https://www.statista .com/statistics/184536/number-of-fdic-insured-us-commercial-bank-institutions/.

2. A P Kamath, "Yodleeing Their Way to the Top," Rediff on the Net, October 30, 1999, https://www.rediff.com/news/1999/oct/30us2.htm.

3. "Total Number of Websites," InternetLiveStats.com, accessed October 8, 2019, https://www.internetlivestats.com/total-number-of-websites/.

4. A P Kamath, "Yodleeing Their Way to the Top."

5. Marc Hedlund, "Why Wesabe Lost to Mint," *Marc Hedlund's Blog*, October 1, 2010, http://blog.precipice.org/why-wesabe-lost-to-mint/.

6. Bobbie Whiteman, "Padma in Bed with Her Baby Daddy! Lakshmi Confirms She Is Very Close Again with Krishna's Father Adam Dell with Intimate Instagram Photo," Dailymail.com, June 18, 2017, https://www.dailymail.co.uk/tvshowbiz /article-4615754/Padma-Lakshmi-bed-baby-daddy-Adam-Dell-Krishna.html.

CHAPTER FOUR

1. "World GDP by Year," Multpl.com, accessed October 8, 2019, https://www .multpl.com/world-gdp/table/by-year.

2. Fabian T. Pheffer, Sheldon Danziger, and Robert F. Schoeni, *Wealth Levels, Wealth Inequality, and the Great Recession*, Research Summary (Russell Sage Foundation, 2014), https://inequality.stanford.edu/sites/default/files/media /_media/working_papers/pfeffer-danziger-schoeni_wealth-levels.pdf.

3. Another paper, by NYU professor Edward Wolff, found that "the richest 10 percent of households controlled 84 percent of the total value" of stocks. Edward N. Wolff, "Household Wealth Trends in the United States, 1962 to 2016: Has Middle Class Wealth Recovered?" (working paper, National Bureau of Economic Research, Cambridge, MA, 2017), 19, https://www.nber.org/papers/w24085.pdf.

4. Carmen DeNavas-Walt and Bernadette D. Proctor, "Income and Poverty in the United States: 2014," Census.gov, September 2015, https://www.census.gov /content/dam/Census/library/publications/2015/demo/p60-252.pdf; Board of

Governors of the Federal Reserve System, "Report on the Economic Well-Being of U.S. Households in 2018," FederalReserve.gov, May 2019, https://www.federalreserve.gov/publications/files/2018-report-economic-well-being-us-households-201905.pdf.

5. Cybele Weisser, "The Rise of the Robo-Advisor," ConsumerReports.org, July 28, 2016, https://www.consumerreports.org/personal-investing/rise-of-the-robo-adviser/.

6. "Good" wealth managers—wealth managers interested in the good of their clients—certainly exist. But not every brokerage is quite so customer-centric. One former advisor told us, "In 2000, when I started my career, I was not concerned as a financial advisor about the overall financial health of my clients; I was concerned about how I could sell them a product. I was told we should be selling this mutual fund, in order to help it score high on rankings, even if it's not a suitable product for the customer."

7. Wealth manager fees have been coming down gradually. In 2000, many private wealth managers were charging 2 percent, and they also charged a commission each time they made a trade on behalf of a client, around thirty-five dollars per trade. Discount brokerages like Charles Schwab and Scottrade began underselling these trading commissions, charging eight dollars, then seven. Then the arrival of online trading platforms like E-Trade pushed trading commissions even lower, a trend completed by the arrival of Robinhood and zero-commission trades.

8. There's an old anecdote about two shoe salesmen at the end of the nineteenth century who each went to Africa looking for possible business opportunities. Soon after arriving, the first one sent a telegram back to his home office: "The situation is hopeless: no one here wears shoes." The second one also sent a telegram: "Amazing opportunity: they haven't got shoes yet!" Where most wealth managers ignored all but the highest-worth individuals (because everyone else was "hopeless"), Betterment saw an "amazing opportunity" and turned it into a business.

9. John C. Bogle, "The First Index Mutual Fund: A History of Vanguard Index Trust and the Vanguard Index Strategy," Bogle Financial Markets Research Center, accessed October 8, 2019, https://web.archive.org/web/20130507033534/http://www.vanguard.com/bogle_site/lib/sp19970401.html.

10. David Thomas, "Passive Investing Vehicles Close the Gap with Active Management," *Forbes*, February 4, 2019, https://www.forbes.com/sites/greatspeculations/2019/02/04/passive-investing-vehicles-close-the-gap-with-active-management/#44bd40705778.

11. Robin Sidel, "FDIC's Tab for Failed U.S. Banks Nears $9 Billion," *Wall Street Journal*, updated March 17, 2011, https://www.wsj.com/articles/SB10001424052748704396504576204752754667840.

12. Dennis Jacobe, "Americans' Confidence in Banks Remains at Historical Low," Gallup, April 6, 2010, https://news.gallup.com/poll/127226/americans-confidence-banks-remains-historic-low.aspx.

13. Though the growth of the robos has been quick and impressive, the incumbent investment companies still manage vastly more wealth. For comparison,

BlackRock, the largest of these incumbents, holds $6.5 trillion AUM; Vanguard holds $5.3 trillion; Schwab $3.3 trillion; and Fidelity $2.4 trillion.

14. Boris Khentov, "Navigating Market Stress: Betterment's Approach to Brexit," Betterment (website), June 27, 2016, https://www.betterment.com/resources /navigating-market-stress-betterments-approach-to-brexit/.

CHAPTER FIVE

1. Gerald Apaam et. al, *2017 FDIC National Survey of Unbanked and Underbanked Households* (Federal Deposit Insurance Corporation, 2018), fdic.gov /householdsurvey/2017/2017report.pdf.

2. Eighty percent of commercial banks and credit unions in the United States use a service called ChexSystems, a reporting agency that tracks bounced checks, overdrawn accounts, and potentially fraudulent bank account activity. These files are shared between banks, and when a person's ChexSystems file shows too many negative reports, banks will "de-risk" the customer, making it hard or impossible for them to open an account at any bank. ChexSystems keeps each reported incident on a person's file until at least five years after the incident: it can take a very long time for bank customers to clear their record.

3. Maria Lamanga, "Overdraft Fees Haven't Been This Bad Since the Great Recession," MarketWatch, April 2, 2018, https://www.marketwatch.com/story/overdraft -fees-havent-been-this-bad-since-the-great-recession-2018-03-27.

4. Like so much of the Great Recession, these new "banking deserts"—communities unserved by any bank—disproportionately impacted the already disadvantaged. Someone living in a low-income census tract is more than twice as likely to live in a banking desert than someone in a higher-income tract, and 25 percent of all rural branch closures happened inside majority-minority census tracts.

5. Jason Richardson et al., "Bank Branch Closures from 2008–2016: Unequal Impact in America's Heartland," National Community Reinvestment Coalition, n.d., https://ncrc.org/wp-content/uploads/2017/05/NCRC_Branch_Deserts _Research_Memo_050517_2.pdf.

6. These aren't just inconveniences. For the poorest people, the "inconvenience" of traveling ten miles comes at a cost—bus fares and lost work—and that's assuming the person is able to travel at all. Additionally, according to the Fed, "access to bank credit, particularly for small businesses, declines as the distance between the bank and borrower grows." See Richardson et al., "Bank Branch Closures from 2008–2016."

7. As if all this weren't bad enough, there is another costly side effect of using a nontraditional lender: because these loans and repayments happen outside of the banking system, they aren't reported to credit agencies—and that means that no matter how good a borrower is at repaying their debt, it won't help them to build up a credit history. As a result, underbanked households have less access to traditional bank credit. Using nonbanking products makes it, in some ways, harder to switch back to using regular banking products.

8. Martha Perine Beard, "In-Depth: Reaching the Unbanked and Underbanked," Federal Reserve Bank of St. Louis, January 1, 2010, https://www.stlouisfed.org /publications/central-banker/winter-2010/reaching-the-unbanked-and -underbanked.

9. For comparison, cable companies now routinely offer download speeds of 30 megabytes per second (more than 500 times faster than those dial-up modems), and gigabyte broadband (1,500 times faster than dial-up) is becoming more and more commonplace.

10. And Steve *did* pay him back.

11. Steve clarified: "I can say we had a call center, but for a long time the office was in my house. We had one person with one phone in a supply closet."

12. Because prepaid cards force the cardholder to budget more carefully than a credit card, in the years since the financial crisis, they have become increasingly popular with the banked as well as the unbanked. According to a 2014 study from the Pew Charitable Trust, 45 percent of the users of prepaid cards also used a traditional credit card at least once during that past year. See The Pew Charitable Trusts, *Why Americans Use Prepaid Cards: A Survey of Cardholders' Motivations and Views*, February 2014, https://www.pewtrusts.org/~/media/legacy/uploadedfiles/pcs _assets/2014/prepaidcardssurveyreportpdf.pdf.

13. The average credit card holder in America carries a balance of $6,348, and approximately 40 percent of these people carry a debt from month to month, accruing interest and, often, fees. The "unbanked" aren't the only ones with banking problems. . . . See The Pew Charitable Trusts, *Why Americans Use Prepaid Cards*.

14. Amazon has recently sought to take Steve Streit's original idea for the Green Dot card and turn it into a tool that *does* allow users to build up their credit. See Kate Rooney, "Amazon Launches a Credit Card for the 'Underbanked' with Bad Credit," CNBC, June 10, 2019, https://www.cnbc.com/2019/06/10/amazon -launches-a-credit-card-for-the-underbanked-with-bad-credit.html.

15. Third, if you count soft rock.

16. Put aside, for a moment, the fact that the availability of broadband and high-speed mobile data networks also favors the wealthy and urban over the poor and rural.

17. OK, the idea of branchless banks wasn't entirely new. There had been a handful of earlier efforts launched with mixed success: First Direct opened as a telephone-only banking service in the UK in 1989, and ING Direct was a popular online-only bank that was growing in popularity in the United States until it was acquired by Capital One in 2010. But both of these were subsidiaries of larger, traditional banks. The neobanks were distinct partly because they were neo— new—and going head-to-head against existing incumbents who already had a head start in terms of capital, customers, and charter.

18. This "leverage ratio" requirement is one reason that tech companies don't always want a bank license, and don't always survive if they do get one: the 15 percent of assets that they keep in their proverbial safe is 15 percent that they cannot invest in the marketplace, and this can handicap them against their competition.

CHAPTER SIX

1. Ismail Einashe and Matt Kennard, "In the Valley of Death: Somaliland's Forgotten Genocide," *The Nation*, October 22, 2018, https://www.thenation.com/article/in-the-valley-of-death-somalilands-forgotten-genocide/.
2. Or, anyway, it's as old as money.
3. "Stock Ticker History," The Stock Ticker Company, accessed October 8, 2019, https://web.archive.org/web/20141225041242/http://www.stocktickercompany.com/stc/history; "Stock Ticker," Thomas A. Edison Papers, Rutgers School of Arts and Sciences (website), last updated October 28, 2016, http://edison.rutgers.edu/ticker.htm.
4. It was the British, not the Americans, who really pioneered submarine cables, in an effort to connect their sprawling empire with faster means of communication.
5. Western Union continued to innovate and reinvent itself for many years. In 1914, they invented the first consumer charge card. In 1923, they unveiled teletypewriters. By 1935, they had invented a way to send images across telegraph wires and began offering the first-ever public facsimile service. In 1943, they invented a way to transmit messages between cities using microwaves instead of telegraph lines. By the 1970s, they were launching satellites into space.

    Eventually, all of these diverse projects were Western Union's undoing: by 1994, the company was overextended and out of cash, and filed for bankruptcy protection. By the end of the bankruptcy restructuring, their money transfer business was the only thing to survive intact.
6. "Find Locations," Western Union (website), accessed October 8, 2019, https://www.westernunion.com/sg/en/find-locations.html.
7. Rural M-Pesa users see their household income increase, on average, between 5 and 30 percent.
8. Toby Shapshak, "Sub-Saharan African Will Have 500m Mobile Users by 2020, Already Has Over Half Mobile Money Services," *Forbes*, July 11, 2017, https://www.forbes.com/sites/tobyshapshak/2017/07/11/sub-saharan-african-will-have-500m-mobile-users-by-2020-already-has-over-half-mobile-money-services/#3dc464262456.
9. Some WorldRemit customers still prefer—or need—to retrieve their money as cash, and the company does provide that as an option. But seven out of ten remittances sent through the platform are digital, end to end, compared to just one in five industry-wide.

CHAPTER SEVEN

1. Satoshi Nakamoto, "Bitcoin: A Peer-to-Peer Electronic Cash System" (white paper, bitcoin.org, 2008), 1, https://www.bitcoin.com/bitcoin.pdf.
2. Eric Hughes, *A Cypherpunk's Manifesto*, March 9, 1993, https://nakamotoinstitute.org/static/docs/cypherpunk-manifesto.txt.

3. The value of gold, meanwhile, has soared since 1993: it's currently around $1,275 an ounce.

4. Nick Szabo, "Bit Gold Markets," *Unenumerated* (blog), December 27, 2008, https://unenumerated.blogspot.com/2008/04/bit-gold-markets.html.

5. Satoshi Nakamoto, "Satoshi Nakamoto's Page," P2P Foundation, accessed October 8, 2019, https://web.archive.org/web/20120529203623/http://p2pfoundation .ning.com/profile/SatoshiNakamoto.

6. In 2014, *Newsweek* launched a search for Nakamoto and determined, "There are several Satoshi Nakamotos living in North America and beyond—both dead and alive—including a Ralph Lauren menswear designer in New York and another who died in Honolulu in 2008, according to the Social Security Index's Death Master File. There's even one on LinkedIn who claims to have started Bitcoin and is based in Japan." Eventually, the article unveiled a man named Dorian Satoshi Nakamoto and named him as "The Face Behind Bitcoin"—a bit of investigative reporting that has been widely discounted—and derided—by the cryptography community. See Leah McGrath Goodman, "The Face Behind Bitcoin," *Newsweek*, March 6, 2014, https://www.newsweek.com/2014/03/14/face-behind-bitcoin -247957.html.

7. If anything, the author of the Bitcoin paper had almost too much expertise: people have suggested that Satoshi Nakamoto might actually be a group of people rather than one single person.

8. Bitcoins are awarded for each block that gets mined—but since all of the miners on the network are contributing toward the ultimate solution to the math problem, the award of those bitcoins is distributed among different miners according to how much "hash rate"—processor power—each of them contributed to the mining of the block.

9. The reward that miners receive for mining was initially set at 50 coins for each completed block, but this value was designed to halve after every 210,000 new blocks—so, as the size of the blockchain grows, fewer and fewer new coins are introduced into circulation. At the time of this writing, the blockchain has a "height" of roughly 580,000 blocks, and mining a new block is worth 12.5 bitcoins. When the block height reaches 630,000, the reward for mining will drop again, to 6.25. Around the year 2140, after issuing 21 million bitcoins, the system will stop generating new currency forever.

10. Not entirely worthless: on May 22, 2010, a computer programmer from Florida named Laszlo Hanyecz made the first known real-life transaction with cryptocurrency when he traded ten thousand bitcoin for two Papa John's pizzas.

    Later, at the highest valuation of bitcoin, those two pizzas would have been worth about $200 million.

    "I don't feel bad about it," Hanyecz later said. "The pizza was really good."

11. In another way, BitInstant wasn't so different from Steve Streit's Green Dot, which sells prepaid cards at many of these same retail locations. Both companies offer financial services to an underserved market by going to where that market already shops.

12. Colleen Taylor, "With $1.5M Led By Winklevoss Capital, BitInstant Aims to Be the Go-To Site to Buy and Sell Bitcoins," TechCrunch, May 18, 2013, https://techcrunch.com/2013/05/17/with-1-5m-led-by-winklevoss-capital-bitinstant-aims-to-be-the-go-to-site-to-buy-and-sell-bitcoins/.

13. Taylor, "BitInstant Aims to Be The Go-To Site."

14. Benjamin Weiser, "Long Sentence Sought for Silk Road Creator Ross Ulbricht," *New York Times*, May 27, 2015, https://www.nytimes.com/2015/05/27/nyregion/long-sentence-sought-for-silk-road-creator-ross-ulbricht.html.

15. Ofir Beigel, "20 Strange Things You Can Buy on Silk Road," 99Bitcoins, last updated January 2, 2018, https://99bitcoins.com/20-strange-things-you-can-buy-on-silk-road/.

16. The report's title reveals the FBI's preference for the prosaic over the poetic: "Bitcoin Virtual Currency: Unique Features Present Distinct Challenges for Deterring Illicit Activity."

17. "Bitcoin History," Bitcoin Wiki, updated September 7, 2019, https://en.bitcoinwiki.org/wiki/Bitcoin_history#Bitcoin_in_2011.

18. This same phenomenon happened again during the Venezuelan bolívar hyperinflation: in 2016 and 2017, as the local currency became relatively worthless, Venezuelans poured their wealth into Bitcoin as a safe repository.

19. Verge Staff, "The Coin Prince: Inside Bitcoin's First Big Money-Laundering Scandal," *The Verge*, February 4, 2014, https://www.theverge.com/2014/2/4/5374172/the-coin-prince-charlie-shrem-bitinstant-bitcoin-money-laundering-scandal.

20. Perhaps if Charlie had been sent to prison in Somaliland instead of the Lewisburg Federal Prison Camp in Pennsylvania, he could have circumvented Western Union by transferring the money via Ismail Ahmed's WorldRemit . . .

21. Nat Ives, "Winklevosses' Cryptocurrrency Exchange Says the 'Revolution Needs Rules,'" *Wall Street Journal*, January 4, 2019, https://www.wsj.com/articles/winklevosses-cryptocurrency-exchange-says-the-revolution-needs-rules-11546599600.

22. Charlie Shrem, "Bitcoin's White Paper Gave Us Liberty—Let's Not Give It Back," CoinDesk, October 20, 2018, https://www.coindesk.com/bitcoins-white-paper-gave-us-liberty-lets-not-give-it-back.

CHAPTER EIGHT

1. Claire Brownell, "Vitalik Buterin: The Cryptocurrency Prophet," *Financial Post*, June 27, 2017, https://business.financialpost.com/feature/the-cryptocurrency-prophet.

2. Daniel McGlynn, "Crypto Bites: A Chat with Ethereum Founder Vitalik Buterin," *Abra* (blog), March 13, 2019, https://www.abra.com/blog/crypto-bites-a-chat-with-ethereum-founder-vitalik-buterin/.

3. "Testimonials from Alumni," The Abelard School, https://www.abelardschool.org/students.

4. "Testimonials from Alumni."
5. McGlynn, "Crypto Bites."
6. Morgen Peck, "The Uncanny Mind That Built Ethereum," *Wired*, June 13, 2016, https://www.wired.com/2016/06/the-uncanny-mind-that-built-ethereum/.
7. Brownell, "Vitalik Buterin."
8. Vitalik Buterin, "Ethereum White Paper: The Next Generation Smart Contract & Decentralized Application Platform (white paper, ethereum.org, 2013), http://blockchainlab.com/pdf/Ethereum_white_paper-a_next_generation_smart_contract_and_decentralized_application_platform-vitalik-buterin.pdf.
9. Peck, "The Uncanny Mind That Built Ethereum."
10. Matthew Braga, "Change Agents 2016: Vitalik Buterin, Ethereum," *Canadian Business*, October 13, 2016, https://www.canadianbusiness.com/innovation/change-agent/vitalik-buterin-ethereum/.
11. Buterin, "Ethereum White Paper."
12. Peck, "The Uncanny Mind That Built Ethereum."
13. "Crypto Token Sales Market Statistics," CoinSchedule, accessed October 8, 2019, https://www.coinschedule.com/stats.
14. Edward Robinson and Matthew Leising, "Blythe Masters Tells Banks the Blockchain Changes Everything," *Bloomberg Markets*, September 1, 2015, https://www.bloomberg.com/news/features/2015-09-01/blythe-masters-tells-banks-the-blockchain-changes-everything.
15. Robinson and Leising.
16. Even Blythe's dismissals, though, were thoughtful: "I was sympathetic to the view that the advocates of Bitcoin were espousing—which was that the financial sector had not served the world well in the financial crisis. The concept of placing one's trust in financial intermediaries had clearly failed the world to a degree. . . . [But my] reaction to [the Bitcoin philosophy] was, 'Well, I'm not sure this is what the world needs; we've got big enough problems with money laundering and terrorist financing and sanctions.' The notion of central banks and/or governments losing control of the monetary policy of their economies, because of the advent of a new form of money supply (that, by the way, was inherently deflationary by design because of the finite amount of bitcoin that will ever come into existence, or most other cryptocurrencies that will ever come into existence)—I just didn't see that as being something we needed."
17. Robinson and Leising, "Blythe Masters Tells Banks the Blockchain Changes Everything."
18. Robinson and Leising.
19. Hugh Son, Hannah Levitt, and Brian Louis, "Jamie Dimon Slams Bitcoin as a "Fraud," Bloomberg, September 13, 2017, https://www.bloomberg.com/news/articles/2017-09-12/jpmorgan-s-ceo-says-he-d-fire-traders-who-bet-on-fraud-bitcoin.
20. They did soup up the technology in 2016 to allow for T+2 trading—but still, if you think about Moore's Law, in technological years, 1994 was a long time ago. For perspective, that was also the year of the cutting-edge 100 MB Iomega Zip drive.

21. "CHESS Replacement," ASX, accessed October 8, 2019, https://www.asx.com
    .au/services/chess-replacement.htm.

22. Swati Pandey, "Australia's ASX Set to Lead in Blockchain for Public Companies,"
    Reuters, January 22, 2016, "Distributed Ledger Technology could provide a once
    in a generation opportunity to reduce cost.

23. Tae Kim, "Jamie Dimon Says He Regrets Calling Bitcoin a Fraud and Believes in
    the Technology Behind It," CNBC, January 9, 2018, https://www.cnbc
    .com/2018/01/09/jamie-dimon-says-he-regrets-calling-bitcoin-a-fraud.html.

CHAPTER NINE

1. Alyson Shontell, "Jamie Dimon: Silicon Valley startups are coming to eat Wall
   Street's lunch," *Business Insider*, April 10, 2015, https://www.businessinsider
   .com/jamie-dimon-shareholder-letter-and-silicon-valley-2015-4.

2. Jackie Fenn and Marcus Blosch, "Understanding Gartner's Hype Cycles" (Gartner
   Research, 2018), https://www.gartner.com/en/documents/3887767
   /understanding-gartner-s-hype-cycles.

3. It's maybe ironic that Betterment used technology to gather up a collection of
   lower-wealth individuals and bundle them together in much the same way that
   banks, for the prior decade, had been bundling up mortgage bonds. Now, they've
   been built into big enough piles that their collective worth is enough to warrant
   a bank's efforts.

4. In 2014, an industrious writer at FiveThirtyEight with perhaps too much time on
   his hands calculated an approximate value for that expanded affluence: if Michael
   Banks had invested his tuppence, instead of spending it to feed the pigeons, it
   would have accrued compounded interest for 104 years and would be worth almost ten pounds sterling. How's that for a sense of conquest? See Walk Hickey,
   "Mary Poppins Was Right. Go Ahead and Feed the Birds, Michael," FiveThirty-
   Eight, August 27, 2014, https://fivethirtyeight.com/features/mary-poppins-50th
   -anniversary-tuppence/.

5. SoftBank Robotics America, "HSBC Bank and SoftBank Robotics America Partner to Bring Humanoid Robotics to Fifth Avenue U.S. Flagship Bank Branch," PR
   Newswire, June 26, 2018, https://www.prnewswire.com/news-releases/hsbc
   -bank-and-softbank-robotics-america-partner-to-bring-humanoid-robotics-to-fifth
   -avenue-us-flagship-bank-branch-300672008.html.

6. SoftBank Robotics America.

7. S. C. Stuart, "Dancing (and Banking) with Pepper the Robot in Beverly Hills," *PC
   Magazine*, April 19, 2019, https://www.pcmag.com/news/367499/dancing-and
   -banking-with-pepper-the-robot-in-beverly-hills.

8. Stuart.

9. Kurt Schlosser, "Can a Robot Spice Up the Retail Banking Experience? HSBC's
   'Pepper' Is Now on the Job at Seattle Branch," *GeekWire*, March 12, 2019, https://
   www.geekwire.com/2019/can-robot-spice-retail-banking-experience-hsbcs
   -pepper-now-job-seattle-branch/.

10. Stuart, "Dancing (and Banking)."

11. Ron Shevlin, "How Much Do Banks Spend on Technology? (Hint: It Would Weigh 670 Tons in $100 Bills)," *Forbes*, April 1, 2019, https://www.forbes.com /sites/ronshevlin/2019/04/01/how-much-do-banks-spend-on-technology -hint-chase-spends-more-than-all-credit-unions-combined/#1ae22bbb683a.

12. Adam Lashinsky and Jonathan Vanian, "What Big Banks Say about Being 'Screwed'—Data Sheet," *Fortune*, June 21, 2019, https://fortune.com/2019/06 /21/big-banks-change-data-sheet/.

13. Goldman Sachs, "Goldman Sachs to Become the Fourth Largest Bank Holding Company," press release, September 21, 2008, https://www.goldmansachs.com /media-relations/press-releases/archived/2008/bank-holding-co.html.

14. If this all seems a little too earnest or populist for the bank once referred to as "a great vampire squid wrapped around the face of humanity," consider what it is that banks do: they seek out undervalued opportunities and try to capitalize on them before anyone else beats them to it. Goldman's earnest, customer-first ethos happens to be what they think is best for their bottom line. See Matt Taibbi, "The Great American Bubble Machine," *Rolling Stone*, April 5, 2010, https:// rollingstone.com/politics/politics-news/the-great-american-bubble-machine -195229/.

EPILOGUE

1. Wall Street sometimes throws Netflix into the group and refers to them, collectively, as the vampiric "FAANG."

2. Jun-Sheng Li, "How Amazon Took 50% of the E-commerce Market and What It Means for the Rest of Us," TechCrunch, February 27, 2019, https://techcrunch .com/2019/02/27/how-amazon-took-50-of-the-e-commerce-market-and -what-it-means-for-the-rest-of-us/; Kurt Wagner, "Digital advertising in the US is finally bigger than print and television," Vox, February 20, 2019, https://www .vox.com/2019/2/20/18232433/digital-advertising-facebook-google-growth -tv-print-emarketer-2019; Associated Press, "Apple, Amazon, Facebook, Alphabet, and Microsoft Are Collectively Worth More Than the Entire Economy of the United Kingdom," *Inc.*, April 27, 2018, https://www.inc.com/associated-press /mindblowing-facts-tech-industry-money-amazon-apple-microsoft-facebook -alphabet.html.

3. On the one hand, this would be an incredibly disruptive new model. On the other hand, it's not new at all: Sears Roebuck did it, offering financing for customers who wanted sewing machines or bicycles. Ford did it to help its customers buy cars. And, as we've seen, General Electric did it to sell appliances and grew its financing arm into the division that eventually became Margaret Keane's Synchrony Bank.

4. Both Apple Pay and Google Pay still link back to a user's traditional credit card or bank account—for now.

INDEX

Accel Partners, 118
Acorns, 62, 87
aggregation, 46–52
agile methodology, 77–78
Ahmed, Ismail, 105–9, 111–14, 117–18
AIG, 158
Airbnb, 10–11, 153
Aldermore, 101
Alibaba, 192
Amazon, 4, 94
  as data aggregator, 164
  and Green Dot card, 202n14 (ch 5)
  influence of, 188, 189
  loans to vendors of, 37
  1-Click purchasing on, 9
  possible financial services from, 182,
    189–92
  users' trust in, 54
Amazon Lending, 191
American Banker, 24
American Express, 4, 5
Amex, 175
angel investors, 59
Angry Birds, 9–11

APIs (application programming
    interfaces), 51–52, 102
Apple
  App Store, xxxiii, 9
  Clarity Money app, 62–65
  influence of, 188, 189
  iPhones, xxix–xxxiii, 9, 97
  possible financial services from, 182,
    189–92
Apple Pay, 191, 208n4 (epilogue)
application programming interfaces
    (APIs), 51–52, 102
apps, 187–88
  actions taken with, 60
  for iPhone, xxix–xxxiii
  mentality for, xxxii–xxxiii
  payment information in, 11, 12
  see also specific apps
Ariely, Dan, 60
Arora, Anil, 46–47, 49, 51, 52
artificial intelligence, 60, 63
Aspiration, 101
Associates First Capital Corporation,
    100

Atom Bank, 101
AT&T, xxi
Australian Securities Exchange (ASX),
    161–64
Austrian school of economics, 124–25

Back, Adam, 130
Baldwin, James, 92
Balkin, Jeremy, 172, 173
banking culture, 29
banking deserts, 91, 201n4 (ch 5)
bank-level data security, 5
Bank of America, 98, 103, 176
banks, 89–103
    aggregating customer data for, 48–52
    Big Tech's threat to, 188–90
    branchless, 99, 115, 202n17 (ch 5)
    brands of, 54
    communication among, 6
    and credit cards for kids, 94–95
    credit cards from, 18
    disrupted narrative of, 169–71
    and double-spending problem, 127–28
    Early Warning Services venture in, 13
    entry into blockchain by, 157–64
    during financial crisis, 190
    for fintech customers, 89–90
    fintech partnerships with, 181
    following financial crisis, 91, 168
    infrastructure costs for, 18, 21
    innovation by, 6, 162, 168, 171–73
    as intermediaries, 18–19
    investment, 33–34, 174–76
    lending by, 19–20
    margin structure of, 64
    mobile banking, 97–103
    online, 99–103, 179–80
    and prepaid cards, 95–97
    reactions to fintech revolution in,
        165–86
    regulation of, 41, 98–100, 174–76,
        192, 202n18 (ch 5)
    reserves of, 34, 198n2 (ch 2)
    risk assessment in, 22, 157
    small business loans from, 35
    and subprime mortgage crisis, 33–34
    technology budgets of, 173
    trust in, 21, 34, 79
    UK neobanks, 101
    and "un-/underbanked" Americans,
        90–92, 201nn3, 6, 7 (ch 5)
    white-label, 102–3
BankSimple, 101
Barre, Siad, 105, 106
behavioral economics, 60–61, 70
Betterment, 76–84, 207n3 (ch 9)
Big Tech/Big Four, 188–92
BillGuard, 60
Bitcoin, 124–26, 132–45
    and blockchain, 154–56, 204nn8–9
        (ch 7)
    Buterin and, 148, 149
    and crypto-anarchists, 139–42
    finance industry's rejection of, 159–61
    and hyperinflation, 205n18 (ch 7)
    programming language of, 150–51
    and proof-of-work system, 133
    regulation of, 140–42, 144
    unstable value of, 141
Bitcoin Foundation, 136, 143, 149
BitInstant, 134–39, 142, 143, 204n11
    (ch 7)
BlackRock, 81, 201n13 (ch 4)
Blankfein, Lloyd, 176
blockchain, 132–33, 147–64
    banks' entry into, 157–64
    and Bitcoin, 154–55, 204nn8–9 (ch 7)
    Buterin's work on, 149, 151
    and creation of cryptocurrencies,
        154–56
    disintermediation with, 154
    Nakamoto's version of, 150, 151
    permissioned, 163–64
    potential uses of, 150
    proof of work-based, 150
    and smart contracts, 151–52
b-money, 130
Bogle, John C., 74–76
Bond Street, 180
Bonneville Bank, 100–101

Braintree, 7–13, 168–69
Brexit vote, 83
Broverman, Eli, 77
Buffett, Warren, 83, 158
Buterin, Dmitry, 147, 149
Buterin, Vitalik, 147–53, 155

Casey, Michael, 153–56, 163, 164
Charles Schwab, xxxvii, 200n7 (ch 4),
    201n13 (ch 4)
CHESS system, 163
Chevron, 185
ChexSystems, 201n2 (ch 5)
Chime, 101
Cirrix Capital, 39
Citigroup
    and banking expenses, 98
    in consumer banking, 176
    services of, 103
    tech budget of, 173
    and VerticalOne, 48
    and Yodlee, 49
Clarity Money, 60–64, 180
ClearBank, 101
Clear Channel, 93, 94
Cleary Gottlieb, 17
Community Reinvestment Act, 32
consumer advocacy, 62–65
consumer financing, 183, 184
credit, origin of, 183, 184
credit bureaus, 22, 26
credit cards
    average balance on, 202n13 (ch 5)
    from banks, 18
    and double-spending problem, 127–28
    information on, 4–5, 9–11
    and peer-to-peer lending, 28
    "private label," 185
    for young people, 94–95
Creditex Group, 159
Credit Karma, 23–27
credit scores, 22–27
creditworthiness, 22–27, 37
Cruttenden, Jeffrey, 85–87
Cruttenden, Walter, 85–87

cryptocurrency(-ies), 121–45
    of banks, 180
    Bitcoin, 124–26, 132–45, *see also*
        Bitcoin
    Ethereum and creation of, 154–55
    of Facebook, 191
    Gemini, 144
    and privacy, 126–27
    and proof-of-work system, 130–31,
        133
    regulation of, 140–42, 144
    and schools of economics, 123–25
    tokens, 155–56
    and trust in money, 128–30
CVS, 134
Cydia, xxi, xxii
Cypherpunk Manifesto, 126
Cypriot financial crisis, 141

DailyCheckout, 122–24, 134
data
    access to, 45–46
    aggregation of, 46–52, 164
    of Big Tech, 190
    processing of, 53
    use of, 49–53
    value of, 164
data modeling, 36–38
data security, 5
debit cards, 5, 95–97
Dell, Adam, 56–65
    on banks, 173, 174
    Goldman's software purchase from,
        180
    on possible Big Tech financial services,
        189, 191
Dell, Michael, 57, 58
Digital Asset Holdings, 159, 161, 163,
    164
Dimon, Jamie, 64, 161, 164, 165, 181
Discover, 4, 5
disintermediation, 18–21, 154
distributed ledger technology, 132–33,
    161, 163
Dodd-Frank Act, 80

Donahoe, John, 12, 13
Donovan, John, 16
Dread Pirate Roberts, 140, 142
Dropbox, 10–11, 153
Duane Reade, 134

Early Warning Services, 13
eBay, 4, 36–37, 94
EcoCash, 117
e-commerce, 4, 7–14. *see also* mobile
    shopping; online shopping
economic cycles, 167
Edison, Thomas, 110, 182
Ellison, Larry, 17
emojis, 13–14
Equifax, 22
Ether, 155
Ethereum, 151–55, 157
Ethlance, 154
E*Trade, 85, 200n7 (ch 4)
Experian, 22

Facebook
    angel investment in, 59
    as data aggregator, 164
    influence of, 188, 189
    innovation motto for, 40
    and LendingClub, 27–29
    possible financial services from, 182,
        189–92
    users of, 38, 79
    users' trust in, 54
Fair Isaac Corporation, 22
Ferguson, Niall, 60
FICO Scores, 22–23, 27, 39
Fidelity, 81, 201n13 (ch 4)
Fidelity Go, 180
Fidelity Investments, 180
Final, 180
financial crisis (2008), 31–34, 67–68, 79,
    184, 190
financial industry, xxxvi–xxxvii
    customer pain points in, 178–79
    innovations in, 72, 167–68, 182
    predatory practices of, 54

and psychology of customers, 70
    regulation of, 192
    rejection of Bitcoin in, 159–61
    work environments in, 184–86
    see also banks; *specific topics*
Finovate Conference, 15–16, 23, 55
fintech(s)
    and agile methodology, 78
    and banks, 89–90, 181
    and banks' narrative, 169–71
    big banks' reactions to, 165–86
    conflicting histories of, 166
    culture of, 29
    and 2008 financial crisis, 31–32
    innovation stories in, xxxvi–xxxvii
    Quicken as, 44
    timeline for, xv–xxii
    worldwide number of, 181
    see also specific topics and companies
First Direct, 202n17 (ch 5)
Flint, John, 173
Ford Motor Company, 100, 208n3
    (epilogue)
fractured banking model, 49
Fraser, Alexander G. "Sandy," 43
Freeman, Jay, xxi
friction, 3–4
Friedman, Milton, 124
Friedman, Rich, 177

Gap, 185
Gates, Bill, 103
GE (General Electric), 182–85, 208n3
    (epilogue)
GE Capital, 182–85
Gemini, 144
General Electric (GE), 182–85, 208n3
    (epilogue)
Gnosis, 154
GoBank, 101–2
GO.com, 94
Goldman Sachs, 56, 64–65, 98, 174–80,
    208n14 (ch 9)
Golem, 154
Google, 164, 182, 188–92

Google Pay, 191, 208n4 (epilogue)
Great Recession, 67, 91
Green Dot, 96–97, 100–103, 202n14
    (ch 5), 204n11 (ch 7)

Hansell, Saul, xxxiii
Hanyecz, Laszlo, 204n10 (ch 7)
Hargeisa, Somaliland, 105–7
hawala, 108–9
Hedlund, Marc, 56, 58
Hirani, Sunil, 159, 160
housing bubble, 32, 67, 68
HSBC, 171–73
Hughes, Eric, 126
Hughes, Nick, 115

ICOs (initial coin offerings), 156
I-Gen, 95–96
Inala, Sam, 46
inflation, 71, 129, 205n18 (ch 7)
ING Direct, 78, 202n17 (ch 5)
initial coin offerings (ICOs), 156
Intuit, 44, 49, 52, 56, 103
investing, 67–87
    behavioral economics in, 70
    with Betterment, 76–84
    and financial crisis, 67, 68
    free stock trade services, 170
    in mortgage-backed securities, 32–33
    passive, 74–76, 82–83, 87
    by peers, *see* peer-to-peer lending
    robo advisors, 81–84
    saving money vs., 71
    in stock market, 71–76, 162–63
    using round-ups for, 86–87
    via Facebook, 28–29
    wealth managers for, 72–74
investment banks, 33–34, 174–76
iPay, 7
iPhones, xxix–xxxiii, 9, 79, 97
Ismail, Omer, 174–80
It's a Wonderful Life, 19–20

Jefferies, 39, 41
Jobs, Steve, xxix–xxxiii

Johnson, Eric, 60
Joseph, Michael, 115, 116
JPMorgan, 173, 176
JPMorgan Chase, 98, 103, 157–59, 180

Kabbage, 35–38
Kagan, Noah, 52
Keane, Margaret, 182–86, 190, 192
Keynes, John Maynard, 123–24
Keynesian economics, 123–24
Kickstarter, 153
Kortina, Andrew, 1–7
Kumar, Srihari Sampath, 46
Kupper, Elmer Funke, 163

Lakshmi, Padma, 58
Laplanche, Renaud, 15–21, 27–31, 39–41
Lehman Brothers, 31, 33, 157–58
lending
    by banks, 19–20
    and FICO Scores, 22–23
    mobile mortgage loans, 59–60
    peer-to-peer, *see* peer-to-peer lending
    small business loans, 35–38
    and subprime mortgage crisis, 31–34
LendingClub, 15–21, 27–31, 34–35,
    39–41
Libra, 191
Lin, Ken, 23–27
Lincoln, Abraham, 110
LinkedIn, 54
Lowes, 185

Mack, John, 39
Magdon-Ismail, Iqram, 1–7
Marcus, 64–65, 179–80
Mastercard, 4, 5
Masters, Blythe, 157–61, 164, 180–82,
    192, 206n16 (ch 8)
Masters, Danny, 159
McQuown, John, 157
Metro Bank, 101
Microsoft, 52
Mint, 45–46, 52–56, 58, 60
mobile banking, 97–103

mobile payments, 13
mobile remittance, 114–19
mobile shopping, 9–13, 187–88
money, xxxvi
  attitudes toward, 61–62
  emotional nature of, 61
  saving, 62–64, 70–71
  trust in, 128–30
  see also specific topics
money hackers, xxxvi
Monzo, 101
Moore's Law, 9–10, 97
Morgan Stanley, 175
The Moron Test, 9
Morris, Hans, 39
mortgage lending, 31–33, 59–60
Mortiz, Sir Michael, 98
Motorola, xxx
Moven, 101
moving money, 1–14
  and emoji-based social feed, 13–14
  mobile shopping, 9–13
  removing friction for, 4–10
  see also remittance
M-Pesa, 114–17
MTN, 117
mutual funds, 74–76
My Campus Post, 1

Nakamoto, Satoshi
  and Bitcoin, 125–26, 132, 133, 144, 155, 156
  and blockchain, 145, 150, 151
  identity of, 132, 204nn6–7 (ch 7)
Nascentric, 45
Nelson, Gareth, 134
New York Stock Exchange, 71
N26, 101

OakNorth, 101
online banks, 99–103, 179–80
online shopping, 4–5, 92
OpenTable, 61, 62
Oracle, 17
Owen, Sean, 77–78

passive investing, 74–76, 82–83, 87
Patzer, Aaron, 43–46, 52–54, 56
payment gateways, 4–5, 12–13
PayPal, 12–13, 142, 169
PCI compliant technology, 4–5
Pearson's Law, 60
PeerStreet, 35
peer-to-peer lending, 15–41
  and creditworthiness of debtors, 22–27
  disintermediation for, 18–21
  and financial crisis, 31–34
  and power of social media, 21, 27–29
  regulation of, 29–31, 41
  return on, 34–35, 39
peer-to-peer (P2P) services, 12
Pepper (robot), 171–73
personal finance management, 43–65
  consumer advocacy in, 62–65
  and use of customer data, 49–53
  user-centered design in, 53–62
  and venture capitalism, 57–59
Petralia, Kathryn, 35–38
Plaid, 87
prepaid cards, 95–97, 202n12 (ch 5)
privacy, 126–27
Prosper, 16, 17, 31
P2P (peer-to-peer) services, 12
Putorti, Jason, 52–56, 60

Quicken, 44, 45

Radix, 154
Rajan, P. Sreeranga, 46
Rangan, Venkat, 46
Ready, Bill, 7–13
regulation
  of banks, 41, 98–100, 174–76, 192, 202n18 (ch 5)
  of cryptocurrency, 140–42, 144
  Dodd-Frank Act, 80
  of investment banks, 174–76
  of peer-to-peer lending, 29–31, 41
  by SEC, 29–31, 40
  of tech companies, 192

remittance, 105–19
 digital platform for, 113–14
 fees on, 111–12, 118
 fraud in, 112–13
 hawala system for, 108–9
 by migrants, 107–10, 113–14
 mobile, 114–19
 with M-Pesa, 114–17
 by wire transfers, 109–11
Revolut, 101
risk assessment, 22–27, 37, 157
Ritchie, Dennis, xxxii
Rite Aid, 95
Robinhood, 170, 200n7 (ch 4)
robo advisors, 81–84
Rocket Mortgage, 59–60
Rokr phone, xxx
Roth Capital, 85

Safaricom, 114–16
Samid, Yaron, 60
Satyavolu, Ramakrishna "Schwark," 46
saving money, 62–64, 70–71
Schwab, 81
Scottrade, 200n7 (ch 4)
Sears Roebuck, 208n3 (epilogue)
Securities and Exchange Commission
    (SEC), 29–31, 40
securitization, 30–33
Sequoia Capital, 98
7-Eleven, 134
Shawbrook Bank, 101
Shrem, Charlie, 121–25, 133–39,
    142–44
Silicon Valley, 40, 165–68, 184
Silk Road, 140, 142, 143
Singh, Sukhinder, 46–50, 52, 56, 189, 190
Skee-Ball, 9
small business loans, 35–38, 198n8 (ch 2)
smart contracts, 151–52
smartphones, xxx–xxxiii, 9, 12, 187–88
social media, 21, 27–29, 38
social network, of early fintechs, 168–69
social news feed, 7
SoFi, 35

SoftBank Robotics, 171, 172
SoftPay, 135
software bots, 46–48, 50–51
Splunk, 184
Starling Bank, 101
Stein, Jon, 68–70, 73–74, 76–80
stock market
 current bull market, 82–83
 and financial crisis, 67, 68, 79
 free trading in, 170
 households' control of value in, 199n3
    (ch 4)
 investing in, 71–76, 162–63
Storj, 155–56
Streit, Steve, 90, 92–98, 100–102
subprime mortgage crisis, 31–34
subscriptions, 62–63
Summers, Larry, 39
Synchrony, 182, 184–86
Szabo, Nick, 129–31, 151

Tandem, 101
TCV, 118
TechCrunch40, 54, 55
TechCrunch Disrupt, 79–80
Tencent, 188
Thiel, Peter, 59, 153
Thompson, Ken, xxxii
Tide, 101
Tigo, 117
tokens, 155–56
TransUnion, 22
TripleHop Technologies, 17
Troubled Asset Relief Program, 33
trust
 in banks, 21, 34, 79
 and cryptocurrency development,
    128–30
 and customer pain points, 178–79
 in fintech, 81
 in money, 128–30
 of users, in providing information, 54

Uber, 10–11, 103, 153
Ulbricht, Ross, 142

United Nations (UN), 112–13
Unix, xxxii
Upgrade, 40, 41
upwork, 153

Vanguard, 81, 201n13 (ch 4)
Vanguard 500 Index Fund, 76, 78
Venmo, 2–7, 11–13, 168
venture capitalists (VCs), 57–59, 118, 181
Ver, Roger, 136, 143
VerticalOne, 48
Visa, 4, 5
Vodafone, 114, 115
von Mises, Ludwig, 124

Walgreens, 134
Walmart, 102, 103, 134
Warren, Elizabeth, 54
wealth managers, 72–74, 200nn6–8 (ch 4)

WeChat, 188, 189, 192
Wei Dai, 130
WeiFund, 154
Wells Fargo, 98, 176
Wesabe, 56
Western Union, 109–11, 143, 203n4 (ch 6)
widgets, xxx
Wilde, Oscar, xxxvi
Winklevoss, Cameron, 137–38, 143–44, 149
Winklevoss, Tyler, 137–39, 143–44, 149
wire transfers, 109–11
WorldRemit, 113–14, 117–19, 203n9 (ch 6)

Yodlee, 46–52, 87

Zelle, 13, 180
Zuckerberg, Mark, 28, 40, 137, 191